T0418479

INDIGENOUS KNOWLEDGES AND HIGHER EDUCATION IN CANADA

Indigenous Knowledges and Higher Education in Canada explores the intricate relationship between Indigenous knowledges and the evolving landscape of higher education in Canada, revealing their profound influence in shaping institutional policies, practices, and cultures. Grounded in decolonial perspectives, the book addresses the persistent struggle within universities to confront ongoing colonialism and achieve systemic change.

Focused on shifts in institutional governance, policy, teaching, research, innovation, and culture, the book draws on extensive document analysis and personal narratives of Indigenous individuals across various Canadian universities. Embracing a decolonial perspective, it underscores the resilience of Indigenous communities in challenging traditional paradigms of higher education. The book reveals how, through critical grassroots efforts, Indigenous peoples are reclaiming their rightful place in academia, reshaping institutional dynamics from the ground up. It argues that the emergence of Indigenous knowledges within academia is the result of proactive and ongoing efforts by Indigenous individuals asserting their presence in Canadian higher education.

Ultimately, *Indigenous Knowledges and Higher Education in Canada* advocates for a path of decolonization through intentional learning and unlearning, envisioning a future where Indigenous voices and perspectives are authentically centred in the fabric of academic discourse and practice.

MERLI TAMTIK is the associate dean of graduate programs and research and an associate professor of educational administration at the University of Manitoba. She serves as president of the Canadian Society for the Study of Higher Education and as an elected member of college in the International Public Policy Association.

Indigenous Knowledges and Higher Education in Canada

MERLI TAMTIK

UNIVERSITY OF TORONTO PRESS
Toronto Buffalo London

© University of Toronto Press 2025
Toronto Buffalo London
utppublishing.com

ISBN 978-1-4875-4289-4 (cloth) ISBN 978-1-4875-4291-7 (EPUB)
ISBN 978-1-4875-4290-0 (paper) ISBN 978-1-4875-4292-4 (PDF)

Library and Archives Canada Cataloguing in Publication

Title: Indigenous knowledges and higher education in Canada / Merli Tamtik.
Names: Tamtik, Merli, 1974– author
Description: Includes bibliographical references and index.
Identifiers: Canadiana (print) 20240495853 | Canadiana (ebook) 20240495861 |
    ISBN 9781487542900 (softcover) | ISBN 9781487542894 (hardcover) |
    ISBN 9781487542917 (EPUB) | ISBN 9781487542924 (PDF)
Subjects: LCSH: Critical pedagogy – Canada. | LCSH: Indigenous
    peoples – Education (Higher) – Canada. | LCSH: Indigenous peoples –
    Canada – Intellectual life. | LCSH: Indigenous peoples – Study and
    teaching – Canada. | LCSH: Decolonization – Canada. | LCSH: Education,
    Higher – Canada. | LCSH: Education, Higher – Social aspects – Canada.
Classification: LCC LC196.5.C2 T36 2025 | DDC 370.11/5–dc23

Cover design: Mark Rutledge
Cover image: Red Buffalo Skull, Marlyn Bennett/Wawate Ikwe

We wish to acknowledge the land on which the University of Toronto Press operates. This land is the traditional territory of the Wendat, the Anishnaabeg, the Haudenosaunee, the Métis, and the Mississaugas of the Credit First Nation.

University of Toronto Press acknowledges the financial support of the Government of Canada, the Canada Council for the Arts, and the Ontario Arts Council, an agency of the Government of Ontario, for its publishing activities.

 Canada Council Conseil des Arts
for the Arts du Canada

 ONTARIO ARTS COUNCIL
CONSEIL DES ARTS DE L'ONTARIO
an Ontario government agency
un organisme du gouvernement de l'Ontario

Funded by the   Financé par le
Government   gouvernement
of Canada   du Canada

 Canadä

Dedicated to people fighting for self-determination

Contents

Tables and Figure

Tables

Figure

Acknowledgments

I would like to acknowledge the Treaty 1 territory, the ancestral homeland of the Red River Métis nation, where I work and which I continue to benefit from in my life and academic career as an uninvited guest and settler on these lands. I hope that this book represents my modest contribution to broader institutional change in Canadian higher education that respects and empowers Indigenous communities in their self-determination efforts. It is with deep gratitude that I acknowledge the individuals who made this work possible. First and foremost, I am deeply grateful to my participants, who generously shared their time, knowledges, and experiences by engaging in this work with me, connecting with me, sharing their wisdom, teaching me, and supporting this project in various other ways. Your wisdom, guidance, and support have been invaluable, and I hope I have upheld the role of a respectful listener. I would like to express my thanks to my Indigenous colleagues at the University of Manitoba, including Drs. Laara Fitznor and Frank Deer, who shared their time and insights during this journey. I am also indebted to the peer reviewers whose thoughtful comments and guidance significantly contributed to the refinement of the book manuscript. Their insights were imperative in grounding and strengthening this book, pushing me towards criticality and deeper self-reflection in my writing. My family, Emilie and Taavi, have been the rock that I was able to lean on during the extensive writing process. Their encouragement, and various discussions we had during our walks and car rides, helped me immensely to keep my focus and stamina. Finally, I must acknowledge the financial support that made this research and publication possible. This work received funding from the Social Sciences and Humanities Research Council of Canada, as well as through Scholarly Works Grants from the Faculty of Education, at the University of Manitoba.

Aitäh! Ekosani! Thank you!

INDIGENOUS KNOWLEDGES AND HIGHER
EDUCATION IN CANADA

Prologue

Indigenous peoples and their knowledges have become a powerful catalyst for change in Canadian higher education, calling for profoundly different ways of doing research, engaging with teaching practices, and participating in university governance. Significant and growing scholarship has emerged from Indigenous authors on Indigenous pedagogies (e.g., Fitznor, 2005; Louie et al., 2017); Indigenous student achievement (e.g., Ottmann & Jeary, 2016; Parent, 2017; Pidgeon, 2019); research paradigms (e.g., Battiste, 2007; Kovach, 2021; Smith, 1999; Wilson, 2008); curriculum and programming (e.g., Donald, 2009; Louie et al., 2017; Ottmann & Pritchard, 2010); and institutional leadership, governance, and policy (e.g., Brunette-Debassige, 2021; Kuokkanen, 2019; Staples et al., 2021). These Indigenous scholars have built a distinct body of rich scholarship that centres knowledges emerging from land, individual experiences, community relationships, and spiritual connections and that flows from Indigenous theoretical frameworks and methodologies. This scholarship is self-standing, yet fundamentally different from western knowledge traditions. Mainstream higher education institutions have struggled to accommodate Indigenous epistemologies. There is a consensus that Canadian higher education institutions have not served Indigenous communities well because of the ongoing impact of colonialism and Eurocentric knowledge hierarchies embedded in universities (e.g., Cote-Meek & Moeke-Pickering, 2020; Smith, 2019; Tuck & Yang, 2012). The inherent struggle to reconcile western and Indigenous epistemologies and knowledge hierarchies within higher education reflects the broader societal momentum arising globally among equity-seeking groups. Movements such as Black Lives Matter, Missing and Murdered Indigenous Women and Girls (MMIWG), and Idle No More have emerged as powerful platforms advocating for equity and social justice. The work of the Truth and Reconciliation Commission of Canada has activated the reconciliation imperative and brought renewed political attention to the debates around Indigenous experiences. All these developments have pushed Canadian higher education institutions to take stock of their relationships with Indigenous peoples and Indigenous knowledges at large.

While there seems to be an agreement around supporting equity, diversity, and inclusion in higher education, there is an unresolved struggle to address the ongoing impact of colonialism within universities. Institutional efforts to address issues emerging from Eurocentric knowledge hierarchies have resulted in universities' uneven and fragmented approaches to Indigenous perspectives, experiences, and engagement with institutional change at large (see Andreotti de Oliveira et al., 2015; Gaudry & Lorenz, 2018; Stein, 2020). There has been an explosive growth in the number of institutional Indigenous strategies, action plans, and performance reports developed to prioritize Indigenous knowledges and experiences as part of institutional equity efforts. Universities are competing to hire Indigenous faculty from a limited pool of applicants. Territorial land acknowledgments have become default practice at any public event. However, the backdrop to these efforts is still the dominant Eurocentric knowledge frameworks that keep perpetuating the same institutional structures and practices that academia is trying to change. Overall, higher education institutions have been put in a vulnerable position where the relevance of their traditional knowledge frameworks and institutional policy contexts is under close scrutiny, and there is confusion over how to move forward.

Activities around Indigenous knowledges have been typically framed in mainstream media to celebrate universities and their senior administration for Indigenization efforts. New policy initiatives featuring Indigenous experiences are triumphantly highlighted as "record-setting," whereby universities are seen as taking "a momentous step" in leading change, "setting new directions" or "entering a new era" (Samson, 2020; UBC, 2020). The work of Indigenous knowledges and communities has remained somewhat invisible and strongly overshadowed by competing narratives describing the heroic efforts of universities in working with Indigenous communities towards reconciliation. These narratives tend to overlook and minimize decades of ground-up work that Indigenous communities have spearheaded in order to advocate for a meaningful change in Canadian post-secondary education. This situation is an illustration of what Indigenous scholars describe as cognitive imperialism (Battiste, 2000) or epistemic ignorance (Calderón, 2014; Kuokkanen, 2007a), which tends to marginalize and silence anything other than the dominant Eurocentric intellectual traditions. While there is will and evidence of institutional efforts towards transforming the mainstream university, more needs to be done at the systemic level for higher education institutions to participate in a meaningful change.

The main purpose of this book is to examine the institutional transformations that have occurred in Canadian higher education in relation to Indigenous knowledges. The research questions that guide this volume are the following: *How have Indigenous peoples and knowledges changed Canadian universities? What has changed?* This book specifically examines the changes in institutional governance and policy, research, teaching, and innovation but also examines institutional climates that are essential in shaping the policy–practice interface. The analysis highlights the individual perspectives and experiences of Indigenous faculty members working in Canadian universities as they contribute to this transformation. The book approaches institutional change through a decolonizing lens, hoping to provide stronger theoretical and practical guidance that may support institutional processes in this work. My personal inner struggle as a non-Indigenous author learning and writing about Indigenous knowledges is a reflection of this larger epistemological conflict that Canadian universities must resolve in order to move forward on the path of equitable institutional change.

Positionality: Uncomfortable Confrontations

A starting point for any non-Indigenous researcher to acknowledge Indigenous perspectives is to unpack and confront their own individual power and privilege. This typically happens through inner critical reflection, which is often an uncomfortable and difficult process. Yet, examining one's possible bias is necessary for recognizing one's own role in maintaining violent colonial structures in academia and in society at large (Absolon & Willett, 2004; Styres, 2019). Furthermore, the naming of one's location and positionality has epistemological value to Indigenous peoples because it allows others to understand where you come from and examine the value frameworks you represent. This process helps to establish relationships and builds trust (Wilson, 2008). As Margaret Kovach (2021, p. 146) pointed out, engaging with "the act of critical self-locating, we are given occasion to analyse the power dynamic that flows between the researcher and the participant." The author noted that self-location connects the personal, cultural, and social aspects of the self and serves as a decolonizing strategy (Kovach, 2021). It is only after scholars carry out such personal and institutional examination that they can be in a position to engage with Indigenous knowledges.

My personal confrontations with privilege and power take me back to my childhood growing up under the Soviet colonial regime, my academic training within Eurocentric knowledge frameworks, and then my professional career within predominantly white Anglophone academia in Canada. The most eye-opening part in this inner reflection has been identifying the differences between my personal experiences and those of Indigenous scholars, while trying to avoid drawing surface-level parallels or falling into "me-too-ism" as per Aveling (2013, p. 3), which may occur with such comparisons. Another obstacle for me was to decide how much personal revealing is enough to be meaningfully accountable to Indigenous communities in Canada without oversharing and overshadowing. Below, I share my uncomfortable confrontations that position me as a settler but an ally to Indigenous peoples living in Canada. In this process, I try to be intentional in articulating differences when discussing experiences.

I grew up in the northeastern part of Europe in what was then the Soviet Republic of Estonia. A bit of socio-political background is appropriate to understand my positionality in relation to where I come from and how I have experienced power. Between 1940 and 1991, Estonia, once an independent country, was annexed and operated under the Soviet communist regime. During several decades, the Soviet regime exercised cultural assimilation, determined to change the ethnic composition of Estonia by bringing in Russian settlers and attempting to merge both Russian and Estonian cultures into one Soviet culture. Estonians as a cultural group were violently displaced through a series of repressions, with thousands of people being deported against their will by the Soviet regime, executed, and imprisoned. My grandmother was one of them but managed to come back after several years spent in Siberia. As a result of the Soviet occupation, the Russian population in Estonia grew from about 23,000 in 1945 to 475,000 in 1991, which had damaging effects on people, culture, and language across generations. Scholars have argued that the violent practices of the Soviet regime, continuous cultural assimilation, and removal of people from their lands are colonial behaviours and should be confronted as such (see Annus, 2011; Schorkowitz, 2019). Today, the population of Estonia remains small – about 1.3 million people, with less than 700,000 Estonian speakers. Safeguarding the Estonian language is of utmost importance to Estonian people, as our language is closely connected to Estonian identity. Protecting the language equals safeguarding the freedom and independence of the country. Kaljundi (2022) has argued that Estonian identity is characterized by a unique intersectionality where, on one hand, people identify as Europeans and, on the other hand, as Indigenous people connected to a particular land. Being situated in a European borderland and surviving decades of trauma caused by the Soviet colonial regime have built a strong political desire to belong to Europe. Yet, culturally, Estonians have maintained their distinct traditions, ceremonies, and deep connection to land, which make them physically and culturally native to that area. While this history of occupation, attempts at cultural assimilation, and formal removal of independence for decades shares some powerful similarities with Indigenous experience, it is still fundamentally different. Estonians were never subject to the racial discrimination, complete removal from their lands, or erasure of knowledge epistemologies, language, and culture that Indigenous communities in Canada have been experiencing to this day.

Growing up, I didn't perceive whiteness as a marker of privilege in a homogeneous, white-only society. Race often remains as a blind spot in my experiences even today. There was no formal difference between social classes, either, because communist ideology prescribed everyone to be equal. Power and privilege were possible to gain primarily through relationships and personal connections and were manifested through having access to goods that were otherwise out of reach – being able to buy exotic fruits, such as bananas or pineapples, or a pair of shoes imported from outside of the Soviet republics. Opposition to an authoritarian regime gets manifested often through practising refusals (Tuck & Yang, 2014). A memory from my childhood surfaces, where I was in a bus with a few Russian grandmothers who had picked up their grandchildren from school and were riding home. Their hair was coloured purple, and they laughed loudly with their golden teeth shining through. They spoke Russian with entitlement and were ordering other passengers to answer them in Russian only. Those demands were met with silence and people's refusal to engage. The grandmothers loudly stated that all Russians must be honoured for bringing freedom to Estonia. Our truth was the opposite – they took our freedom from us. We were natives of these lands, and they were the uninvited settlers who didn't want to leave. Protecting Estonian culture, traditions, and language was the silent practice of resistance among Estonians when I was growing up. For eleven years, I was an active member of an Estonian folk-dance group and participated in a school choir that was an important connection to our cultural heritage during the totalitarian regime. Never did I think of myself as becoming a settler who benefits from living and working on the lands that belong to others – the

Indigenous peoples in Canada. That thought is troubling and deeply uncomfortable to me.

I have experienced education as serving as a powerful political tool. Education can lead to a better life, but it can also be used to maintain power and form citizens loyal to the government. In school, we learned the Soviet version of Estonian history, where any connection to independence or political freedom was erased or silenced. History teachers could get fired for introducing materials about Estonian independence or national self-determination. Soviet values and ideology were systematically built in through media and films that pitched Soviet heroes against the West. When I went to school, all instruction was in Estonian, but the Russian language became mandatory from Grade 3. Older students were immersed in military/citizenship education, preparing for the looming war coming from the West. The curriculum included lessons on how to assemble a gun (a timed activity that didn't tolerate long nails as a fashion statement) and strategies to escape nuclear bombs by pulling on gas masks and running to the school basement. There was always the thrill of suffocating, as some masks had defects. We were taught to align with the Soviet ideals through curriculum and textbooks determined by the government. In order to succeed in life, one had to assimilate and follow the rules. Estonians were lucky to maintain their schooling in the Estonian language, which wasn't the case for Indigenous peoples of Canada and has led to loss of language and cultural diversity. This has been another uncomfortable realization where I have seen education as serving as a direct tool for assimilation, creating obedience while strengthening the power of some groups over others.

When I graduated from high school, Estonia gained back its political freedom. It was the time of Estonian cultural renaissance, a new awakening and rebuilding of one's country politically, economically, socially, and culturally. Education was then and is still viewed as a core value among Estonians, who see it as a path to a better life but now in the hands of an independent country. It was anticipated that I would go to university, and I was the first person in my family to graduate with a university degree. With borders opening up, I was able to take advantage of an opportunity to be accepted by the University of Toronto with a full scholarship. Coming to Anglophone western academia from a society that had transitioned from communism to liberal democracy within a few short years was a major adjustment on all fronts. I was older compared to most of my classmates, as I had family responsibilities and a previous administrative career. My knowledge was primarily grounded in Eurocentric frameworks but in the works of Russian thinkers who were unfamiliar names in Canadian academia. Furthermore, my whole schooling had followed the Soviet scientific realm with quantitative methods, and I had never been exposed to qualitative research. I was used to a lecture style without challenging professors. Group assignments scared me, and I saw them as a waste of time. My confidence took a hit, as the linguistic and epistemic realms that I had known had been overthrown. My language skills didn't measure up, and I had no knowledge of Canadian academic research culture or expectations. I felt like a true imposter among others. I wonder now if this feeling is slightly similar to what Indigenous students may experience when they come to pursue their degrees in Canadian universities, planted in a system that doesn't recognize their familiar ways. Language was my number one issue. While I had relatively good English skills, I had never written an essay in English. I was absolutely thrilled when I received my final mark in my first graduate course. It was an A–. I teared up from happiness, reflecting on all of my struggles as an international student, away from my people and my family, operating in a completely unfamiliar academic environment. This mark was an immense boost to my self-confidence, and I was grateful. I started to wonder whether maybe I could actually do academia. Walking in the hallway, cheerful and happy, I ran into a classmate who was crying, a copy of her final essay in her hands. What had happened? I approached her. She told me that she had practically failed the course, showing me her A–. Apparently, this was the bare minimum everyone was expected to get in the graduate program. I was stunned – all of my feelings of victory faded, and my achievements were suddenly minimized and belittled. However, this encounter taught me that context matters, and slowly I started to realize the privilege that some students (in my view, Anglophone Canadians) had and took for granted, without noticing any systemic barriers others had to struggle with. As a white student, I didn't have to face the issue of race. I had the advantage of being able to put in more work and overcome my language barrier to level the playing field a bit compared to others.

While I studied at one of the top universities in Canada, the gaze and focus of scholarship was outwards, primarily international. This suited me well as an international student, and I felt that I could contribute to the conversations. During my studies, there was hardly any exposure to Indigenous peoples or their histories or knowledges. To my knowledge, none of my peers identified as Indigenous to Canada. Residential schools were mentioned maybe once, in one of my course readings. At the time, I didn't realize the significance of such silencing of Indigenous peoples and knowledges, not realizing my own contribution to this silencing. Canada had been good to me, and it emphasized multiculturalism as a core value, a discourse that worked well with my Estonian cultural pride. I couldn't associate Canada with cultural erasure. Now I find it surprising that I didn't dig deeper into the topic then, as I could have easily drawn parallels to the feelings of being native to a place, yet almost losing one's lands and culture. I was too subsumed in my own personal survival, trying to settle and make it in academia. After all, I had given up so much to come here. For years I was completely oblivious to the cultural genocide that was ongoing in Canadian society.

My deeper critical inquiry into Indigenous peoples and their experiences in Canada began during the end of my PhD studies, when I had comfortably settled. There were regular lectures and events held among the Estonian community in Toronto about the history of Soviet occupation in Estonia, cultural genocide, and language loss. We shared pride over survival and our continuing connection to the fatherland. I started to draw connections with the history of the Indigenous peoples of Canada, slowly coming to realize the extent of the ongoing ethnic and cultural erasure. Most comments among the Estonian community compared Indigenous experience with Estonian settler experience, equalizing it within the narrative of multiculturalism whereby hard work was leading to results. It overlooked the systemic, structural issues around white privilege, race, the supposed superiority of Eurocentric knowledge systems, and decades of cultural assimilation. My reality check came when I interviewed for a professor job at the University of Manitoba, triumphantly presenting my publication record and speaking about my research agenda focused on innovation policy. When it was time for questions from the audience, a senior Indigenous professor raised her hand, asking: "This is all fine and well, but what have you done for Indigenous peoples in Canada?" I was completely thrown off my throne, as I mumbled something about Estonia, safeguarding one's language, and drawing parallels with the Indigenous experience. I knew the answer fell short but, more importantly, this question was a true awakening for me, a personal confrontation as a settler, challenging my privilege as I interviewed for a position in a Canadian university that operated on Indigenous lands. This question has stayed with me until today, when I am still trying to formulate my answer.

Working at the University of Manitoba, I learned about the Treaties and the lands that belong to Anishinaabeg, Ininiwak, Anisininewuk, Dakota Oyate and Dene peoples, and the Red River Métis. For me personally, working there meant digging deeper into the cultural richness and learning about the history of Indigenous communities living on these lands. I also reflected on my own Estonian cultural background and my personal privilege as a white person taking space in Canada as a settler and uninvited guest on Indigenous lands. Winnipeg, Manitoba was the perfect place for these reflections, as many of the institutional activities were centred on Indigenous experience. Several of my colleagues identified as Indigenous, and I had regular conversations with them, slowly building relationships. The situation was like day and night compared to my Toronto experience. In Manitoba, I was able to attend many events, workshops, and training sessions with rich opportunities to learn about Anishinaabe and Cree cultural teachings, driven towards the topic by my own personal interests. I volunteered to go to Northern Manitoba and serve as a practicum supervisor in the rural towns of Gillam and Churchill to get a better sense of the communities there. My interest didn't go unnoticed, and I started to be invited to serve on student committees that examined Indigenous topics, where I worked with Indigenous faculty. Through these relationships, I gradually built deeper insights into Indigenous knowledges and feelings of personal appreciation and gratitude. Being gradually more exposed to critical scholarly work by Indigenous authors, I started to see the power imbalances created by the colonial system in Canada. I realized the extent of the cultural genocide that had taken place, while none of it was exposed at a larger international scale. I was also starting to slowly realize the difference between my own experience and ongoing Indigenous colonial oppression. Only by digging deeper into the critical literature on white privilege did I start to see myself as part of the problem – performing as an oppressor in relation to Indigenous peoples, continuously enjoying the privileges gained from occupying Indigenous lands. It was a stark, unpleasant realization, as my childhood memories of Soviet oppression and my feelings of anger came to the surface. I felt a direct conflict between and increasing discomfort with my own lived experience and then settling in and working in Canada.

On this journey, I have made many mistakes and taken missteps in conversations; the learning is ongoing. I remember the same colleague who asked me the difficult question during my job interview giving me another (friendly) push when I once walked into her office empty-handed, wanting something. She gently commented, "This is something you might want to learn about, when you're approaching Indigenous people. You have a protocol of a gift offering, and mine is tobacco. Otherwise, you are just plunking yourself in!" I almost collapsed from embarrassment in her office. Turning red all over my face, I had mental flashbacks of my mom's wisdom, reminding me to always bring gifts to people to establish a relationship, a connection that was essential when operating under the Soviet regime. Gift giving was a familiar practice to me but something I completely came to ignore after settling in Canada. There have been many other occasions when I feel

I have made mistakes. There have also been occasions of rejection or silencing on the part of Indigenous peoples towards my well-intended efforts of support. I completely understand and respect their position. The situation is delicate; I myself feel fragile and uncomfortable, realizing my power and the privilege that comes from my whiteness and training in Eurocentric academia. I think those feelings are the main point of these uncomfortable conversations that may hopefully lead to deeper learning. I know these are the dilemmas other non-Indigenous peoples are facing in the process of supporting the work of Indigenous communities. While rejection can be part of the experience, it is part of the learning experience.

Tuck and Yang (2012) critically described various narratives in which white settlers free themselves from responsibility and from work towards reconciliation and decolonization. "Colonial equivocation," which they describe as "homogenizing of various experiences of oppression as colonization" (Tuck & Yang, 2012, p. 17), is one of them. My story of positionality has revealed my personal connections with experiencing privilege that comes from whiteness and from being a settler who works in the Eurocentric academic system. There is also marginalization that comes from my background of experiencing power through Soviet authoritarianism and from my social class and cultural background as a non-Anglophone immigrant woman living in Canada. These connections are not linear but intertwined and complex with conflicting dilemmas. They feature feelings of discomfort as I realize my struggles around being native to Estonia yet settling on Turtle Island; around safeguarding one's language and culture yet assimilating to Anglophone Canada; around recognizing the privilege of working on Indigenous lands but not wanting to give it up. Realizing those intersections, limitations, and personal dilemmas in relation to Indigenous experiences is important in departing on my decolonial learning journey. Guided by the advice of my Indigenous colleagues, in which they have pointed out that fighting systemic, structural colonialism is the responsibility of all of us but particularly of non-Indigenous people, I have actively looked for ways in which I can be part of the solution and not the problem. I am hopeful that my work may contribute to this in small ways by speaking to non-Indigenous groups working in academic spaces and beyond. Hence the book.

Settler Responsibilities

My personal journey of learning about Indigenous perspectives has been a bumpy road filled with unexpected twists and turns. It has revealed some crucial lessons that non-Indigenous peoples, especially settlers in Canada, should consider when aspiring to be allies to Indigenous communities. The following perspectives on settler responsibilities emerged from my experience and may serve as a useful starting point for others. While not an exhaustive list, these suggested actions are intended to start the process of enhancing one's understanding of Indigenous experiences:

- Accepting colonialism and one's role in it. This process begins by reflecting deeply on one's own life journey and experiences and recognizing any privileges and biases one may hold, while making comparisons across Indigenous experiences to highlight differences. While this process may evoke discomfort, it is an integral part of the decolonial learning and should be embraced. The focus is educating ourselves on colonialism as an ideology, its underlying premises and historical impact. This then leads to noticing the pervasive presence of colonial structures around us that continue to suppress Indigenous peoples. Throughout this process, one's own complicity in perpetuating these inequitable structures, often through being silent, becomes visible. An essential part in the process is learning about and acknowledging the traditional lands of Indigenous peoples, with active consideration of ways in which those lands can eventually be returned to their rightful owners.
- Advancing one's understanding of Indigenous knowledges. Developing cultural competence involves delving into Indigenous epistemologies, knowledge frameworks, histories, cultural protocols, and languages. This effort enhances one's ability to engage respectfully and ethically with Indigenous community members. While books are great resources, nothing beats personal experience. It is worthwhile to make an active effort to attend lectures, workshops, and events, visit Indigenous communities, and engage in meaningful conversations. Often, person-to-person interactions prove to be the most influential in shaping norms, as these interactions foster relationships that are difficult to ignore. Practising active listening skills during these interactions is vital for deepening our understanding of Indigenous experiences in Canada.
- Prioritizing Indigenous knowledges through practice. As faculty members, administrators, researchers, or students, we possess powerful tools in our hands for supporting Indigenous perspectives through our teaching and learning practices, program development, research endeavours, leadership roles, and service commitments. As settlers, we have a responsibility to help create supportive environments for Indigenous students, staff, and scholars by advocating for the availability of resources, mentorship

programs, scholarships, and culturally relevant services. We have the means and access to promote and elevate Indigenous voices and perspectives within the university context, whether in meetings, conversations, classrooms, or interactions with various stakeholders. This may involve supporting Indigenous-led initiatives and projects, participating in curriculum development, incorporating territorial land acknowledgment in our course outlines, and incorporating materials authored by Indigenous scholars into course curricula.

- Engaging in policy change. Advancing institutional policy change is a critical aspect among settler responsibilities. This involves questioning, challenging, and changing the norms grounding our institutional policies and practices that sustain colonialism and perpetuate inequity within the university operations. These efforts encompass advocating for the recruitment of Indigenous faculty, promoting Indigenous representation in university decision-making processes, establishing programmatic cohorts for Indigenous students, and facilitating the growth of Indigenous departments or research centres. It is important to contribute to the creation of an institutional climate where Indigenous individuals can see themselves as integral to university operations and where both students and faculty feel valued and safe in expressing their perspectives and opinions.

- Participating in settler advocacy. As an ally, we need to stand in solidarity with Indigenous peoples, supporting their rights, and advocating for equitable and just treatment. This can be done by making an effort through everyday interactions to openly challenge institutional and societal structures, decisions, and practices that persist in marginalizing Indigenous experiences. When feasible, we can actively engage with local Indigenous communities and build relationships rooted in ethicality, respect, and reciprocity. An important aspect of advocacy work is engaging in critical conversations with one's own non-Indigenous community members to share perspectives, insights, and knowledge. Since knowledge is socially constructed and interactions with others play a pivotal role in this process, such conversations may provide an important mechanism for influencing norms beyond academia.

Our position as settlers is delicate, as our goodwill can be easily misunderstood or even rejected. This is understandable, as the intergenerational harm inflicted upon Indigenous communities is not easy to mend. While our focus is on empowering Indigenous voices, we must be mindful not to overstep boundaries by inadvertently silencing these voices when attempting to speak in support of Indigenous perspectives. Mistakes are inevitable, but it is crucial to approach them with the spirit of respect, mutual understanding, and ethicality, and to learn from these experiences.

Ethical Considerations

Ethicality is paramount when engaging with Indigenous communities in research. Centring on ethicality helps to disrupt colonial relations in research and support the spirit of respect, relevance, reciprocity, and responsibility (Kirkness & Barnhardt, 1991). Ownership, Control, Access, and Possession (OCAP) principles, developed by First Nations communities, assert that research data should remain with Indigenous communities. OCAP serves as a decolonizing framework, securing accountability and ethicality in the research process. The Indigenous community involved in this project – Indigenous faculty members working in universities – was an organizational, not a territorial, tribal, or interest-based community. This distinction is important, as it sets standards for research ethicality, including formal Ethics procedures set by the organization (university) that I had to follow. However, as Kovach (2021) noted, there is currently limited infrastructure in Canada to fully comply with OCAP. Being bound by formal organizational procedures made following the community data ownership, access, control, and possession guidelines problematic, as there are currently no formal data repositories in universities for storing relevant data that are accessible to Indigenous communities. While I shared interview transcripts with individual participants and worked with them on the analysis, the data, as a collective, stayed with me as a researcher. My project started pre-COVID, and the interruptions caused by the global pandemic had an impact on my intentions versus lived reality, particularly on the front of collaborating with the participants in my data analysis. Instead, I had to heavily rely on the scholarship centring on Indigenous conceptual frameworks and decolonizing methodologies (e.g., Kovach, 2021; Smith, 2021; Wilson, 2008). I recognize these realities and have tried to mitigate these limitations in the writing process to the best of my knowledge, but I have also tried to make these limitations clear to my readers. The key aspect is that these barriers or limitations have been carefully considered and accounted for. While I recognize potential barriers in this complex process, I aim to share the steps that I followed to make sure the research was conducted from a place of responsibility and respect as an ongoing effort. While I followed ethicality in formal organizational protocols, consideration of ethicality started much earlier with relationship building, learning about the history, and reflecting on my own role in the research process. I am drawing on Kovach's framework – 1) researcher preparation; 2) research preparations; 3) meaning-making of gathered knowledges; and 4) reciprocity and dissemination: giving back (Kovach, 2021, pp. 54–9) – in describing my steps to ensure research ethicality.

Preparation of myself. This project grew gradually, driven by my personal experiences in academia and informal conversations that have occurred over the years with my Indigenous colleagues. I have been part of the Canadian higher education system for over fifteen years, and I have observed the institutional change occurring in academia in relation to Indigenous knowledges. During that time, I have witnessed formal discussions around Indigenous topics in departmental and faculty meetings, hiring committees, and university senate work. I also have participated in informal hallway conversations where frustration and anger have been shared with me. There were comments made towards non-Indigenous peoples to step up, start educating themselves, and stop living on Indigenous peoples' backs. I think my own positionality and lived experience with an oppressive regime has helped with this openness and with being perceived as someone who may share similar perspectives on oppression. At the same time, I have experienced some confusion on the part of my non-Indigenous colleagues, and myself, when we have been unsure of the actions needed or have had difficulties with deciding how to best support Indigenous colleagues. These encounters have led me to reflect on my role, understanding, and responsibility as someone working in a system that struggles to engage in meaningful institutional change when it comes to decolonial approaches to Indigenous knowledges. Overall, I have heard articulated the need to engage in better-informed critical learning and meaningful action. I see my small role in contributing to this by engaging with a decolonizing lens and speaking to my own people – the non-Indigenous community in higher education.

My engagement with learning about Indigenous cultural traditions began when I started my academic career at the University of Manitoba, a while before I even considered this research project. As a recent settler in Canada, I didn't have any cultural connections to Indigenous communities. The relationship formation has unfolded organically over the years. My initial preparation consisted of reading relevant literature by Indigenous authors and putting this scholarship to work in my coursework with students. I purposefully attended talks and workshops where Indigenous faculty presented on their research. Some of these included workshops on Indigenous land-based education, on cultural teachings such as the Medicine Line (Mashkiki Beshibii'igan) or Sweet Grass Braiding (Wiingashk). The cultural teachings I was most closely exposed to came from the Anishinaabe and Cree. Many of these events took place at Migizii Agamik, the Indigenous Student Centre at the University of Manitoba, which helped me to connect with both students and faculty informally following the public events. I volunteered to serve as a faculty advisor at practicum sites that allowed me to spend some time in the rural communities of Gillam and Churchill in Manitoba, which have high Indigenous populations. I also was able to visit an on-reserve school at Fox Lake Cree Nation. I made connections to the urban Indigenous youth community, attending community-initiated weekly meetings at the Bell Tower, situated in the North End of Winnipeg. In academic circles, I was looking for relevant opportunities to attend conferences and sessions on the topic of Indigenous scholarship. I joined the Canadian Association of Studies in Indigenous Education to build my knowledge further and support the work of the organization. All of these activities provided me with some exposure to and deeper insights into Indigenous history, culture, and experiences, in which the colonial reality of repressive societal structures became more and more clear to me.

Preparation of the project. Formulating the scope and nature of this research project took me a while. I initially decided to examine faculty's innovation and entrepreneurship activities, which now serve as one chapter in this book. The project organically took a different path and broader scope, which reflects my learning journey. Early preparations for the research project involved decisions over research questions, theoretical frameworks, and methodology. I am very grateful to my Indigenous colleague Professor Frank Deer, Kanienkeha'ka from Kahnawake and Canada Research Chair in Indigenous education, who was willing to support me in this process, providing insights, guidance, and direction. Frank reviewed my proposal, gently guiding me in my decisions. I did consider using Indigenous methodology (e.g., storytelling) but decided to stay in my own epistemological realm with document analysis and a narrative approach with semi-structured interviews. The project was submitted to the Indigenous Adjudication Committee for SSHRC Tri-Council funding. I received funding but also supportive feedback from the Indigenous committee members, which was a further signal to me about the importance of this work.

The next step was to gain approval from the institutional Ethics Review Board. Getting approval required several rounds of revisions, mainly concerning the recruitment process for participants and clarification on participants' veto rights in data sharing. As part of the process, I needed to delve into the Tri-Council policy statement on Ethical Conduct for Research Involving Humans (TCPS2), including training in Module A9 on Indigenous peoples, to gain deeper knowledge of the processes of conducting research ethically with Indigenous peoples. The protocol also included individual consent forms whereby potential participants were assured of their voluntary participation, anonymity, and voluntary withdrawal option. While Indigenous members serve on ethics boards, these communities are still grounded in Eurocentric intellectual knowledge frameworks, and the final decision about the suitability of a project is largely made by the dominant cultural group. With the intention to engage and support Indigenous students, I sought to hire Indigenous students to work with me. This ended up being an incredibly difficult task. I was reminded by one of my research participants: *"Something our institutions have to recognize is that our Indigenous students, that come to university, tend to be older and have more responsibilities. They've got the weight of the world on their shoulders"* (interview, December 18, 2018). That comment spoke volumes about Indigenous students' being in a survival mode in universities, not having the mental or physical capacity to take on more tasks than what's needed. I ended up hiring one Indigenous student short-term and then a non-Indigenous student from a Native studies department for a longer commitment.

The interviews took place in person over a twelve-month period in 2018–19. In approaching my research participants, I first reached out to people I knew and had already developed relationships with, communicating the nature and the purpose of my project by email. These people knew me through working together in academic settings, advisory committees, and professional organizations or through attending conferences together. In a couple of cases, I was vouched for by people who knew and trusted me and who referred me to other potential participants. I was able to connect with faculty I had had previous relationships with; those that I had not met before tended not to respond. There was one faculty member who was willing to meet with me, connecting with my Estonian identity, which aligned with their best friend's, but then decided to withdraw, citing overwhelming workload. This is where the role of relationships, trust, and previously formed connection become an apparent deciding factor in participation. As all of the interviewed faculty members were active researchers themselves, there was a certain familiarity with the process and protocols, and no one questioned or withdrew from the study at a later stage. In most cases, I sensed enthusiasm towards the project, and people were appreciative of my asking about their experiences. We often shared similar experiences, since I was relatively new to Canada and academia. In order to address the asymmetrical power relations emerging from different positionalities, I aimed to be respectful and reflective in the research process. To respect cultural protocols, I had tobacco with me and offered it as a token of appreciation when it was welcomed. I also started out the conversations by sharing my own story to partly address the power hierarchies potentially emerging in those interactions. My initial interview protocol, with pre-determined research questions, a tape recorder on the table, and required consent forms passed around, somewhat impacted the sincerity of the moment and led me to doubt the appropriateness of such an approach. Archibald (2008) described a similar experience, where she concluded that the ethical responsibility and trust towards the participants becomes more important than institutional procedures. Instead, researchers must understand the limits of the permission and not abuse the permission or knowledge received. As a result, I decided to send the consent forms with interview questions in advance and didn't press on them during the actual meeting.

Meaning-making of interviews. Ethicality (axiology as per Kovach, 2021) in meaning-making becomes particularly relevant when interpreting the thoughts or stories shared by participants grounded in Indigenous ontologies and epistemologies. As Iseke-Barnes (2009) noted, misrepresentation of stories can start dominating mainstream understandings, oversimplify Indigenous spirituality and worldview, and end up in racist representations of Indigenous peoples and stories. I became aware that, while one may be meticulous in composing transcripts or sharing summaries, the moment ideas get captured in written words, their interpretive meaning can change. When they are taken out of their cultural or political contexts, they can represent a simplistic or stereotypical way of approaching what was said. There may be layers of hidden meanings in the sharing process that can never be included in the written word. Therefore, in any research conducted by non-Indigenous researchers with Indigenous communities, there may be components that do not adhere to the true ethicality or cultural protocol that is required.

In order to be highly careful with capturing the meaning of the conversations to the best of my abilities, I learned to be purposefully flexible in allowing the conversations to go in directions that were important to the participant. That way I was able to grasp, in an unrestricted way, the context and ideas that were meaningful to the story and experience. Archibald (2008) described that as a respectful way of conducting interviews, leaving the power with the participant to say what is needed.

Immediately after the interviews, I wrote down notes relevant to the context or my thoughts that emerged during the interview. These notes included relevant events prior to the interview that may have impacted the meaning of the shared knowledge. For example, one interview was conducted shortly after the murder of Colten Boushie, which drove the conversation towards the themes of justice, fairness, and colonialism. I also documented the names or authors who were mentioned, which I researched to fully grasp the suggested meaning. I was able to engage with some of the cultural teachings my conversation partners offered to me, which further allowed me to expand on the stories that were shared with me. For example, during one of the interviews, I was offered the chance to taste a "weegas root" or "rat root," used as a traditional medicine to fight off a cold, which was bitter as hell. In another interview, I was shown a collection of incredible rock art as a cultural teaching. Through these experiences, I was able to create connection and deeper levels of understanding beyond what was being physically said. I also shared interview transcripts with my participants, offering them an opportunity for a follow-up meeting to discuss the meanings and elaborate on aspects that needed clarifications. My participants had the opportunity to remove sections of their transcripts or add information to them at a later time. I also provided them with the opportunity to highlight thoughts that they definitely wanted to be included in the book. Unfortunately, there was a significant delay due to COVID interrupting the overall workflow, including my ongoing connection with some of my research participants. Coming back post-pandemic, I was mindful not to burden my participants more than was absolutely necessary, yet to leave the door open if there was interest for further connection. I was intentional in limiting any additional mental or physical labour associated with this research, being mindful of the many sorts of service requests that Indigenous faculty are regularly bombarded with. Still, several of my participants took the chance to connect over the project post-COVID, reviewing what was said and reminiscing about their thoughts and ideas shared then. I hope my efforts to work from a place of respect and responsibility in capturing the meanings in a way that was least invasive to the participants had the results I intended.

Reciprocity and dissemination. This project taught me to let go of my initially formulated plans, theoretical perspectives, and methodologies. It also demonstrated clearly the need to shift my initial research focus away from western concepts of institutional change and to dig much deeper into the colonial structures of academia. This research was part of my personal growth process to reframe my Eurocentric perspectives, situate myself within a decolonial reality, deconstruct the dominant norms that academia has been operating on, and start anew. I think the decolonial lens in this project has allowed the reciprocity in my work to come forward and support my meaningful engagement as a non-Indigenous ally.

Results from this research have been disseminated through appropriate scholarly venues, such as academic journals and conferences, in which I have applied a decolonial lens and advocated for further criticality in decolonizing work related to higher education. I am making an intentional effort to incorporate the knowledge I have gained into my course contents to align better with the idea of education being the core mechanism of transformative change. I try to be intentional in taking on graduate students with Indigenous backgrounds and participating in advisory committees on the topic, if asked or invited. Knowledge hierarchies can only change if we are examining the political processes and interrupting white, non-Indigenous spaces in a meaningful way. I agree with Aveling's (2013) statement that, for non-Indigenous researchers, engaging with Indigenous knowledge means primarily constructing conditions of support that help with efforts of Indigenous self-determination. After all, decolonial work supporting Indigenous knowledges should not be left only on the shoulders of Indigenous peoples.

Styres (2017) noted that the creation of ethical spaces is a journeying process that begins by making a conscious and at times uncomfortable decision to move into unfamiliar territory. Ethical spaces that occur through purposeful journeying directly lead us to consider and shift previously held assumptions and paradigms. It's a learning process that is not fixed but rather fluid and interconnected, continually evolving and changing. Haig-Brown (2010, p. 927) called this process "deep learning" about the cultural protocol, language, and historic and social context through relationships and collaboration with people developed over time. In my case, this learning process is only starting to unfold and continues beyond this book.

Participants

Ten participants in the study were working as either tenured or tenure-track academics in universities across four different provinces – Alberta, Manitoba, Ontario, and Saskatchewan. Nine identified as Indigenous peoples of Canada and one noted Indigenous ancestry. The participants described their membership in relation to the following: Anishinaabe, Cree, Haudenosaunee, Mohawk, Ojibway, and Métis. I am intentional about not revealing the specific tribal affiliations that my participants represented, or the specific universities involved, as this might compromise their anonymity. One of the participants has passed away since the interview, and one has now retired. At the time of the interviews, all participants worked in 15 research-intensive universities (often referred to as U15). There were two participants who shared their experiences with working in both the university and the college sector. At the time of the interviews, five participants had recently (within the past year or two) started a tenure-track appointment at the rank of assistant professor and five held tenured appointments at either the associate or full professor rank. All participants worked in the fields of social sciences and humanities – more specifically in education, social work, kinesiology, and sociology. Two of my participants held formal leadership roles in their universities that allowed them to provide perspectives on the leadership aspect of institutional changes. All of the participants were actively involved in various kinds of committee work at the faculty or university level, which formed a significant part of their workload. While one of my research participants was potentially open about revealing their name in the book, in the interest of coherence, I decided not to attach specific names to the quotes but rather use interview dates instead.

Decolonial Methodology

I situate my work methodologically within the qualitative paradigm of the western intellectual tradition, applying a decolonizing lens to my research methodology. Kovach (2021, p. 31) noted that western qualitative research is relational and interpretive and, thus, can offer "a bridge for understanding" of Indigenous paradigm. As a non-Indigenous researcher, I have realized that I am not in a position to engage with Indigenous methodologies, as these require Indigenous epistemologies that form a barrier to non-Indigenous researchers. Some say that non-Indigenous researchers should not be involved in Indigenist research at all (Aveling, 2013). Others believe that it's not a question of identity but of the nature of the research and the research methodologies used (Haig-Brown, 2010; Kovach, 2021). Kovach (2021) stated that not all Indigenous-focused research requires Indigenous methodologies. However, the danger of applying western theoretical and methodological approaches is that they may generate work that subsumes all Indigenous knowledges within the dominant Eurocentric frameworks, perpetuating the same hierarchies of knowledge that one is fighting against. This is where decolonizing methodologies become essential.

A decolonizing methodology is needed because it focuses on Indigenous–settler relationships and seeks to interrogate the power that continues to marginalize Indigenous peoples through ongoing colonialism and the dispossession of lands (Nicoll, 2004). There are invisible power dynamics embedded in research with Indigenous groups, and critical decolonial approaches may help to break down such hierarchical barriers. A decolonizing approach also helps to bring to light the non-European epistemes that are necessary to reconceptualize the western notion of what counts as valid knowledge in the higher education context. Smith (2021) argued that decolonizing methodologies allow for deeper thinking about the roles that knowledge, knowledge production, knowledge hierarchies, and knowledge institutions play in decolonization and social transformation, and thus they may trigger learning and change. Thambinathan and Kinsella (2021, p. 3) proposed and described four approaches that I used as a qualitative non-Indigenous researcher framing my work within decolonizing methodologies: (1) exercising critical reflexivity, (2) reciprocity and respect for self-determination, (3) embracing "Other(ed)" ways of knowing, and (4) embodying a transformative praxis. Decolonial methodology requires that a researcher is constantly aware of their own biases as a means of consistently locating themselves in their research (Battiste, 2013a). A positionality statement is one small part of it. Critical reflexivity needs to be carried out throughout the whole research process, including theorizing and data analysis. Addressing ingrained power dynamics and reflecting on my own role in the research process helped me to move towards a process of learning that shaped my theorizing and data analysis approaches. Battiste (2000) noted that decolonizing research means centring the work on community voices in the research process through listening. Listening also implies accountability and active commitment to growth that goes past this research project. I try to activate this aspect in my book (particularly Part I) but also in my everyday teaching, student advising, and service engagements. Embracing other ways of knowing means re-imagining how we construct, produce, and value knowledge and considering how such work may subscribe to the dominant discourse of the other, shaped by imperial and colonial ideologies. Respecting participants' cultural protocols is an important consideration in this process. The work of Jimmy et al. (2019) provides a starting point for universities and non-Indigenous individuals in terms of their roles and responsibilities in this journey towards institutional change. The authors highlighted braiding as a promising approach that would help to establish harmony between two epistemologically and ontologically different knowledge systems. Braiding is premised on respecting the continued internal integrity of both sides that would open opportunities for a continuous journey towards engagement and collaboration. The authors also mentioned the importance of developing the stamina, flexibility, and humility to sustain collaborations and relationships through difficulties associated with long-term work on colonial legacies from both sides. A transformative approach to research involves reflexivity, community engagement, reciprocity, and action. It opens spaces in academia for decolonizing research, methods, practice, and discussion.

This book builds on extensive document analysis (institutional academic plans, Indigenization strategies, government statistics, media reports, and news articles) and features specific examples of change as shared through the stories of Indigenous individuals (faculty members) working in various Canadian universities. For my interview method, I started out with a semi-structured interview protocol, but, as noted earlier, it changed organically to a narrative conversational approach, which better suited the knowledge epistemologies of my research participants. The conversational method found in Indigenous methodology is different, as it is linked to tribal knowledge and situated within an Indigenous paradigm (Kovach, 2010). In my work, conversation is understood as a non-structured method of gathering knowledge that combines reflection, story, and dialogue, allowing for the participants to guide their experience (Kovach, 2010), but it emerges from the western paradigm. A conversational narrative approach is characterized by relationality, which is a pillar of the Indigenous paradigm and is helpful when engaging with research involving Indigenous participants. In these conversations, I was intentional about honouring the values of respect, relevancy, reciprocity, and responsibility as part of my ongoing efforts to remain ethical in research.

For analysis, I did use thematic analysis of the interview transcripts, drawing themes that were relevant to the various chapters of the book. I was mindful in considering the Indigenous conceptual framework described by Kovach (2021, p. 47) focusing on 1) Indigenous Epistemology (beliefs about knowledge creation); 2) Indigenous Ethics (axiological premises); 3) Indigenous Community (land and place); and 4) Experiencing Self in Relationship. This framework allowed me to pull focus on the themes that were relevant to self-determination, which forms a focal point of such work. Guided by the suggestions of my participants but also by the writing of Iseke-Barnes (2009), who reminded authors that, by privileging some aspects of the story and dismissing others, they decide which parts of a culture are admissible into the mainstream readership and which are not, I decided to include a range of quotes that were directly relevant to the Indigenous conceptual framework featured in Part I of the book. These themes focusing on the idea of change towards self-determination are foundational for Indigenous communities. As it stands, this section allows these quotes to speak for themselves. This facilitates a personal relationality and meaning-making process between the participant and the reader, creating connection and relationship that allow readers to learn from the participants and take the wisdom from the quotes that speak individually to them based on where they are in their learning journey. Other quotes shared across the chapters were selected based on the importance that I assigned to them in relation to the chapter topics. I am mindful that my personal lens is biased, and my interpretations might not have grasped the full extent of the meaning shared with me. I would like readers to be aware of that.

Terminology

A section on terminology is necessary in this book to provide a better introduction to the language used. For example, the term "Indigenous" is used broadly to denote individuals who self-identify as First Nation, Métis, or Inuit of Canada, recognizing that no individual Indigenous experience is similar to another and that there are major differences between and among Indigenous peoples. I also use "peoples" intentionally in the plural. From a decolonizing perspective, it is important to respect the diversity of the over 60 different Indigenous nations in Canada, which enrich our society with their languages and cultures. However, as Kuokkanen (2007a), Battiste (2000), and others have pointed out, it is also important to recognize that Indigenous peoples share the experiences of colonialism, as well as fundamental values and ways of viewing the world. I use the term "Indigenous knowledges" in the plural to acknowledge the shared commonalities but also differences across Indigenous ways of knowing and being. I am avoiding using the term "aboriginal" in this book, as it has often been associated with deficit-based perspectives in policy work and scholarly literature. My attempt is to move away from this language and support the use of the word "Indigenous" instead. The term "aboriginal" is used only when it is included in the original titles of policy documents, scholarly writings, or program titles or when participants used it in their reflections. An important distinction is made between the words "western" and "Eurocentric." "Western" is used in contrast to "Indigenous" to distinguish two fundamentally different epistemologies and ontologies of knowledge. "Eurocentrism" in this book is a used as a value-based term, denoting the inherent bias and dominance of power in mainstream knowledge systems that stem from historically favoured western civilizations. It denotes attitudes, behaviours, and normative beliefs that frame mainstream knowledge as the superior knowledge system in society.

Purpose and Organization of the Book

There are three main reasons why I wrote this book. *First,* this book is guided by the intention to highlight the power of Indigenous knowledges, which remain on the sidelines of mainstream higher education spaces. There is a need to create a stronger narrative to balance the dominant storyline about institutional equity in relation to Indigenous knowledges featured by higher education institutions and the media. In this book, I share a decolonizing perspective that centres the role of Indigenous faculty in working from within towards structural change in higher education. This book is intended to make a contribution to the realm of higher education by highlighting the daily work of Indigenous individuals in shifting institutional norms in Canadian universities. *Second,* there is a personal responsibility involved. I have been gifted with conversations where personal stories have been shared with me in the hopes of supporting learning from these experiences. As such, I feel responsibility for taking action by sharing the message among non-Indigenous people to work together to strengthen and promote institutional change embedded in Indigenous perspectives. This responsibility comes from what I have learned in this process and from my engagement with Indigenous faculty. Indigenous individuals are still directly dependent on the knowledge hierarchies and institutional structures in academia that shape their experiences. It is our place as non-Indigenous researchers to create conditions that would allow these hierarchies to break down and eventually lead to a broader structural and systemic change in academia. *Third,* as a professor in the area of educational administration, I am painfully aware of the limited scholarly literature on this topic. As such, this volume provides an analytical approach to examining the current changes in the higher education sector driven by Indigenous peoples and their knowledges. The book is intended to be used as a conversation starter in university classes around Indigenous knowledges and organizational change. The purpose of the book is to provide theoretical insights into the processes of institutional change from decolonial perspectives and to examine the colonial structures creating ongoing struggles for many. Furthermore, the book takes a strength-based perspective, aiming to highlight the work and resilience of Indigenous individuals to challenge the traditional functions, delivery, and purpose of academia, gradually transforming Canadian higher education. The voices of Indigenous individuals carry the reader through the book while they share their personal perspectives on institutional change.

The central argument of this book is that the emergence of Indigenous knowledges in Canadian higher education has materialized in significant institutional change. The change has not occurred solely as a result of the altruistic efforts of universities to accommodate diverse needs or do the responsible, equitable thing by Indigenous peoples. The change has occurred because of gradual and persistent work on the part of Indigenous communities – faculty members, students, staff, knowledge keepers, and community members at large. This book argues that every individual and their effort has mattered and made a difference in the normative change occurring in higher education today. Daily acts, whether they have been perceived as little victories in impacting the thinking of particular students or as larger gains in decision-making structure or as even individual failures against a rigid system, have been meaningful and mattered. The change has often been manifested as smaller changes in local contexts that often get overlooked and left unnoticed. However, ultimately those little steps carve a path towards systemic and structural shift in institutions that have been resistant to change. The book is about identifying, illuminating, and drawing attention to these individual episodes that have created a foundation for a bigger momentum occurring in Canadian higher education.

This book is divided into two parts. Part I contains a selection of quotes by Indigenous faculty addressing the values grounded in Indigenous experience around self-determination. The purpose of this section is to highlight individual lived experiences through personal voices and to show how a different, parallel storyline may exist next to mainstream educational narratives within the structures of the university. Guided by an Indigenous conceptual framework (as per Kovach, 2021) and organized around the four main themes of 1) prioritizing decolonization, 2) returning control, 3) rebuilding capacity, and 4) connecting to land, the core values of Indigenous self-determination get captured. This section of the book creates a personal relationship between the reader and the participants through their perspectives and voices. This section provides an opportunity to reflect on these voices and learn from them.

Part II is composed of nine chapters, each focusing on a distinct aspect of Indigenous knowledges in relation to institutional change. The part starts with an overview of the Canadian university as a colonial construct to set the stage for the critical decolonial approach in this book. The chapter on Indigenous knowledges focuses on the knowledge politics that create the power hierarchies shaping work in academia. The chapter on theoretical perspectives presents the theoretical underpinnings of institutional change from decolonizing perspectives. The chapter argues that Indigenous peoples, drawing from Indigenous knowledges, have managed to create pressures that affect normative beliefs in organizations, leading to transformations in individual attitudes and collective norms. The chapter introduces a decolonial framework that may guide institutional efforts in working with systematic change embedded in learning processes. The next chapter discusses changes in institutional governance structures and developments of policy frameworks (hiring and employment, admissions and programming). Institutional climate is essential in transformative change, and the following chapter discusses key strides made on that front. Aspects like territorial and land acknowledgments, cultural ceremonies, the involvement of Elders and knowledge keepers, and the nature of physical spaces on campus are discussed from a critical perspective. In this chapter, the disconnect between the featured organizational norms and actual lived experiences is emphasized. The next chapter focuses on the role of Indigenous teaching pedagogies in higher education settings. The chapter also provides an overview of the developments in Indigenous programming and issues emerging from mandatory coursework requirements, sharing faculty perspectives on the topic. The next chapter discusses changes in research practices. The chapter focuses on the issues around ownership and control of research data and ethical codes for conducting research with Indigenous communities. The next chapter reveals Indigenous perspectives on innovation, which has largely been an overlooked area of scholarly research. The chapter problematizes the mainstream understandings of innovation and points out how Indigenous innovation should be approached from a learning perspective that focuses one's gaze on past histories. The final chapter draws together the key ideas presented in this book. This concluding chapter emphasizes the main argument for the power of Indigenous knowledges by highlighting successes and summarizing the gains made in Canadian academia. The chapter ends by providing some perspectives for institutions to consider when moving forward on the path towards broader structural and systemic change in Canadian higher education. Overall, the book highlights the idea powerfully proposed by Absolon and Willett (2004), whereby Indigenous peoples have survived and continue to thrive as peoples while their knowledges evolve, including in higher education spaces.

PART I

Empowering Quotes

These empowering quotes were shared by research participants and go beyond the materials included in the chapters. These thoughts form a necessary starting point of reflection for the reader when considering the need for institutional change. Guided by the foundations of the Indigenous Conceptual Framework (see Kovach, 2021), the quotes bring forward Indigenous voices and experiences organized around four central themes: prioritizing decolonization, returning control, rebuilding capacity, and connecting to one's roots. These quotes also centre on the active ground-up advocacy efforts towards self-determination that often have been overshadowed or silenced in the processes of institutional change in Canadian higher education.

Prioritizing Decolonization: Perspectives on Power, Voice, and Advocacy

HAVING AGENCY AND INITIATING CHANGE

We've pushed people to think ... we've been the environmental consciousness. We've been the spiritual consciousness. We've been the cultural consciousness. We've been the consciousness of what happened through colonization – decolonizing consciousness. (Interview, 9 March 2018)

I'm like the horse fly. I'm always bugging the system, bugging them to be more inclusive, to bring Indigenous perspectives, to bring an increased Indigenous presence – bodies of people who have Indigenous knowledges, backgrounds, and heritages – through any work I've done at university. (Interview, 9 March 2018)

There is a resurgence of Indigenous knowledge as a voice, which I think has pushed the politics. /... / I think the TRC has also raised voices in regards to that. (Interview, 3 December 2018)

I believe in working with diplomacy, I believe in being diplomatic and tactical, but I also believe in being bold, and direct, and saying what needs to be said. (Interview, 9 March 2018)

I don't take a lot of those things personally – I never have – but I will challenge things more head-on than I would in the past. (Interview, 9 March 2018)

Now we're in a different era, and a different way right now. Do I think it's going to last? No, I don't, but I think there will be good advances made. There will be another place that we sit in terms of how Canadians see Indigenous peoples. It's going to be a different place, a good place. (Interview, 10 April 2019)

When Indigenous people have been allowed to, you know, have some input, there's some good things that come out. But, there's always the non-Indigenous side that's fighting with Indigenous people. Indigenous people have to fight, even just to have a seat at the table in most instances. Even on our own lands! (Interview, 18 December 2018)

I always say, it's like that old saying, "If you're not part of the solution, then you're part of the problem." So, we can't just sit back, you know, write about things, unless we're really willing to make a change. (Interview, 22 November 2018)

THE DESTRUCTIVE POWER OF COLONIALISM

A lot of people look at Indigenous issues – even the term "Indigenous issues" could be problematic – but people [are] looking at the high rate of Indigenous children in care, high rate of Indigenous people in the prison system, and not realizing that the problem is with those systems themselves. But from an Indigenous perspective and a non-Indigenous perspective, those high rates are a problem. Is it the Indigenous problem or the colonial problem? (Interview, 14 February 2018)

Residential schools definitely broke the ties between generations. And we had people who came out of those schools broken, not speaking their language, [with an] inability to communicate with the generations before them. But, I think, that's slowly coming back. There's a resurgence in that. (Interview, 18 December 2018)

From an Indigenous perspective, the power of colonization has been very destructive, obviously, to our cultures. And the driving rationale is to not let that continue, is to not let ongoing colonization occur within the society. And I think it's a very, very lofty and difficult task, but I think it's necessary if we want to not repeat the past. We have to understand that that was a process that is still ongoing today. In order to be better and do better, we have to critique what's going on now so as to then not keep repeating it. (Interview, 4 December 2018)

I said, to me, that's normal – making people feel uncomfortable, or they're choosing to be uncomfortable with what I bring into the knowledge: stuff around white privilege, around critical thinking, pedagogy, which calls us to be mindful about who we are and our social identities, and what privileges we hold or [do] not hold in society, and how society views us. (Interview, 9 March 2018)

I came to know who I am as an Indigenous person through university. Because, when I was a young person, growing up in care, I was ashamed about being Indigenous. /... / It wasn't until I was in university, when I started to study the effects of colonization on Indigenous people, where I saw my family reflected in that understanding that I came to know. (Interview, 18 December 2018)

I'm standing in my truth. I'm a little upset because there were things taken away from me, as a young person. My language. (Interview, 12 December 2018)

We've experienced this [colonization] for 500 years. Others, they're just coming into it. So, we have a lot to offer ... When we go places and we talk about our experiences, we can tell people what to avoid, you know, or what to look for, or these types of things – what you don't want to happen. (Interview, 22 November 2018)

Sharing Power

And, really, all the institutions that exist in Canada should incorporate Indigenous ways of knowing, being, and doing. And that means moving over and sharing power. So, that's a pretty hard concept for people to digest. (Interview, 18 December 2018)

If you want to share knowledge, you have to make space for our knowledge, as well. So, if you can take away our land, at least, you know, make some space to include our knowledge in your university curriculums, and it's going to impact everyone. (Interview, 18 December 2018)

Any time things shift and power shifts, all of a sudden, people want to be part of that. So, we do have a piece of that that's happening, where I think people claim some Indigenous heritage. This is a place where I can get monies, I can get some status. And so there's a lot of identity politics around funding. (Interview, 3 December 2018)

If they [university administration] want the community to take us seriously, we need to have meaningful partnerships, whereby they have actual power, where the university itself is not holding all the power. And the Indians are, of course, you know, fumbling around, trying to scramble around, trying to fit into the system. (Interview, 14 February 2018)

Moving Forward Together

We have to understand many things about each other, but I don't have an exclusive view of it. I don't think it just stops at Indigenous peoples. I think, in order for this country to be strong, we have to understand each other, period. (Interview, 10 April 2019)

The moment we're honest with ourselves that it's the same darn world and that both philosophically and in terms of mutual respect, we're in the same bloody boat and we park the tribalism, I think we'll be better off. (Interview, 9 March 2018)

There is tension within the Indigenous community on campus about how, you know, do you work with the institution and try and make change, or you just continually critique it from the outside and hope you can blow it up and start over again? (Interview, 3 December 2018)

Decolonizing is a big part of our journey here. You and I can decolonize – okay, I shouldn't do it by myself. You should also do it. All of my students should do it. Everybody in this faculty should do it. (Interview, 9 March 2018)

My understanding of broader issues related to power and dynamics and social issues has evolved. Whenever I get frustrated around someone, when I see someone who is not quite understanding, or has the same understanding, I always have to remember that I was at that point at one point in my life as well. (Interview, 4 December 2018)

I encourage students to consider shifting their paradigms from primarily western-dominant privileged frameworks, to be inclusive of Aboriginal Indigenous frameworks, and to recognize the difference and recognize also the overlap – there are spaces of overlap and things that come together. (Interview, 9 March 2018)

Non-Indigenous people have to learn to be a little bit more uncomfortable with the realities that we have experienced as Indigenous people because a lot of things were taken away from us. And our knowledge that exists, the knowledge that has come forward thus far, it is beautiful. (Interview, 18 December 2018)

We need more Two-Eyed Seeing. And maybe that means having two Presidents – one that represents the non-Indigenous way of seeing and one that represents the Indigenous way of seeing. (Interview, 18 December 2018)

Returning Control: Perspectives on Institutional Structures, Community, People

CONNECTING TO COMMUNITY

My heart is with my community. (Interview, 14 February 2018)

I have deficits myself, as a person who's been removed from my community. I've had to claw my way back to my community, basically, you know, to re-establish relationships with family members, and there's still, there's still a long way to go, right. Because non-Indigenous systems have been pretty effective in disconnecting Indigenous people from family, community, culture, language, land. (Interview, 12 December 2018)

There are pockets across this country of [Indigenous] communities who have gotten it together, beaten poverty, which really sucks many communities down into a morass that is very difficult to get out of. But there are a lot of lights across this country that I think really demonstrate that communities are making on their own terms. Not really necessarily how other people want or expect, but what's important to their communities. (Interview, 10 April 2019)

There's people out there doing very creative and innovative things despite the obstacles and the challenges, and I think we can't say, well, like many of my students, "I didn't get band funded, so I'm not going to university." Ehhh, heard of student loans? Man, you go and get a student loan in the first year, and you go back to your community and say, "You know what, I took on this personal expense. I have skin in the game. I'm really serious about going to school, and I sure hope my community is going to support me in doing this." ... So, if you are interested in it, you will do it, you will do whatever it takes. If there is support, not support, you will find a way, because it's important. (Interview, 10 April 2019)

Freddy [Fred] Carmichael, Gwich'in fellow, very humble, very down to earth, and he loved flying. He saw planes go by one time up in the North – he was raised on the land – and he saw a plane go by and he said, "I'm gonna fly one of those one day" [paraphrased]. He became the first Gwich'in pilot in the Northwest Territories, and he had three businesses. /... /And, what I think really made Freddy's effort memorable and an example of success was his attitude towards his community, his customers – always had a big heart, always has a big heart to the needs of the community, and supported them whenever and however he could. (Interview, 10 April 2019)

Disrupting Structures and Cycles

I think of my son, he's seen me leading a reasonably healthy life; he's never seen me drunk, or any of that. He's never gotten into that lifestyle, you know. And so, I think for him, maybe, you know, we stopped that cycle in our family, the cycle of abuse and these types of things. Trauma. (Interview, 22 November 2018)

There can't be reconciliation without justice. (Interview, 14 February 2018)

There is a student lounge now, you know, for students. The late [name of an Indigenous scholar], who was with me in education at the time, who was head of Aboriginal Student Services – they were in the basement, which was pretty damp. She fought to get the Aboriginal Student Lounge, to get them out of the basement. There should be nothing in the basement for Indigenous people, she said. (Interview, 22 November 2018)

As an Indigenous person, I've been taught the western ways of knowledge, right. But I've also been taught how to use western knowledge in a way to help benefit Indigenous people. (Interview, 12 December 2018)

I will say this, we are the ones who did change the logo [name of the university], and I know there's an ongoing fight now to change the name, [name of the team], for the sports team. But we did get the logo removed in my time, with our group. (Interview, 22 November 2018)

One day we had our department meeting, and I complimented this faculty member on this beautiful winter jacket he was wearing. It had this beautiful artwork on the bottom. So – and he knows how I feel about residential school issues, and stuff, right – so, I said, [name], I say, "I love your jacket. It's a beautiful jacket. Where'd you get it from?" He said, "Oh, my wife made it." He said, "she learned how to sew in residential school." I looked at him and I said, "Funny, I learned how to sew at home." [Laughs] I mean, what can I say, right? He's like, literally, he's trying to jab at me on how Aboriginal people learn skills in residential school that they would not have learned otherwise. I said, "Don't give me … that bunch of bullshit." You know, I said, "Don't give me that"./… / So, those are a lot of tidbits of interactions I've had. (Interview, 9 March 2018)

So, at this meeting, [name of the faulty member] pipes up. He says, "I'm doing student practicum supervision at one of the high schools." He said, "I noticed the teacher was doing this novel study on Indian in the Cupboard*." The moment he said that, my body just … and I'm waiting for the onslaught, okay. This little expression, you know. And he seemed happy; he's sharing like he knows stuff about Aboriginal community. [Laughs] He said, "I noticed that the students [were] responding, and I noticed a couple of Aboriginal students were not engaging." So, I had to say something – so I can make a choice to ignore and feel angry in the trauma of what he just said, because this happens so often, and then I thought I have to speak up. I said, "When I hear that's still happening in our modern-day school classrooms, that somebody is teaching a racist novel like* Indian in the Cupboard*, I want to give a metaphoric slap to the idea." That's exactly what I said. I said, "We have to move beyond that." I said, "If they're using it as a poor example of a novel of, you know, looking at issues around equity and justice. … " I said, "You know, Indians aren't just objects to be played with whenever you want to." So, I went on, and on, and on. So that was that.* (Interview, 9 March 2018)

ENABLING PERSPECTIVES OF STRENGTH

We need to talk about the things that we have done that we are proud of, our resilience in facing these obstacles, these challenges. And what I would add to the idea of our resilience is the story of people who have not followed the same path as everybody else, and include that in the story, so that our young people can see themselves in those stories and can see a way to move forward, to move on. (Interview, 10 April 2019)

IndSpire is an Indigenous scholarship program. They highlight national Indigenous role models every year. They have different people supporting their programs financially. By highlighting Indigenous role models across the country, I think it is important to the youth to see these role models and understand why Indigenous education is important. (Interview, 14 February 2018)

I happen to be on an Indigenous Council for SSHRC. It's an advisory council. I know that they've done a lot of work. I was shocked when I went to the meeting a couple of weeks ago in Ottawa. So, there were about eight of us, Indigenous scholars of different levels. And some of them are famous, famous. Marie Battiste is one. Jo-Ann Archibald is another. Just people I just recently used in my thesis, and it was just stunning to see them sitting there asking me questions. (Interview, 14 February 2018)

I think in my work people are very humble and don't necessarily see themselves as leaders. They don't necessarily see what they're doing is having an impact, not only in their own community, but across the board for other Indigenous communities and also for Canadians, to battle stereotypes, to combat prejudice, to shake people up, to realize that there's a lot of value in our communities and our people. (Interview, 10 April 2019)

I think the contribution we bring, in terms of changing people, shape shifting, and changing their attitudes, is a big – to me – a big transformative one. (Interview, 9 March 2018)

Rebuilding Capacity: Perspectives on Indigenous Knowledges, Healing, Scholarship, and Emphasis on Youth

On Indigenous Knowledges

It's important to understand that our knowledge is just as relevant as western knowledge. And the thing is, we haven't even tapped into all of the knowledge that Indigenous people have./… / What if, in one of those Indigenous persons, is the cure for cancer or, you know, the cure for any of the diseases that exist on this earth are in our culture? (Interview, 18 December 2018)

There is no form of Indigenous spirituality, for example, or ceremony, or even cultural gathering, that doesn't involve music or art, or both. So, it's an easy buy-in. It's interesting. It's fun. It's exciting. And, it's good information./… / I think music and art is one of the biggest fillers of the soul. (Interview, 14 February 2018)

I think it's having a mindset that believes that Indigenous knowledge is relevant – I think that's a big part of it. And not simply stories, not simply just fables, or whatever, you know, but the knowledge itself is relevant. (Interview, 22 November 2018)

I talked about that one journey, when you travel from your mind to your heart and you bring them together, when you can bring your heart and your mind together, then you're standing in your truth. (Interview, 12 December 2018)

ON REBUILDING KNOWLEDGE

Indigenous ways of knowing and being offer something different, and I think people have become intrigued about that. And, so all that, coupled with everything else that's going on around awareness around colonization, you know – let's push forward this moment in time. Yeah, there seems to be real momentum. (Interview, 4 December 2018)

There's a resurgence of our culture. It's informed by some of our Elders, who are still alive, that can share the little bit of the knowledge that they've been able to still acquire and use that in a way that builds towards evolution, a new way of understanding our culture and our people. (Interview, 12 December 2018)

I'm proud to be a part of a U15 institution that does have Indigenous scholars deliberately recruited for the purposes of causing learning in their respective disciplines, in the areas that are important to Indigenous achievement. (Interview, 9 March 2018)

Indigenous knowledge resurgence is happening at so many different levels. (Interview, 10 April 2019)

ON HEALING

Most of our ceremonial life today is based on healing, and it wasn't that big an issue, healing, because we didn't have that much to heal from. (Interview, 22 November 2018)

Humour is the other one, because you see me laughing a lot. Humour is very important because, I tell you, if I didn't have humour, I would be a basket case, somewhere at some institute. [laughs] That's what happens to a lot of our people. Yeah, they lose the humour as a healing tool, and they have a hard time laughing things off, working through some of the issues. (Interview, 9 March 2018)

He [a leader in the community] said, "We haven't actually done anything for a year as the people heal, my staff heal" [paraphrased]. And I thought, wow! To be sensitive to people, and giving them space to get back on their feet. (Interview, 10 April 2019)

ON STRENGTHENING INDIGENOUS SCHOLARSHIP

I would like to see Indigenous researchers encouraged in research, given opportunities. I think we're going to that stage right now of having lots of opportunities to do research in various ways and have it financially supported. But I also feel like we have to not fall into a trap of expecting anything, because you have to work hard. (Interview, 10 April 2019)

I've taken a different approach to kinesiology, a more physical, mental, spiritual, and emotional approach to it, you know. More holistic approach to these things. And maybe that's my contribution to the field. (Interview, 22 November 2018)

My research agenda is associated with Indigenous languages. I am studying public schools' success and initiatives in the area of Indigenous language education, which is becoming more and more a topic in the public sector. I am studying Cree language issues in the North and community initiative in those areas. I am also interested in spirituality and religion, how it relates to language and Indigenous peoples, generally speaking. (Interview, 9 March 2018)

I don't know whether my research was completely original because, again, it was such a process of coming to know – coming to know myself but then also coming to know the literature and coming to know the ideas that were out there. (Interview, 4 December 2018)

Success for me has been the fact that I could give public presentations, talk to Indigenous entrepreneurs across the country about what they're doing in their communities, and how it's important, what impacts they have seen. Also, the opportunity to share in my classes some of the case studies that I have come across in my research, so that students are more sensitive to the nature of Indigenous economies – the fact that it actually exists is important. Many Canadians aren't aware of the level, the complexity, the breadth, the depth of activity that is going on in Canada. (Interview, 10 April 2019)

One that's important to me and that I think most about in the work that I do is a retelling of history being brought to non-Indigenous people. That's the kind of work I engage in, and that, I think, I find the most rewarding. (Interview, 23 November 2018)

In a school, the principal is saying, "The big problem with our language is we don't have books. We don't have any books, and so our kids can't learn the language." I said, "Well, what did we do for 10,000 years?" You know, that's how our minds have been imperialized by western education. We can't even think outside of the context of a book to teach our kids language, when it's been spoken for, you know, 10,000 years, or something, you know. (Interview, 22 November 2018)

On Building Capacity among the Youth

Young people need to have that support and that vision to see that they are capable of making change because that's what we've always done, and we have not all done it the same way. That's part of why we survived – we've done it in ways that made sense where we were. (Interview, 10 April 2019)

I am always drawing on Justice Murray Sinclair's words that education is the key to reconciliation, and I strongly feel that way because I feel that the students in the courses we are teaching will be educating the future leaders. (Interview, 14 February 2018)

I think, for me, in education, we have the best possible place to change people in their thinking through because we're in education. We have the framework to do that, right. So, I use it to the best way possible. (Interview, 9 March 2018)

In interesting, more subtle ways, Indigenous students come and speak to me about issues, and I … what I really do like, I like the networking that is happening now./… / It's starting to create a synergy where I actually meet more people and know more people, and that's a good thing, but, I mean, it can bring more things your way, as well. (Interview, 23 November 2018)

Something our institutions have to recognize is that our students, our Indigenous students that come to university, tend to be older, and our Indigenous students tend to have more responsibilities. They've got the weight of the world on their shoulders. (Interview, 18 December 2018)

INNOVATIVE EXAMPLES

There are people who work in making Indigenous video games. I think there's one that's really beautiful called **Never Alone,** *made by a group out of Alaska. I bought it for my kids, and it's actually one of the traditional stories being retold. The character is a little boy who is running through a storm, and then his dog, or his wolf, is running with him throughout the game. It's a beautiful game.* (Interview, 23 November 2018)

Jarrett Martineau on the radio, who is able to blend the traditional with the very new – and you see what's being done in music as well, and all kinds of things – so, he plays a music on CBC Radio that's … it's quite a vast and diverse blend of traditional to contemporary, and different genres of music that are being made by Indigenous peoples. (Interview, 23 November 2018)

I've talked with some people around – you know, the areas that a lot of Indigenous people were interested in initially were social work, education, nursing, because those are the people that, you know, came into the communities, and people aspired to that. I actually think that those [professions] are going to start to decrease. Now it's going to be, you know, the entrepreneurs, the scientists, and things like that. (Interview, 3 December 2018)

Connecting to Roots: Perspectives on Identity, Community, Relationships, and Land

EXAMINING INDIGENEITY

So, where Indigenous peoples can carve their own space and innovate with free rein, without having to worry as much about majority society's perceptions of what Indigeneity is, that's what I like the most. (Interview, 23 November 2018)

In the late 60s/70s, an Elder would say something, and you would take that and you would hold onto it verbatim, you know, as complete truth. And you wouldn't explore anything else. And I find this generation is much more inquisitive now, and they're willing to challenge, you know, in a sense, some of the doctrine that had been taught. (Interview, 22 November 2018)

We have a romanticized notion of Indigeneity, but it's that old one from pre-contact times. The really existing Indigenous peoples nowadays are seen as culturally contaminated. They're the disappointment. You don't live up to our ideals of Indigeneity … / …/ There's that backlash and that kind of scrutiny that comes from a non-Indigenous society. It's something that can actually harm the feeling of security one gets, to allow for a culture change and cultural discussions. (Interview, 23 November 2018)

As Indigenous people, we are not stuck in time. Our culture is not frozen. It evolves with every generation, you know, so, even though Indigenous, some of our knowledge has been broken, there is still a lot of knowledge that is still here. Like, it went underground for a bit, right, because it was outlawed to practise. So, there is a lot of protection of some of that information. (Interview, 18 December 2018)

I grew up with nothing. I didn't grow up in poverty, but I didn't grow up middle-class, that's for darn sure. I grew up with my language. I grew up going to the longhouse. I grew up amongst Indigenous people, so what have I missed? What do other people know that I don't? I don't know. (Interview, 9 March 2018)

EXPERIENCING LANGUAGE LOSS

Residential schools definitely broke the ties between generations. We had people who came out of those schools broken, not speaking their language, [with an] inability to communicate with the generations before them. (Interview, 18 December 2018)

When my mother was alive, we spoke our language./ … / We spoke Ojibwe. I know some words, but I don't speak because I haven't had – as a child separated from my community and my family, you don't have a chance to speak. (Interview, 18 December 2018)

Indigenous people who come to our university are trying to keep our culture alive through language. So, they [universities] offer language courses. Those are fundamentally important to our people. (Interview, 18 December 2018)

My grandparents had those experiences they don't talk about much, for being called the dirty Indian or dirty half Indian and what have you. So keeping the language alive wasn't a ... wasn't a priority. In fact, language was something that they just kind of kept hidden. (Interview, 24 November 2018)

I speak Kanyen'kéha, but I'm losing it quickly because I have nobody to talk to. (Interview, 9 March 2018)

Reclaiming One's Identity

For a lot of our Indigenous people, when they make that connection between who they are as an individual, all the harms that were done to Indigenous people, and how it impacts them – when they reconnect with knowledge, they become a more whole person. And their successes are all that much more possible because they've reconnected their spirit with who they are as an Indigenous person. (Interview, 12 December 2018)

Many Indigenous people are trying to get back to themselves. We're trying to find who we were again because we've lost our way. We've lost our way. (Interview, 14 February 2018)

There's a saying that that's the longest journey you can take is from your head to your heart. And, quite often, a lot of people only think with their head, I mean, especially in universities. We're taught to think with our head, and we often disregard our heart and our emotions, right. (Interview, 18 December 2018)

If we are operating from the perspective that you are only Indigenous if you go into the lodge, which means you participate in ceremony and you are traditional, I think that hinders the reality of who we are as Indigenous people. I remember Satsan Herb George, from the West Coast. He's the head of, I think it's Indigenous Governance Centre something. Anyway, I met him; we were at a presentation, I think at York University. One of the things that he shared was, he said, "We need to tell a different story." (Interview, 10 April 2019)

I love hearing people's stories. There's lessons that come out of these stories that they share with us. And the beauty is in the person finding that lesson for themselves. /... / I think, in the process [of storytelling], they come to a better understanding of themselves. (Interview, 18 December 2018)

Identity Struggles

My thinking is primarily, socially and Indigenously, Cree. When I start shift-ing how I use words, I know I'm thinking in Cree – my Cree is leading. It's how we end up using language and how we talk about certain things. So, in that sense, I'm in that third space. I'm not 100% Indigenous, Cree, as long as I'm speaking English, talking about plucking feathers off a goose in English. So, that's the tension. So, I think a lot of Indigenous people live in both worlds and in this in-between space. (Interview, 9 March 2018)

Respecting Land

These lands made us who we are. (Interview, 18 December 2018)

My social interaction and development has been Cree-based and land-based. / ... / Indigenous people have primacy on this land, this territory. / ... / So for someone suddenly to realize that the land that they live on has been stolen and taken is not a comfortable feeling. They're going to resist that. I get it. (Interview, 9 March 2018)

If you don't respect Indigenous people, how will you respect the environment, because we are the environment, we are the land. (Interview, 9 March 2018)

Using tobacco is for praying, for showing gratitude, for giving thanks, you know, to acknowledge the reciprocity of what the land gives us and what the Earth gives us – that we just don't willy-nilly accept it, or take it for granted, because the moment you take something for granted, you forget the initial value of it, of our health and well-being and sustenance. (Interview, 9 March 2018)

When I go and I pick rocks, I put tobacco down. I thank the earth because – this is a piece of Mother Earth sitting on my desk. They're millions of years old, and they have spirit. And I only pick rocks when I get – I feel the spirit in that rock. (Interview, 18 December 2018)

A lot of these kids who have been in care, they've never stepped foot in these lands. So, if someone was, say, from Peguis First Nations, they're a member of

Peguis, but they have never actually been to that community. So, I found that really interesting, that disconnection of young people from land. (Interview, 18 December 2018)

My father wanted to continue farming even though he was a teacher, so we always actually kept the land, and he was happy to keep and have land and have cattle in the same … on the same farm where my mother grew up. (Interview, 23 November 2018)

Building Relationships

It's good to develop relationships. And that's really important. That's what we teach in our program, is that relationships are key to everything that you do and relationships are sacred. (Interview, 18 December 2018)

I'm separated from all the people that are important that would have probably helped if I had stronger relationships with my family, but I didn't. (Interview, 12 December 2018)

We need those relationships to develop between non-Indigenous academics with our Indigenous populations. /… / And, so, we need to bridge the knowledge between Indigenous people and non-Indigenous institutions. (Interview, 12 December 2018)

PART II

Colonialism and University

We have to agree that our schools have been very colonial by Christianizing, Europe-anizing, Englishizing. I really have a hard time with the ongoing colonization, push-ing, converting, trying to convert my people. It's a painful history and presence of colonization.

(Interview, 9 March 2018)

It is imperative to start the conversation on Indigenous knowledges in Canadian higher education by examining the broader context of set-tler colonialism and its ongoing impact on Indigenous communities. Without examining the conditions of coloniality, it would be difficult to understand the increasing calls from Indigenous scholars for radical transformations of higher education (Andreotti de Oliveira et al., 2015; Battiste, 2001; Simpson, 2016; Tuck & Yang, 2012). It is widely acknowl-edged that higher education institutions play a key role in a country's social and economic development. Through research and innovative knowledge creation, universities and colleges secure trained profession-als for Canada, support the country's economic competitiveness, and improve overall well-being for people in Canada. While upholding the Canadian socio-economic system, universities simultaneously sustain the nation-state's laws, policies, and other informal structures of power. While these structures of authority may seem appropriate and uncon-tested, they have been highly oppressive to the Indigenous peoples of Canada, removing them from their lands, diminishing the value of their knowledges, and erasing any opportunities to reclaim sovereignty. Tak-ing control and forcibly exploiting resources are practices of colonialism that universities are part of and continue to perpetuate as ongoing sites of colonial domination. This may be an unsettling reality, as colonial-ism typically tends to be associated with past historical conquests by European empires, events that happened a long time ago. Canadians are used to enjoying the image of their country as a friendly diplomat that is known globally to embrace different cultures and people. As Regan (2011) noted, Canadian national history is characterized by a glorified narrative of a peacemaker, rather than an asserter of violence over Indigenous lands. Violent Indigenous histories are in direct conflict with that positive image, and so people actively want to disassociate from them. However, choosing to overlook the violent past and presenting the narrative of colonial conquest as innocent discovery of uninhabited lands erases the past of Indigenous peoples and bolsters the unequal power structures in the present (Regan, 2011). Universities as institutions of state authority have played a central role in cementing narratives and knowledge frameworks that exclude other ways of knowing.

The core idea of a university is the pursuit of knowledge. A stream of critical scholarship has emerged in Canada (e.g., Archibald, 2008; Battiste, 2000, 2013a; Battiste & Youngblood, 2000; Brunette-Debassige, 2021; Cote-Meek & Moeke-Pickering, 2020; Fitznor, 2017; Kovach, 2009; Pidgeon 2016, 2019; Wilson, 2008) that interrogates the role of the university and its relevance to Indigenous peoples, knowledges, perspectives, and experiences. The argument is that the pursuit of knowledge in regard to Indigenous perspectives has been largely absent in the mission of university. A cross-cutting theme in this strand of literature is the historical assertion that universities were established and are still operating as colonial institutions, promoting Eurocentric knowledge frameworks and endorsing hegemonic hierarchies of knowledge. The response to such critique has varied. Universities struggle to resolve the dilemma of supporting the pursuit of knowledge and responsively serving Indigenous communities, which may essentially require a complete restart of the university. As Jones (1998) reflected, the idea of the university may take on different forms depending on the influence of the state, the value placed on education, and the influence of a dominant culture. According to the critical perspective, the dominant ideology that continues to shape the idea of the university in Canada to date is settler colonialism.

Settler Colonialism

Being referred to as a *settler* may cause mixed emotions, including discomfort and feelings of rejection. Yet Styres (2019) argued that accepting this term is necessary to mark the distinction between Indigenous peoples of a particular place and those who have roots somewhere else. The original settlers were of various European origins. They brought with them their laws, customs, and educational practices and applied those to Indigenous peoples and, later, to everyone else who has come to Canada (Vowel, 2016). In today's context, *settler* is a relational term that marks the complex relationship between Indigenous peoples and others who have moved or continue to move to Canada. Today the term applies to most who live on Indigenous peoples' traditional territories and continue to benefit from the privilege gained through previously established colonial relationships.

The starting point for understanding settler colonialism is thinking about colonialism in general terms. Colonialism is an ideology, a set of beliefs, that works through direct or indirect acts of authority over peoples, lands, and knowledges. Scholars have emphasized that colonialism is not a historical occurrence or a single event; it is an ongoing and continuous structural process (Tuck & Yang, 2012; Wolfe, 2006). One of my research participants commented that "*colonization comes from an ideology of violence. It's harmful to both non-Indigenous and Indigenous people*" (interview, 12 December 2018). Canadian history is grounded in settler colonialism, which is a distinct form of colonialism that centres on land. Veracini (2010, p. 1) defined settler colonialism as "a specific mode of domination where a community of exogenous settlers permanently displace to a new locale, eliminate or displace indigenous populations and sovereignties, and constitute an autonomous political body." The main asset associated with settler colonialism is land ownership, which in Canada was claimed by exercising hegemonic political authority. Settler colonialism works through normalizing the societal structures that are oppressive to Indigenous peoples without questioning their premises. Instead, settler colonialism assumes these structures are customary and common sense. Tuck and Yang (2014, p. 813) emphasized how "settler colonialism must cover its tracks, and does so by making its structuring natural, inevitable, invisible, and immutable." Sometimes settlers tend to present themselves as guests on Indigenous lands, but the real intention is never to leave (Stewart-Ambo & Yang, 2021). A belief is created that immigrants and their descendants belong to these lands, as they have worked hard for them and, thus, these lands belong to them (Ellermann & O'Heran, 2021). Once land is acquired and settled, the existing culture gets changed (Barker, 2012). Simpson (2004), among others, has pointed out how uprooting Indigenous cultural practices, spirituality, and ceremonial life has destroyed Indigenous languages, and outlawing traditional Indigenous governance systems has created irreversible damage to Indigenous society.

Colonial practices against Indigenous peoples continue today, some in a slightly different form. Veracini (2010) pointed out that contemporary modes of colonialism tend to be more invisible, as they are ingrained in our everyday functioning and largely normalized through collective power. Therefore, it may be difficult to notice and address the more subtle forms of colonial presence that occur in educational institutions today. Education has been the core pillar reinforcing settler colonial ideology. There is a wide range of critical works that document how education continues to preserve colonial ideology in contemporary contexts (e.g., Calderón, 2011; Sabzalian, 2019; St. Denis, 2011). Reinterpretation of history is a central mechanism of settler colonial practice. Calderón (2011) examined how the civic education curriculum in schools favours settler narratives and actively delinks settler dominance from the historical genocide of Indigenous peoples; this curriculum treats Indigenous peoples as minorities on their lands and not as sovereign tribal nations. Sabzalian (2019) discussed how the narrative of multiculturalism, central to Canadian values, embraces only limited cultural aspects of identity (music, foods, costumes), purposely overlooking the political identities of Indigenous people as sovereign citizens of tribal nations. Dion (2007) described how public schooling actively contributes to knowledge abstraction, cementing stereotypes about Indigenous peoples. The author shared how "dominant stories that position Indigenous peoples as romanticized, mythical, victimized, or militant Other enable non-Indigenous people to position themselves as respectful admirer, moral helper, protector of law and order" (Dion, 2007, p. 331). Framing Indigenous groups as cultural others encourages the social division of groups as equal minorities that need to compete for limited resources and allows participation only on certain conditions, primarily for entertainment purposes. Starblanket (2019) described how misinterpreting history through a distorted explanation of the meaning of numbered treaties reinforces the narrative of settler land claims. Treaties tend to be interpreted as historical events where Indigenous peoples supposedly consensually surrendered their lands to settlers. The perspective that treaties are an integral part of the Indigenous political framework intended to govern the coexistence of peoples in a shared space is overlooked (Starblanket, 2019). As one of my research participants noted: "*Sharing doesn't mean you take away our rights. Sharing doesn't mean you take away our kids. Sharing doesn't mean you take away our land and force us on these small parcels of land*" (interview, 12 December 2018). These are just a few examples of how educational institutions create the dominant narratives and minimize the rights of Indigenous peoples to their lands in the larger framework of settler colonialism.

The dispossession and exploitation of Indigenous lands remains central to the issue of settler colonialism today (Veracini, 2010). Land ownership is directly relevant to higher education, as universities constantly benefit from operating on Indigenous lands. While territorial land acknowledgments have become an important practice in public events among universities, most people in non-Indigenous society still tend to think of themselves as Canadians who are the rightful, established owners of the Canadian territory. This dominant narrative created throughout colonial history is strong and has distorted the contemporary understandings of the rights of those living in Canada. As Tuck and Yang (2012) noted, addressing this foundational aspect of settler colonialism requires the repatriation of Indigenous land and life, an effort that should be at the centre of any social justice work happening in higher education. To counterbalance the dominant settler colonial narrative, it is imperative to support scholarship that explicitly attends to questions of land and to critically examine the issue of citizenship formation as a colonial practice in relation to Indigenous sovereignty and self-determination (Sabzalian, 2019).

Forced assimilation, in which schools have played a crucial role, is another well-identified practice of settler colonialism. It was exercised directly through the residential schools era with tragic consequences, resulting in active resentment of any forms of public schooling by Indigenous peoples. Today, forced assimilation of Indigenous youth continues in a more subtle form through standardized curriculum and limited programming, grounded in Eurocentric knowledges, both in schools and higher education institutions. Grosfoguel (2013) argued that, in the higher education context, scholarship in most disciplines in the social sciences has not changed much from the colonial era and draws almost exclusively on the work of scholars and journals from a few countries in Western Europe and the United States. The expected standard is to follow an objective and neutral knowledge paradigm whose individualistic values and meritocracy conflict with Indigenous perspectives of the relationality of knowledges (Brayboy, 2005; Masta, 2019). The reality of being rewarded for individualistic efforts when competing against each other forces Indigenous students to let go of their cultural integrity and replace it with mainstream academic knowledge in order to get a university degree (Brayboy, 2005). By denying the opportunity for knowledge alternatives to exist, universities support settler colonial ideology and engage in indirect assimilation practices.

Erasure as a mechanism of settler colonial ideology works through processes of elimination. Efforts to eliminate Indigenous cultures, identities, and consciousnesses, permanently replacing them with those of settlers, are typical of settler domination (Wolfe, 2006). Erasure works against Indigenous peoples by deleting any rights to a self-determining sovereign nation with its own political and economic systems (Ellermann & O'Heran, 2021; St. Denis, 2011). Scholars have argued that elimination presents itself in educational spaces through reduction of the power of Indigenous peoples (e.g., limiting access to programs or career opportunities), proclaiming western-dominated thinking as the unescapable norm, and challenging the legitimacy of Indigenous knowledge frameworks (Masta, 2019, Simpson, 2004). These processes are typically interrelated. Reducing power is present in the limited representation of Indigenous peoples in various positions in post-secondary education contexts. Power is also reduced when Indigenous peoples are constructed as the cultural other. Otherness works through minimizing the value and importance of Indigenous knowledges, allowing limited Indigenous voices in decision making, and dismissing alternative opinions. Calderón (2014) recalled that settler colonialism incorporates aspects of territoriality that rely on ideas of cultural and biological superiority. It operates through systemic exclusion of and discrimination against anything other than Eurocentric knowledge. The superiority of Eurocentric knowledge is the current reality in the pedagogical and methodological approaches applied in higher education, which tend to include Indigenous knowledges, epistemologies, and scholarly works only minimally (Henry et al., 2017a). Battiste (2016, p. 120), a Mikmaq professor and education scholar, has called this "cognitive imperialism that positions some groups in power and others to be exploited and marginalized." In institutional environments where settler colonial ideology has determined the curriculum, pedagogy, and institutional priorities, opportunities for meaningful change remain limited.

Silence is a hidden form of colonialism that works towards Indigenous erasure. Silence is a convenient way of doing nothing and staying quiet and indifferent, which allows for colonial structures to stay intact. In higher education, silence may occur through the materials and readings faculty members choose to include in their course syllabi. It translates into availability of course offerings on Indigenous topics or of faculty who are available to teach with authority about the issues and concerns that are fundamental to Indigenous peoples (Henry et al., 2017a). Sabzalian (2019) stated that educational institutions' overlooking and remaining silent about ongoing colonization threatens feelings of belonging for Indigenous youth and limits their visioning of their future as Indigenous peoples. A concept closely related to silence is epistemological ignorance (Calderón, 2011, 2014; Kuokkanen, 2007a). Calderón (2014) argued that intentional ignorance and lack of critical engagement with alternative knowledges protect the dominant ways of knowing. Authors have observed an active interest in not knowing or not making an effort to know, which helps to mask ongoing violence and position settlers as innocent bystanders in settler colonial frameworks, resisting meaningful change (Lees et al., 2021). By remaining silent on Indigenous elimination, non-Indigenous peoples become complicit in the ongoing processes of settler colonialism. Daniels (2011, p. 212) observed that "working against the silences involves informing ourselves as educators, reflecting on our own identities, and bringing in critical materials to our classrooms." As Hirji et al. (2020) noted, it is our collective responsibility, not only the responsibility of Indigenous community, to work towards challenging the pervasive structures of colonialism that present themselves in the Canadian university system.

Neoliberal market-centred ideologies have further paved the way for the contemporary practices of settler colonialism. Viewing higher education as a private commodity, universities are developing trained human capital for the knowledge economy while holding on to institutional rights to land and property and focusing on the accumulation of various resources to compete in global markets (Shahjahan, 2011). Reaching excellence through innovation and forced competitiveness through performance metrics have become the indicators measuring the success of higher education institutions. Academics are encouraged to align themselves with such market logics, which privilege individual competitiveness, business and audit culture, and standardization and metrics. Universities, faculty members, and students alike are "incentivized" to focus on hyper-productivity and high returns on investment (Brown, 2015). Excellence and innovation have become norms in higher education that drive organizational change (Maeße, 2017). In universities, as in other societal institutions, discourses of liberalism, meritocracy, neutrality, and objectivity help to mask colonial structures, leading to inequity and unacknowledged bias (Dlamini, 2002; Kobayashi, 2018). The increased emphasis on recruiting more fee-paying international students and catering to their needs as an income-generating pool competes with the institutional priorities of Indigenization (Beck & Pidgeon, 2020). Indigenization often lacks the profile, perceived benefits, and organizational support that internationalization receives. In the light of neoliberal ideology, Indigenous values and lifeways are seen as risky, since they are inconsistent with the materialistic needs of neoliberal logic (Wilson, 2013). Indigenous knowledges tend to be grounded in history and look at the past rather than forward, which contradicts neoliberal values. Yet, Indigenous scholars have underscored that economic growth has boundaries and that the western framing of innovation has led to massive exploitation of human and land-based resources, resulting in widening inequities among individuals and enhanced racism (Battiste, 2000; Smith et al., 2018). All these structures and dominant value frameworks constitute foundational limits within the Canadian academy that make engaging with, advocating for, and strengthening Indigenous knowledges a difficult task.

Historical Context and Indigenous Advocacy Work

The relationship between schooling and Indigenous peoples in Canada is complex and characterized by colonial violence and cultural genocide that have led to the loss of cultural heritage and the removal of rights to self-determination. State-forced assimilation practices against Indigenous peoples have been the direct mechanism of domination in Canadian history. Forced assimilation started with early education initiatives in the 1600s by European settlers who focused on "civilizing" Indigenous peoples through schooling and religious conversion. One of the earliest accounts of formal schooling comes from New France (now the Quebec area) where Jesuits founded the Collège des Jésuits in 1635 for the purpose of converting Indigenous peoples to Christianity (Wilder, 2013). The establishment of educational institutions on Indigenous lands created tensions from the beginning, as these establishments contributed to the displacement and attempted removal of Indigenous peoples from their living environments (Debassige & Brunette-Debassige, 2018). When the Canadian government was formally established in 1867, the Constitution Act granted the provinces control of education systems, while the federal government was allocated responsibility over Indigenous peoples: "Indians, and Lands reserved for the Indians" (Constitution Act, 1876, Section 24). Later, the Indian Act (1876) became the main governing document (still currently in place) that initiated violent assimilation policies through schooling. Government-sanctioned residential schools were established in the early 1800s across Canada, and the last one did not close until 1996. It is now well documented that the purpose of the residential schools was to destroy the cultural, political, and social institutions of Indigenous peoples (Pidgeon, 2019). Within these schools, thousands of Indigenous children would die and tens of thousands would endure horrifying experiences of physical, sexual, emotional, and psychological abuse. For the children who made it out of the school system, scepticism towards Eurocentric education has remained, not only in their own lives but also in the lives of their children, who are faced with the intergenerational trauma that Canadian society is accountable for. In 2013, a Canadian study conducted among Indigenous youth reported that 57% of First Nations respondents who were currently enrolled in or had graduated from post-secondary institutions "do not trust the education system" (Restoule et al., 2013).

The only path for Indigenous peoples to a formally recognized higher education degree with job prospects has been through the Canadian post-secondary education system. Meanwhile, universities have been complicit in asserting land ownership claims and reinforcing nation-state laws and Eurocentric knowledges at the expense of Indigenous peoples since the 1700s (Coulthard, 2014). Jones (2013) noted that the assumption that forcing Indigenous populations to accept western European values, cultures, customs, and religion was necessary for their success was the core public policy idea guiding Canadian post-secondary education. Access to higher education for Indigenous peoples was provided largely on the condition that they give up their treaty rights and reject their culture, language, and customs, which meant forced assimilation to Canadian society. In reality, very few Indigenous Canadians gained access to higher education until the 1960s (González & Colangelo, 2010; Pidgeon, 2019). Settler colonial ideology has worked in education through restricting access and forcing foreign values while cementing settler national ideology. Brunette-Debassige and Viczko (2022) recalled that this is not unique to Canada; higher education institutions around the world have been maintaining the power of dominant knowledge systems while excluding marginalized groups and voices.

This gradually growing dominance has led to resistance and bottom-up advocacy work from Indigenous groups. There have been continuous and growing calls for change among Indigenous communities, indicating the importance of self-governance through education. In the early 1970s, Indigenous peoples started to make political statements articulating their human right to autonomy. One of the earliest documents that included education in policy advocacy was the *Wahbung: Our Tomorrows* paper (1971) by the Manitoba Indian Brotherhood (now the Assembly of Manitoba Chiefs). *Wahbung* was a local-level position paper presented to the federal government. This document was a response to the government's white paper on Indian policy, which recommended the removal of the special status of Indians for the purpose of achieving equality. *Wahbung* underscored the inherent right of First Nations people in Canada to design and have full authority over their health, education, and child and family services systems, informed by First Nations worldviews, laws, and approaches. The paper advocated for both self-governance over Indigenous-led higher education programs and widened access to mainstream higher education institutions that could support Indigenous knowledges across various disciplinary fields. Local discussions around the role of education in Indigenous self-determination were emerging across Canada around this time, and these perspectives were summarized by the National Indian Brotherhood in 1972 when they released a policy document titled *Indian Control of Indian Education*. This document was a powerful attempt to draw political attention to state-led assimilation practices for Indigenous communities across Canada that occurred through education. It pointed out the absence of fundamental parental rights for Indigenous parents to make autonomous decisions about their children's education, in contrast with other parents. The document also emphasized that the fundamental concept of local control over education didn't extend to Indigenous peoples within the provincial education systems. The document articulated core principles for Indigenous participation in mainstream education, including higher education, to the federal government (National Indian Brotherhood, 1972). Decades later, the government commissioned work to address the concerns raised by the Indigenous community. In 1996, the *Royal Commission on Aboriginal Peoples Report* was released. It pulled together extensive research gained through community consultations and examined historical and contemporary relations between Indigenous and non-Indigenous peoples in Canada. The scope of its recommendations on social and cultural issues included the proposed establishment of an Indigenous peoples' international university, the development of educational programs to support Indigenous self-government, and public education initiatives to promote cultural sensitivity among non-Indigenous people. With little political will from the federal government, these recommendations were never fully implemented. In 2002, another important political statement was made through the *Final Report of the Minister's Working Group on Education*, commissioned by the federal Department of Indian Affairs and Northern Development Canada, focused on First Nations education. The report included a section with specific recommendations for the post-secondary education sector. The recommendations involved the need to improve access for Indigenous peoples to post-secondary education and to establish equitable representation of First Nations individuals among faculty and on senior governing boards. The recommendations also included the requirement to develop First Nations post-secondary institutes. Racism towards Indigenous peoples as a pressing societal issue was raised, pointing to the need for mainstream higher education institutions to take an active role in addressing this (Final Report of the Minister's Working Group, 2002). In 2010, an updated and adapted version of the 1972 document titled *First Nation Control of First Nation Education* was released. Key elements of this update included requests for language immersion for First Nations people, applying holistic and culturally relevant knowledge principles in curricula, support for well-trained educators, inclusive leadership, parental involvement, and making decisions with close involvement of First Nations communities. As a response, the Harper government introduced Bill C-33, the First Nations Control of First Nations Education Act in 2014, which was essentially envisioned as a replacement for the Indian Act. Yet, the process grounding the document was highly problematic, with the federal government acting on its own without meaningful consultations with Indigenous peoples. The document was quickly rejected by Indigenous communities, as it was seen as increasing the control of the federal government as opposed to enhancing the self-governance of Indigenous peoples. The most recent and impactful policy advocacy work has occurred through the work of the Truth and Reconciliation Commission (2008–15), which documented the experiences of residential school survivors. The final report of the Truth and Reconciliation Commission (TRC), *Calls to Action*, gathered their experiences and provided a list of recommendations to Canadian society for reconciliation (TRC, 2015). A set of action items in this report is directed towards (higher) education institutions, including increased access to and attainment within education for Indigenous peoples, focusing on culturally relevant learning. Resulting from the work of the Truth and Reconciliation Commission, efforts towards the Indigenization and reconciliation of academia have now become an integral aspect of the Canadian post-secondary sector (Gaudry & Lorenz, 2018). These processes have been rationalized and built around the broader societal discourse of equity. In the few years since the release of the TRC's final report, many Canadian universities have begun transformations centring on increasing senior Indigenous leadership positions, initiating changes to Indigenous student supports, and adding programming that is reflective of Indigenous studies – all with a view to being responsive to one or more of the TRC's *Calls to Action* (Deer, 2020). After decades of advocacy work, there is movement occurring towards incorporating Indigenous perspectives within higher education.

In parallel with political developments, specific actions have been taken to establish formal autonomous higher education institutions for the Indigenous peoples of Canada. The first recorded Indigenous-controlled formal higher learning institution is connected to the Blue Quills First Nations College in Alberta, dating back to 1865. The institution was housed in a former residential school beginning in 1930. It is now a community-owned academic and training institution operated and owned by the people of the seven area First Nations in Alberta. Blue Quills First Nations College became University nuhelot'įne thaiyots'į nistameyimâkanak Blue Quills in September 2015. Other developments among Indigenous post-secondary institutions include the First Nations University of Canada (est. 1976, name change 2003), which has operated in collaboration with the University of Regina (semi-independently) and is now managing three campuses within the province of Saskatchewan in Prince Albert, Regina, and Saskatoon. Other examples include the Gabrielle Dumont Institute of Native Studies and Applied Research (est. 1980) in Saskatchewan (Dorion & Yang, 2000), the Nicola Valley Institute of Technology (est. 1982) in British Columbia (Billy

Minnabarriet, 2012), and Yellowquill College in Manitoba, founded by the Dakota Ojibway Tribal Council in 1984. However, funding for Indigenous-governed institutions remains a significant barrier (Stonechild, 2006). Robinson (2023) argued, based on the case of Indigenous-controlled post-secondary institutions in British Columbia, that publicly funded Indigenous post-secondary institutions (such as Nicola Valley Institute of Technology) have guaranteed government funding and are, thus, facing less financial insecurity. Federated institutes (such as Wilp Wilxo'oskwhl Nisga'a Institute) or community learning centres (like Cariboo Chilcotin Weekend University) are in a much more vulnerable financial situation (Robinson, 2023). Nevertheless, Robinson (2023, p. 406) argued that Indigenous post-secondary institutions should be seen as "leaders in decolonization and reconciliation" for their inherent partnerships with Elders and community, demonstrating Indigenous control over Indigenous education and having significant impact on student identity. As Pidgeon (2016) noted, most Indigenous students are enrolled in predominantly white institutions and, thus, rely on a mainstream higher education system. The alternative, an Indigenous-planned and-controlled system of higher education in Canada, is currently not a reality but rather a vision to work towards.

As a result of various kinds of advocacy work, the rate of Indigenous students pursuing higher education in Canada has been increasing. Gradually rising participation of Indigenous individuals began in the 1960s with the establishment of Native Education and Native Studies programs in Canadian public universities (Battiste & Barman, 1995; Castellano et al., 2001; Stonechild, 2006). The first Native Studies program was established at Trent University in 1969, and the University of Manitoba and Brandon University followed suit in 1975 (Taner, 1999). Today there are over a dozen more (Stein, 2020). Additional student support services for Indigenous students have sometimes been provided (Pidgeon & Hardy Cox, 2005). However, Stonechild (2006) has described significant discrepancies among the Indigenous programs, policies, and student services offered across Canadian higher education institutions. He argued that these services have sporadically been initiated by Indigenous and non-Indigenous faculty or staff, or whenever the provincial government has provided targeted funds for such services (Stonechild, 2006). Funding has been a major barrier for the Indigenous population to access mainstream higher education. The fundamental contestation between the federal and provincial governments, centring on confusion over whose jurisdiction it is to fund the higher education of Indigenous students in Canada, has had detrimental effects on access to and schooling of Indigenous students, as Pidgeon (2019) described. The number of Indigenous students in Canadian higher education institutions remained low for decades. In 1969, it was estimated that 125 Status Indians were enrolled in Canadian universities (Stonechild, 2006). The enrolment of Status Indians grew steadily through the 1970s, when the federal Post-Secondary Student Support Program helped to increase access. Yet, the funding levels have been capped and are not in alignment with the increasing costs of tuition, accommodation, and living. This has led to students taking fewer courses or working, and thus extending their time to degree completion (Pidgeon, 2019). Shanahan (2015) noted that while many Indigenous people regard post-secondary education as a treaty right, the federal government has viewed its involvement through funding more as a matter of social policy than a legal obligation.

As this brief historical overview suggests, Indigenous participation in Canadian higher education institutions has been limited, conditioned by government funding, and impacted by various assimilation practices. Furthermore, the openness of Canadian post-secondary institutions to engage with Indigenous communities and develop culturally relevant programs and support services has been sporadic. Various bottom-up political attempts to establish control over Indigenous (higher) education have led to some success, helping to increase awareness and support through Native Studies programs. The importance of Indigenous knowledges has most recently emerged in connection with the Truth and Reconciliation Commission, which has positioned higher education institutions as key stakeholders on the path of reconciliation.

Representation and Documented Experiences of Indigenous Peoples in Academia

The impacts of ongoing settler colonial ideologies are evident in the limited availability of representation data. More is known about the documented experiences of Indigenous faculty members and students. Overall, numeric data on Indigenous peoples in higher education are highly fragmented. There are several reasons for this. Individuals may choose not to disclose their Indigenous identity because of potential discrimination. Institutions may opt not to report on Indigenous peoples individually, as representation numbers tend to be so small. As a result, information on Indigenous peoples may be presented together with that on other racialized individuals. Data are absent on intersectionality, including non-binary gendered data (Brunette-Debassige, 2021). There are limited comparative data between the university and college sectors, particularly when student numbers are concerned. There is also an absence of information on Indigenous staff members and their experiences.

Representation. The Indigenous population in Canada has increased over the years, reaching 1.8 million people, which is 5% of the total population in Canada (Statistics Canada, 2022). Previous studies have indicated that there are over 45,000 academic staff working in the Canadian post-secondary education sector, approximately one-third of whom are women (Canadian Association of University Teachers [CAUT], 2018a; Smith, 2017). Indigenous faculty make up only 1.4% of the faculty positions across Canadian universities (Statistics Canada, 2016a). Their representation among college instructors is slightly higher at 3% (see Table 1). Inuit are the least represented Indigenous group at only 0.03% of faculty in universities and 0.18% in colleges. Métis representation among instructors is 0.54% in universities and 1.2% in colleges. Instructors identifying as First Nations represent only 0.76% of university faculty and 1.5% of faculty in the college sector (Statistics Canada, 2016a). Again, these data are only tentative, as many individuals prefer not to disclose their Indigenous identity. It is also known that Indigenous women professors earn 26.7% less than non-Indigenous women in the Canadian academy (CAUT, 2018a). Indigenous male professors earn 26.3% less than non-Indigenous male professors (CAUT, 2018a). The Canada Research Chair (CRC) program is the most prestigious federally funded research program in Canada. Data on Indigenous faculty members holding Canada Research Chairs positions became available only in 2017, with the nomination numbers fluctuating between 4 and 7 Indigenous Research Chairs each year across tiers and 83 Indigenous-identified chairholders (4.1%) out of 2,026 CRCs in total in 2023 (CRCP, web).

According to Smith (2019), there is also a notable absence of Indigenous peoples in various leadership roles across Canadian universities. A survey conducted by Universities Canada stated that only 2.9% of senior leaders in Canadian universities identified as Indigenous (Universities Canada, 2019). Interestingly, Indigenous women are in the majority of these leadership positions (Brunette-Debassige, 2021). At the departmental chair level, Indigenous women comprised 1.9% of administrators and Indigenous men 1.1%. At the program chair level, Indigenous women were reported to make up 0.3% of administrators and Indigenous men 0.1% of these administrative positions (Smith, 2019).

Table 1. Overview of Indigenous Instructors across Canadian Post-Secondary Institutions

Indigenous Identity	University Teachers	College Instructors	Total Labour Force
Non-Indigenous	98.6	97.0	96.2
Indigenous identity	1.4	3.0	3.8
– First Nations	0.76	1.50	1.98
– Métis	0.54	1.20	1.56
– Inuit	0.03	0.18	0.13
Multiple Indigenous identity	n/a	0.06	0.05

Source: Statistics Canada, 2016a.

The proportion and representation of Indigenous students in Canadian higher education institutions are similarly low, but growing (see Table 2). According to Universities Canada, an estimated 5% of undergraduate students and 3% of masters and PhD students on Canadian campuses self-identify as Indigenous (Universities Canada, 2018). As noted earlier, the issue of little trust in the Canadian educational system, limited access to higher education due to scarcity of funding, and a lack of culturally relevant knowledge incorporated into university programs has kept the attendance of Indigenous individuals in Canadian universities low – 15% of First Nations individuals living on reserve and 23% of First Nations individuals living off reserve, compared to 45% of individuals with non-Indigenous identity (Statistics Canada, 2016b). More specific data are less readily available. Increases in Indigenous student numbers tend to be reported by individual universities. For example, in 2019, the University of Saskatchewan announced that their self-declared Indigenous student body had increased by 7% to a total of 3,320 students (Shewaga, 2019). The University of Regina reported an increase of 5.7% in the number of students who self-identified as First Nations, Métis, or Inuit and declared that these students now comprised 13.2% (close to 1,000 students) of their student population (University of Regina, 2019). A 2021 press release from Laurentian University in Ontario stated that it had over 1,100 self-identified Indigenous learners enrolled (Laurentian University, 2021). Although the total number of Indigenous individuals who have attained university degrees has increased throughout the past 25 years – for example, 3.4% of Indigenous people living on reserve had a degree in 2001 compared to 9.1% in 2021 (Statistics Canada, 2021) – the disparity between Indigenous and non-Indigenous populations with a university degree continues to widen, extending now from 16.7% in 2001 to 27.9% in 2021 for Indigenous peoples living on reserve, and less for other Indigenous

Table 2. Percentage of Indigenous Students and Academic Staff in Canadian U15 Universities

University	Students who identify as Indigenous	Academic staff who identify as Indigenous
University of Alberta	2 to 4.99% (out of more than 40,000 students)	Less than 2%
University of Calgary	2 to 4.99% (out of more than 33,000 students)	Less than 2%
Dalhousie University	2 to 4.99% (out of more than 19,000 students)	Less than 2%
Laval University	Less than 2% (out of more than 45,000 students)	n/a
University of Manitoba	5 to 9.99% (over 2,500 Indigenous students) (out of more than 29,000 students)	Less than 2%
McGill University	Less than 2% (out of more than 39,000 students)	n/a
McMaster University	Less than 2% (out of more than 33,000 students)	n/a
Université de Montréal	Less than 2% (out of more than 67,000 students)	n/a
University of Ottawa	n/a (out of more than 40,000 students)	n/a
Queen's University	Less than 2% (out of more than 26,000 students)	n/a
University of Saskatchewan	10% or more (over 3,400 Indigenous students) (out of more than 25,700 students)	2 to 4.99%
University of Toronto	n/a (out of more than 90,000 students)	n/a
University of British Columbia	Approximately 3% (1,904 Aboriginal students) (out of more than 66,000 students)	n/a
University of Waterloo	n/a (out of more than 42,000 students)	n/a
Western University	Less than 2% (out of more than 40,000 students)	n/a

Source: Indigenous programs and services directory, Universities Canada Online Database (n.d.), and institutional websites.

groups (AFN, 2018; Richards, 2014; Statistics Canada 2023). This disparity is also illustrated by the fact that nearly 30% of non-Indigenous Canadians aged 15 to 64 have university degrees, compared to 10% of Indigenous peoples in the same age group (Davidson & Jamieson, 2018). Comparative data on students for the university and college sectors are absent.

Data on the composition or experiences of Indigenous non-academic staff working in Canadian higher education institutions are practically non-existent. Reports featuring the University of Alberta and their Indigenous librarian program have been published (Carr-Wiggin et al., 2017; Farnel et al., 2018). There is also some information available on Indigenous individuals working in (Indigenous) access, academic summer camps, and recruitment programs (Jungic & Thompson, 2020). However, the exact number and role of Indigenous non-academic staff employed by Canadian institutions are not clear. This limited literature suggests that this is an area in need of further research and institutional attention.

Disciplinary silos. Malinda Smith (2017) has noted that it is the departments and disciplines that often function as gateways, providing or denying people's access particularly to graduate degrees. The data on Indigenous representation across disciplinary fields are fragmented and largely anecdotal. Therefore, it is imperative to draw attention to the issue of disciplinary silos and examine how disciplines tend to strongly uphold colonial knowledge frameworks in academia. Available evidence shows that Indigenous faculty tend to be concentrated in a small number of programs. Social work, education, health, law, and Indigenous studies are the main sites of concentration (Dua & Bhanji, 2012; Henry, 2012; Ontario's Universities, 2020). Gregory et al. (2008) reported that, in 2007, there were only 22 known Indigenous nursing faculty in Canada. Ansloos et al. (2019) stated that, as of 2018, there were fewer than 12 Indigenous people practising and/or teaching psychology throughout Canada, which is alarming considering the need for mental health services among Indigenous communities. An investigation into communication studies departments across Canada revealed that there was only one Indigenous person working as a faculty member there (Hirji et al., 2020). Henry (2012) described how Indigenous studies, the single area where Indigenous faculty typically concentrate, was not considered a true university discipline by some non-Indigenous faculty. This perspective is in alignment with the practice of colonial erasure and delivers yet another instance of the cognitive imperialism prevalent in higher education.

A field that has contributed much to the critical scholarship on Indigenous knowledges is education (e.g., Battiste, 2002; 2005; Calderón, 2006). Education is critically important in driving structural change; thus, Indigenous scholars have actively engaged in identifying ways in which education can become an important vehicle for resisting colonial structures and reimagining alternative ways forward. While there is wide critical engagement among Indigenous researchers in the field of education, there are still fields and disciplines that remain untouched spaces of Eurocentric epistemologies, resisting change. Disciplinary silos where there is a lack of Indigenous (women) representation are prevalent in the sciences, technology, engineering, and mathematics (Smith, 2017). Smith (2017), herself a Black professor in political science, argued that that there is a silence about race and Indigeneity in the constitution of the political science discipline. The composition of political science faculty and leadership in Canadian universities remains overwhelmingly white and primarily male. The author pointed out how disciplines such as political science are complicit in erasing power relations from their essence, thereby reproducing institutions, policies, and processes of the colonial state (Smith, 2017). Hirji et al.'s (2020) examination of communication studies in Canada revealed similar dynamics around the continuing domination of whiteness and refusal to address colonial structures. Smith (2017) concluded that more attention needs to be paid to disciplines as units of analysis and the ways they reflect and represent historical and social realities in relation to diversity and the hierarchy of knowledge.

Experiences. While some Indigenous individuals may be gaining access to scholarships, government-funded research opportunities, or leadership positions, this is not the standard practice. Difficulties that Indigenous peoples face in Canadian universities have been overwhelmingly documented. Indigenous peoples continue to struggle with various structural barriers to finding their voice, legitimacy, and credibility in university contexts (Brunette-Debassige, 2021; Smith, 2019). Indigenous scholars report facing microaggressions, chilly and unwelcoming climates, and resentment from colleagues, which in turn contribute to feelings of self-doubt and tokenism (Bopp et al., 2017; Henry & Tator, 2012). Confronting and resisting colonial structures are shared experiences that cause daily tensions and put pressure on Indigenous peoples. Scholars have highlighted the extra work demanded of racialized (including Indigenous) faculty in order to navigate the institutional whiteness in academia that perpetuates racism (Mohamed & Beagan, 2019).

It has become the task of Indigenous peoples to prove their value to academia, demonstrating how they fit into established norms and structures. An example of this is the rigid, uniform practices of hiring and tenure processes that create epistemological conflicts and are sources of tension for Indigenous faculty. In hiring processes, Indigenous candidates are expected to fit into established positions within rigid disciplinary boundaries and not the other way around. McCaffrey (2013) shared how her community engagement work was pushed to the side in her tenure process, while importance was given only to writing, curriculum work, and course-based evaluations at the expense of her community-based work. The author had to make a case and persuade her committee that her work was valuable before the members would meaningfully consider her contributions as an Indigenous faculty member. This illustrates the difficulties of negotiating Indigenous worldviews around Eurocentric expectations and institutional policies that become barriers for supporting alternative epistemologies.

Authors have documented the intermediary roles that Indigenous peoples constantly need to fulfil owing to this epistemological divide. The "two-world perspective" centring on the Indigenous world and the world of white academia has become characteristic of Indigenous individuals' academic research projects and learning experiences (Kirkness & Barnhard, 1991; Styres et al., 2010). Researchers have identified intermediary roles that call on Indigenous leaders to act as cultural interpreters for Indigenous communities or translate Indigenous worlds for dominant institutional realities. Navigating epistemologically different aspects of knowing may involve translating established educational policies for Indigenous communities or the other way around (Goddard & Foster, 2002; Povey et al., 2022). In an academic context, Corntassel (2011) has asserted that Indigenous peoples doing resurgence work must avoid mediating between worlds, and instead must challenge the dominant knowledge frameworks in academia, confronting ongoing colonial structures in higher education.

Quite often Indigenous peoples are expected to serve as tokenistic advocates for all things Indigenous. Having an Indigenous individual as part of a committee has become a desired criterion for universities to demonstrate diversity in their decision making, yet Indigenous perspectives are hardly listened to. The metaphor of the "Indian in the cupboard" applies here, whereby an Indigenous person is brought out, valued, and paid attention to only when it supports the inherent cause of settler colonialism (Mzinegiizhigo-kwe Bédard, 2018). It is typically the Indigenous scholar who is invited as a guest speaker to explain the impacts of colonialism (Cannon, 2013, St. Denis, 2011). Cannon (2013) argued that having Indigenous peoples remain the token speakers on the topics of racism and colonization removes from non-Indigenous peoples the responsibility of having to think about or engage in matters of structural colonialism or learn about their own role in these processes. Similarly, Indigenous students are often invited to classroom discussions as the experts on Indigenous topics, while they themselves may still struggle to navigate and learn about their Indigenous identity. Indigenous scholars at early career stages are overwhelmingly called on to mentor and support Indigenous students, lead Indigenous programs, serve as liaisons with Indigenous communities, and educate their non-Indigenous colleagues at the expense of their own career progression (Ontario's Universities, 2020). They are tasked with establishing academic forums and support networks designed for racialized and Indigenous students, resolving racist incidents, guiding other faculty and administrators on Indigenous and community protocols, and representing community interests (Hirji et al., 2020). These are all service tasks that take away time needed for research, publishing, developing curriculum, or building community networks. The burdening of Indigenous faculty with a range of service tasks illustrates how structural colonialism works through diluting the attention and energy of Indigenous groups away from efforts towards self-determination in academia.

A different stream of scholarship has described the experiences of Indigenous leaders and administrators in Canadian universities. Lavallée (2020b) argued that universities are eager to promote Indigenous women into senior leadership roles, but in practice they are positioned as "exotic puppets" to be manipulated and pressured under dominant colonial and gendered norms. Brunette-Debassige (2021) similarly addressed the idea of Indigenous women scholars being "lured in" to leadership positions and then critiqued for their input. While Indigenous women leaders feel compelled to serve in order to support their communities, their opinions are often labelled as "radical" and their experiences and advice get dismissed or ignored (Bopp et al., 2017; Brunette-Debassige, 2021, pp. 122–30). Brunette-Debassige (2021) emphasized how Indigenous women leaders must continuously resist settler colonial ideology, while working to develop and implement Indigenous policy. Povey et al. (2022) described how the expectation for Indigenous peoples in leadership roles is limited to bringing traditional culture and community connections to the job, while there is little interest in meaningful structural change. Unequal power dynamics is a theme in university governance literature, with limited Indigenous representation in university boards and senates. Staples et al. (2021) described Indigenous experiences with university governance at Yukon University and noted that the dominant bicameral model of university governance is considered problematic, as it is embedded within a colonial framework leading to an unbalanced institutional power dynamic that overrides the Indigenous voice. Participants in their study highlighted the importance of ensuring that there are dedicated seats for Yukon First Nation representatives on the board of governors and in the senate (Staples et al., 2021).

The scholarship documenting the experiences of Indigenous students in Canadian higher education is growing. The range of Indigenous students' experiences is best understood in terms of students' emotional, intellectual, physical, and cultural encounters within the institution (Pidgeon, 2008). Acts of subtle racism and microaggression play an impactful role in their daily lives and academic achievement (Bailey, 2016). Clark et al.'s (2014, p. 117) study is illustrative in describing the experiences of Indigenous undergraduate students in both Canada and the United States. The authors described how Indigenous students encounter persistent racial microaggressions such as (a) expectations of primitiveness (e.g., "Do you guys live in teepees?"), (b) unconstrained voyeurism (e.g., ridicule, insults, and disrespect based on one's last name or Indigenous connections), (c) jealous accusations (e.g., "The government is paying for your education"), (d) curricular elimination or misrepresentation (e.g., Indigenous issues overlooked, distorted, or superficially addressed), and (e) day-to-day cultural and social isolation (e.g., being the only Indigenous student and not fitting in as a result). The authors called for enhanced cultural competence training from instructors and staff when initiating changes to counteract microaggressions in institutional climates in universities (Clark et al., 2014). The experiences of Indigenous students in higher education are heavily influenced by specific characteristics of the university, including the availability of relevant curriculum and mentors, financial aid, and supportive policy frameworks focused on Indigenous students and their achievement (Pidgeon, 2008).

While there has been overwhelming scholarship documenting negative experiences among Indigenous peoples in Canadian academia, it is important to shift away from the deficit perspective associated with Indigenous peoples. Overall, the focus should be on the resilience and strengths that Indigenous peoples bring with them when navigating colonial structures in academia. Along these lines, Povey et al. (2022) described how collaborative decision making embedded within the internal structure of a faculty has been a helpful initiative for Indigenous leaders. Developing strategic plans and policy documents that centre on Indigenous knowledges was identified as a significant success by their study participants (Povey et al., 2022). Further, Brunette-Debassige (2021) found that when Indigenous women leaders saw meaningful change resulting from their work of resisting colonialism, this made their work worthwhile. There is an overall recognition that the continuous work by Indigenous advocates in confronting and resisting colonial structures in academia is finally starting to make an impact.

Is Academia Finally Starting to Listen?

As noted, the higher education sector in Canada has gradually become more attentive to Indigenous experiences. There is a focused effort among Canadian universities to make a stronger commitment to include Indigenous knowledges, perspectives, and cultures in their teaching, research, and service (Gaudry & Lorenz, 2018). There is also larger political support driving institutional change, so much so that supporting Indigenous knowledges has become an uncontested practice in contemporary higher education contexts. Overall, pressures emerging from Indigenous advocacy work have become impossible to ignore. Several questions arise from this context: Have Indigenous peoples and knowledges started to change Canadian universities? Has academia finally started to listen? Is this change driven by critical decolonial perspectives? Higher education institutions operate as organizations with competing values and diverse dynamics, so there is no one simple answer to this question. Universities are "sites of struggle" (Hampton, 2016, p. 18), expected to respond to the various social, cultural, economic, and political pressures emerging from society to remain relevant. Nonetheless, there is a range of arguments that speak to the need to listen and engage in broader institutional change.

Argument of Indigenous rights. This argument addresses the legal pressures put on Canadian institutions to change. The Indigenous self-determination movement is grounded in the right of Indigenous peoples to freely determine their own political, social, cultural, linguistic, and economic affairs. This right is tied with the legal frameworks of the Canadian constitution, as well as the United Nations Declaration of the Rights of Indigenous Peoples (UNDRIP) internationally. The Canadian constitution states that Indigenous peoples in Canada have the protection of their Indigenous and treaty rights:

> The existing aboriginal and treaty rights of the aboriginal peoples of Canada are hereby recognized and affirmed. (Constitution Act, 1982)

Article 31 of the United Nations Declaration of the Rights of Indigenous Peoples further highlights a rights-based approach to Indigenous knowledges:

> Indigenous peoples have the right to maintain, control, protect and develop their cultural heritage, traditional knowledge and traditional cultural expressions /… / They also have the right to maintain, control, protect and develop their intellectual property over such cultural heritage, traditional knowledge, and traditional cultural expressions. (UNDRIP, 2007)

UNDRIP proclaims basic human rights for Indigenous peoples but also mandates the protection of Indigenous knowledges and heritage (Battiste & Youngblood, 2000). As Canada has now fully endorsed the UNDRIP declaration, it must secure affirmation of the statements made in this document. Both the Canadian constitution and UNDRIP are somewhat controversial documents from a decolonial perspective. While the Canadian Constitution (1982, Section 35) formally recognizes and affirms existing treaty rights, it is sometimes viewed as a colonial document because it was created without the full participation or consent of Indigenous peoples (see Nichols, 2018). Similarly, UNDRIP may be perceived as addressing Indigenous issues within colonial nation-state frameworks that do not fully consider the complex relations between nation-state and Indigenous nations. Therefore, UNDRIP may be seen as a tool for further assimilation of diverse Indigenous groups under colonial structures and systems (see Champagne, 2013). More recently, the Canadian federal government formally renewed its relationship building with Indigenous groups from a more critical perspective, asserting the recognition of Indigenous rights, self-determination, and self-governance (Government of Canada, 2018). While partly contentious, these documents set the legal ground for a rights-based approach to Indigenous self-determination, protecting and developing Indigenous knowledges. The role of higher education institutions is to make sure there are structures in place that protect Indigenous knowledges, including ownership and access, involved in institutional research and other activities.

Argument of changing demographics. This argument speaks to the more pragmatic, functional pressures higher education institutions face. The Indigenous population in Canada is growing. It is estimated that, by 2036, the Indigenous population is likely to exceed 2.5 million persons. The Indigenous population is also nearly a decade younger than the rest of the population in Canada. In 2016, the median age in years for the Indigenous population was 29.1, but 41.3 for the non-Indigenous population (Statistics Canada, 2017). This means that more than 600,000 Indigenous youth will come of age to enter the higher education system with transition to the labour market within the next decade. Nevertheless, the statistics regarding Indigenous individuals attending universities are still quite alarming. In 2017, just over half (53%) of Indigenous adults aged 25 and over, living off-reserve, had earned some form of post-secondary qualification (Statistics Canada, 2017). The difference between Indigenous and non-Indigenous university completion rates had increased to 18.8 percentage points in 2016 (NIEDB, 2019). As demonstrated by these statistics, Indigenous students are becoming a significant part of the student body, supporting the higher education system through their tuition contributions and other fees. Yet, the absence of culturally relevant, Indigenous-led programming is directly impacting the retention and graduation rates of Indigenous youth in higher education (Brayboy et al., 2012). There is a need for the higher education sector to adapt to the changing demographics by opening new programs with relevant supports available for this growing group. In this process, more explicit attention must be paid to Indigenous epistemologies, including tribal sovereignty and self-determination, along with the racism experienced by Indigenous youth (Brayboy et. al., 2012). Such programmatic changes require a normative shift by universities situating themselves within critical decolonial frameworks and tackling their colonial underpinnings in order to make these new programs relevant and meaningful to Indigenous youth.

Argument of contributions to the economy. The economic contributions of Indigenous peoples in Canada have become substantial. The current contribution of Indigenous entrepreneurs and businesses to the Canadian economy is already noteworthy ($32 billion in 2016) (CCAB, 2016). The Indigenous tourism industry alone recorded a $1.7 billion contribution towards annual GDP in Canada in 2017, and there is a goal to increase this amount to $2.2. billion by 2024 (ITAC, 2019). The number of Indigenous entrepreneurs in Canada nearly tripled in twenty years, from 20,195 in 1996 to 54,255 in 2016 (Statistics Canada, 2017). The push towards advocating for a $100 billion Indigenous economy by 2023 in Canada has become a reality (see Indigenomics Institute, n.d.). As Indigenous businesses continue to grow, so do the employment opportunities, wages, and salaries that are attached to their contributions through tax revenues. Post-secondary degrees, training, and knowledge gained through the higher education system help to position Indigenous individuals better for any type of employment or entrepreneurial activity. Lower high school completion rates and limited access to higher education among Indigenous individuals are strongly correlated with poorer economic outcomes, including lower income levels (NIEDB, 2019). Furthermore, suicide rates among First Nations youth (aged 15 to 24 years) across Canada are five to six times higher than among non-Indigenous youth (Kirmayer et al., 2007). These statistics suggest a significant missed economic opportunity for the country. Higher education institutions have a mandate from the governments to provide students with sufficient skills and knowledge for employment and may be held accountable for not doing their part in addressing the issue.

Equity, diversity, and inclusion efforts. A new wave of strategic activities intended to address institutional equity, diversity, and inclusion (EDI) efforts has emerged in Canada (Tamtik & Guenter, 2019). This has been partly triggered by the political pressures put on higher education institutions through the work of the TRC (Deer, 2020). The stark evidence documenting the lived experiences of residential school survivors has revealed the contradiction between this history and the fact that Canadians enjoy the image of being kind, compassionate, and supportive of cultural diversity. The evidence has challenged some of the core beliefs shared among Canadians. Furthermore, the TRC report directly pointed to the violation of Canadian constitutional values of democracy, the rule of law, and respect for human rights and freedoms. It held the dominant cultural group responsible for the harm caused to Indigenous peoples, questioning their role in addressing the ongoing legacies of colonialism within the framework of equity, diversity, and inclusion. Documented evidence from residential school survivors has led to public outcry demanding accountability and action from the Canadian government and their institutions. The discovery of unmarked graves at many former residential schools in 2021 further provided an unforgiving reminder of the tragedies of colonialism and the pressing need for change. Consequently, there has been a renewed commitment among higher education institutions to work towards reconciliation within the larger framework of equity, diversity, and inclusion as they seek to establish a common ground between Indigenous and Canadian values. Decolonization has been gradually added to the list of institutional EDI activities as a crucial pillar of equity work. As a result, people have started to think of decolonial approaches as a required component of undoing the harm done to Indigenous peoples and of settlers' responsibility to address the ongoing legacies of colonialism.

Mission of the university. The idea of the university is that it is both a site of innovative knowledge and also a site of critical discourse. While the idea and purpose of the Canadian university has changed over time (Jones, 1998), the core vision of an institution dedicated to the pursuit of new innovative knowledge remains functionally relevant. Kuokkanen (2007a) argued that openness to various kinds of knowledges is a responsibility of academia. Openness towards Indigenous epistemes, and teaching and learning about them, is not a peripheral issue but part of the academy's mission and reason for existence (Kuokkanen, 2007a). The vision of the university as an institution that aims to serve the broader community and society in general also remains relevant. Consequently, not only the protection but also the advancement of Indigenous knowledges supports the core mission of the university, even if this means tackling the colonial foundations of the institution itself. The work of Indigenous academics has led to affirming and activating that mission. Indigenous knowledges reveal the wealth and richness of

Indigenous languages, worldviews, teachings, and experiences, all of which have been systematically overlooked among educational institutions (Battiste, 2005). The emerging scholarship around Indigenous knowledges creates an impetus for the university to reinforce its core mission but also an awareness around critically assessing how institutional structures work against Indigenous groups. As knowledge is constantly being created and recreated (Battiste, 2005), Indigenous knowledges should be an integral part of this important process, contributing to but also challenging the essence of the university. In this process, universities can fulfil their mission to advance knowledge while also promoting social justice and supporting the well-being of all members of their community.

Conclusion

In order to begin a conversation about Indigenous knowledges, higher education institutions must recognize the core premise that continues to shape their activities and forms the central pillar of their identity–colonial ideology. Settler colonialism works as an ongoing structural process and powerful ideology that maintains the established structures, rules, operations, and power hierarchies that continue to oppress Indigenous communities. Critical scholars have identified a range of mechanisms that work directly or indirectly against Indigenous peoples, including dispossession of lands, reinterpretation of history, and suppressing all attempts at self-determination through assimilation practices, othering, erasure, and silencing Indigenous experiences and knowledge frameworks. Therefore, closely examining these mechanisms, which directly and indirectly present themselves in the daily functioning of the higher education system in Canada, is the first step in any Indigenous or reconciliatory work that universities engage in. While higher education institutions are upholding established norms and structures, they are also uniquely positioned as powerful organizations that can trigger transformational change. As Smith (2017) noted, universities are institutions that can educate about difficult knowledges and contentious issues such as settler colonialism across disciplines and knowledge frameworks, making structural changes possible. There is a range of political, legal, functional, and social pressures that have contributed to increased awareness of decolonization in higher education. By responding to these pressures, universities have started to acknowledge and address the ongoing impacts of settler colonialism. The goal is eventually to create more inclusive and equitable environments for Indigenous peoples and non-Indigenous peoples alike.

Indigenous Knowledges and University

There's amazing knowledge amongst our Elders. It's equivalent to a PhD. For instance, the comment we always hear in our communities is blood memory. We carry the memories of our ancestors. We all do that. And some of us are open to those messages. Some of us are not aware of where our knowledge comes from. But we do have this knowledge that flows through our blood.

(Interview, 9 March 2018)

As universities recognize the importance of incorporating Indigenous knowledges in academia, there is a need to better understand the nature and complexities involved so that it is done respectfully and ethically. Indigenous peoples have always engaged in higher forms of learning. This is understood as a lifelong pursuit of specialized knowledge, gained cumulatively by living one's daily life. Indigenous knowledges are rooted in the lived experiences of a particular community and its philosophies, beliefs, and values, interwoven with spirituality and ceremony (Battiste, 2002; Battiste & Youngblood, 2000; Brayboy & Maughan, 2009; Stonechild, 2006). While recognizing the diversity of Indigenous communities, Battiste (2002, 2016) argued that there are internal consistencies among Indigenous knowledges across diverse communities. Indigenous peoples share relational worldviews whereby ontology (ways of being), epistemology (ways of knowing), methodology (ways of doing), and axiology (ethics of doing) are all interrelated and function through relationships (Hart 2010; Kovach, 2021; Wilson 2008). The centrality of relationships was emphasized by my research participants, one of whom summarized it as follows: *"Relationships are key to everything. Relationships are sacred"* (interview, 12 December 2018). While sharing commonalities, Indigenous knowledges are also uniquely place-based, emerging from a particular land or a region. There is an agreement among scholars that Indigenous knowledge systems cannot be uncoupled from the people, the land, or the ways the knowledge is generated, understood, enacted, and shared (Battiste, 2002; Latulippe & Klenk, 2020; McGregor, 2004; Simpson, 2004). Dei (2000) added that Indigenous knowledges are strongly connected to a long-term residence on the particular land where a knowledge is shaped, and that connection makes the land sacred and essential to one's knowing and being. Dispossession and removal from lands has had detrimental consequences to the survival of Indigenous knowledges, traditions, and languages.

Battiste (2002) argued that Indigenous knowledges should not be defined but rather described. Definitions adhere to the taxonomies and partial methodologies of Eurocentric knowledge and will not align well with Indigenous ways of knowing. Battiste (2002, p. 14) described Indigenous knowledges as follows:

> Indigenous knowledge thus embodies a web of relationships within a specific ecological context; contains linguistic categories, rules, and relationships unique to each knowledge system; has localized content and meaning; has established customs with respect to acquiring and sharing of knowledge (not all Indigenous peoples equally recognize their responsibilities); and implies responsibilities for possessing various kinds of knowledge.

Indigenous knowledges are viewed as a dynamic system of skills, abilities, and problem-solving techniques that embrace the essence of ancestral knowledge and are ingrained in the legacies of diverse histories and cultures (Battiste, 2005; Dei, 2008). My research participant who grew up with Anishinaabe teachings reflected on the changing nature of the purpose and practice of traditional ceremony:

> *You have contemporary teachings now replacing those traditional skills and lessons, how we articulate our stories in a contemporary way. Even how we do our ceremonies and why we do our ceremonies today is different from our ancestors. I look at, for instance, a sweat lodge. Most of our ceremonial life today is based on healing, and it wasn't that big of an issue, healing, before because we didn't have that much to heal from, you know. So, for us, it was traditionally, you know, feeding. Like, a lot of our ceremonies were about feeding, so it was trying to get acknowledgment from spirits that would help us find food to be able to survive, and these types of things.*
>
> (Interview, 22 November 2022)

This reflection illustrates how Indigenous knowledges are dynamic and evolve with time. Daes (1993) has been clear in stating that

Indigenous knowledges are a complete knowledge system with their own concepts of epistemology and their own scientific and logical validity. With their own conceptual and analytic frameworks, Indigenous knowledges stand equal to the western scientific body of knowledge and should be respected as such. There is an agreement that the concept of "Indigenous knowledges" has multiple layers and complex dimensions that are impossible to fully grasp without growing up with these knowledges and without having relationships with the particular community these knowledges emerge from.

While Indigenous knowledges share some epistemological consistencies, it is diversity that truly characterizes them. Indigenous knowledges are extremely rich geographically, culturally, and linguistically. No single Indigenous experience dominates other perspectives, no one heritage informs Indigenous knowledges, and no two heritages produce the same knowledge (Battiste, 2002). In Canada's 2016 census data, more than 70 Indigenous languages and more than 600 unique First Nations/Indian Bands were reported (Census Canada, 2016). This makes it necessary to use the word "knowledge" in the plural form to respect the heterogeneity and to recognize the diversity represented in this body of knowledge. Indigenous knowledges emerge from multiple and collective origins and are shaped by collaborative processes of knowledge creation. Indigenous knowledges emerge from ancestorial relationships found in place (Kovach, 2021), which explains the difference and diversity in their essence. "Indigenous" signals the dynamics embedded in the production, interrogation, and validation of such knowledges, marking exclusive ownership and legal rights, including intellectual property rights, over that knowledge. The exclusive ownership of a particular form of Indigenous knowledge rests with the Indigenous community where it originates, and it is the community's right to determine how, when, and where this knowledge is shared. While there is a growing interest in teaching about Indigenous knowledges in universities, it is essential to acknowledge that the ownership of Indigenous knowledges belongs to Indigenous communities and not the university.

Indigenous knowledges are contextual. They invite nuances, irregularities, and many possibilities within a single body of knowledge. These knowledges are drawn from a variety of sources and aim for a holistic approach to knowing. Castellano (2000) identified three broad aspects of Indigenous knowledges: *traditional knowledge*, which is intergenerational knowledge passed on by community Elders; *empirical knowledge*, which is based on careful observations of the surrounding environments (nature, culture, and society); and lastly *revealed knowledge*, which is provided through dreams, visions, and intuition. Brayboy

(2005), writing from American Indian experience, also distinguished *survival knowledge*, which is formed when academic knowledge is combined with cultural knowledge. This creates a powerful and strategic combination of knowledge that is essential for the resistance and survival of Indigenous groups in the presence of ongoing colonialism. Survival knowledge has emerged as a response to ongoing colonial power dynamics in academia, and its aim is to avoid further harm caused by the systemic marginalization of and discrimination against Indigenous knowledges. Therefore, deep care and carefulness are needed on the part of universities when engaging with Indigenous knowledges so that they do not further damage the essence of those knowledges and the contexts they emerge from.

In view of the complexities involved in Indigenous knowledge systems, it makes more sense to capture a few of the core dimensions of Indigenous knowledges rather than to try to list them all. Unpacking some of these distinct dimensions will help to draw attention to the core values that tend to ground Indigenous experiences. This understanding may be helpful when engaging with the processes of decolonial institutional change.

Land as a Teacher

Indigenous people view land as the first teacher, which forms a primary relationship with the individual. Kimmerer (2013) shared that land teaches reciprocity, obligations, and living in the world in a non-dominating and non-exploitative manner. Asking permission and taking only what is given, while remembering not to take more than one needs, are the core principles forming Indigenous relationships with land (Kimmerer, 2013). Land holds both spiritual and material meaning from which knowledge originates and is gathered (Haig-Brown & Hodson, 2009). The importance of land and one's responsibility to it came forward in my interviews, where a faculty member reflected on being accountable to land: "*It's the importance of being a steward of the land, and to hold Canada accountable for the Treaties that were signed [on these lands]*" (interview, 12 December 2018). The long-term ecological history of the land is like a cloth woven from the threads of stories and ceremonies provided by many different members of the community (Battiste, 2002). Land is always a living, breathing entity. Kimmerer (2013) recalled that harvesting plants is like harvesting nonhuman persons who are vested with awareness, intelligence, and spirit and whose families are waiting for them at home. When one regards plants as kinfolk, another set of harvesting regulations applies that contrasts with the legal regulations emerging from western practices (Kimmerer, 2013). Human identity is regarded as an extension of the environment, grounded in the values of respect, humility, and the idea of giving back. There is an element of inseparability between people and the natural world. According to one research participant: "*My social interaction and development has been Cree-based and land-based*" (interview, 9 March 2018). Indigenous knowledges are inherently tied to land, specifically to particular landscapes, landforms, and biomes where ceremonies are properly held, stories properly recited, medicines properly gathered, and transfers of knowledge properly authenticated (Battiste, 2002, p. 8). Even today, Indigenous peoples continue to depend directly on the natural environment that surrounds them culturally, socially, economically, and spiritually (Castellano, 2000, 2014). Therefore, it is difficult, if not impossible, to engage with Indigenous knowledges in a university setting in the same way as when they emerge in their environmental contexts. A research participant shared: "*My connection to my Indigeneity really revolves around still having that family farm to this day, on the edge of Lake Manitoba First Nation where my mother and her family are originally from*" (interview, 23 November 2018). There is an ongoing conversation occurring between Indigenous peoples and their environment that continues to provide teachings and new knowledge, even in urban settings.

The teachings of land centre on the values of respect and humility towards one's environment. This aspect has grounded the works and activities of Indigenous faculty and students in academia, pushing universities to reconsider some of their mainstream practices. For example, in 2018, the University of British Columbia reported its first PhD dissertation defence by an Indigenous student, Dawn Smith of Nuu-chah-nulth (NCN) territory, that took place on the land in the student's community and not in an office on the university campus (UBC, 2018a). This act of moving the dissertation defence to the community demonstrates respect and ethicality towards Indigenous values and knowledges. The centrality of land as a core value in Indigenous advocacy work has driven change regarding landscaping projects on university campuses by informing decisions on the choice of plants, guiding policies for smudging ceremonies, using Indigenous art in prominent spaces, and increasing engagement in land-based pedagogies in curriculum. Furthermore, advocating for the importance of Elders and knowledge keepers has been helpful in introducing Elder-in-residence programs that have been essential for the success and retention of Indigenous students in higher education, as Elders can serve as a key link between land, knowledge, and community.

The Role of Elders

Elders and traditional knowledge holders play a vital role in the transmission, interpretation, and application of Indigenous knowledges. Elders are symbols of Indigenous culture and knowledge in their very being. They are vital to Indigenous knowledges because of the traditional teachings, ceremonies, and stories they carry (Lavallée, 2009). Elders become Elders through community recognition for what they have learned and experienced in life (Lavallée, 2020a). They have often experienced challenges in their own lives that have led them to deep learning and wisdom, which they can then share with others (Stiegelbauer, 1996). The knowledge carried by Elders varies, as one should expect of any living, dynamic knowledge system that is continually responding to new experiences and fresh insights (Battiste, 2002). As each individual is unique in their experience, learning, and personality, the knowledge of Elders also varies. Each Elder has potentially something different to offer. Some Elders have been deeply immersed in traditional knowledge and ceremonies; others have deeper knowledge of languages. They operate as teachers, facilitators, healers, and guides using ceremony and herbs, but sometimes just talking with an Elder helps to nurture one's body, mind, and spirit (Waldram, 1994). As such, Elders are commonly approached by community members for their insights into difficult decisions ranging from health issues to community development and governmental negotiations (Stiegelbauer, 1996). Elders are often seen as catalysts for Indigenous knowledges, spirituality, and traditions; however, it is the collective experience that shapes their knowledge. In the context of universities, Elders serve as cultural advisors and mentors, helping to guide students, researchers, and faculty in their understanding of Indigenous knowledges. They also play a critical role in the development of Indigenous curricula and programs, ensuring that Indigenous knowledge is shared in a way that is respectful, ethical, and grounded in Indigenous perspectives. The contributions of Indigenous Elders are essential to promoting Indigenous and reconciliatory approaches and the well-being and self-determination of Indigenous communities in academia.

Experience as a Teacher

Knowledge grounded in cumulative lived experience forms a fundamental dimension of Indigenous worldviews. This dimension features the power of the collective that emerges from relationships and centres on intergenerational wisdom as its core value. Battiste (2002, p. 18) stated that the distinctive features of Indigenous knowledges are learning by observation and learning by doing through authentic experiences and individualized instruction. Oral language plays a crucial role in this process. Battiste (2002, p. 2) stated:

> Often oral and symbolic, it [Indigenous knowledge] is transmitted through the structure of Indigenous languages and passed on to the next generation through modelling, practice, and animation, rather than through the written word.

Ceremonies and storytelling are central components of many Indigenous peoples' methods of gaining new knowledge (Archibald, 2008). Stories help to ground people in their lifeways and practices; they help to restore balance and situate one in the circle of knowledge (Kimmerer, 2013). Stories that are both heard and empathetically felt work as guardians of cumulative knowledge and put the onus of understanding their nuances on the hearer rather than the speaker (Brayboy, 2005). Oral knowledge is, thus, a real and legitimate form of data, used as a vehicle for the transmission of culture, knowledge, and power in Indigenous epistemologies (Brayboy, 2005). In higher education institutions, acquiring academic written language and delivering clearly articulated messages have been more important than active storytelling, a norm that has devalued the cultural experiences of Indigenous students (Brayboy, 2005). When Indigenous peoples are denied the right to practise and share their oral knowledge, this can lead to the loss of cultural identity, language, and traditions. It perpetuates the legacy of colonialism, which seeks to assimilate Indigenous cultures to western values and practices. By recognizing and valuing the oral methods of knowing used in Indigenous communities, universities can promote the preservation of Indigenous cultures and knowledge systems and support the self-determination and well-being of Indigenous peoples.

The premise of Indigenous knowledges is that objectivity is grounded in subjectivity. Tewa educator Gregory Cajete (2004) has argued that direct subjective experience, predicated on a personal and collective closeness to nature, will lead to deeply rooted knowledge. Native sciences base their interpretations of natural phenomena on context and create meaning through a multiplicity of metaphorical stories, symbols, and images to explain events in nature. Cajete (2004) argued that Native sciences strive to understand and apply the knowledge gained from participation in the here and now and that they emphasize our role as members of the natural world rather than as people striving to be in control of it. In contrast, Eurocentric knowledge is concerned with objectivity and claims that true scientific knowledge arises from objectivity.

An important aspect of experiential knowledge is that it can be gained through rituals or ceremonies that incorporate dreaming, visioning, meditation, and prayer. Again, key people in this process are Elders and other practitioners who have developed the ability to gain knowledge through spiritual experiences. Learning from such experiences is encoded in community praxis as a way of synthesizing knowledge derived from introspection. Hence, Indigenous knowledges recognize and affirm the centrality of spiritual experiences that lead to new knowledge. In western scientific knowledge such sources are regarded as non-scientific, and their validity is often questioned. Only gradually have universities and higher education institutions become more open to research grounded in experiential knowledge and spirituality. Some examples of defended theses by Indigenous scholars that include dreams, visions, and sacred stories are those by Moses (2012) at McGill University, Farrell-Morneau (2014) at Lakehead University, Christian (2017) at the University of British Columbia, and Fontaine (2018) and Simpson (1999) at the University of Manitoba. In these works, dreams and spiritual experiences have been included to guide the research inquiry as important methodological tools drawing from Indigenous epistemologies.

Relationships as a Teacher

Wilson (2001) noted that the Indigenous paradigm of knowing comes from the fundamental belief that knowledge is relational. Indigenous knowledges are grounded in the vibrant relationships between people, their ecosystems, and other living beings and spirits that share their lands (Battiste & Youngblood, 2000). A research participant summarized this point as follows: *"Who I am is because of my mother, my father, my aunts, my uncles, my grandparents, my siblings, my cousins"* (interview, 12 December 2018). Dion (2007) recalled that Indigenous knowledges are directly attached to community and are accessed through day-to-day work and interaction with the community. Indigenous knowledges are often generated through consensus, cooperation, and collective engagement. In comparison, the western convention of thought typically emphasizes individual status and competition, especially in the era of the knowledge economy. Central to Indigenous perception is the belief that the world comprises an infinite web of relationships, which extend and are incorporated into the entire social condition of the individual. Social ties apply to everyone and everything, including the land. Knowledge is shared with all creation, including animals, plants, the Earth, and the whole cosmos.

The centrality of relationships comes forward through language. Rather than using nouns for objects, the Indigenous worldview describes interactions (e.g., in Cree, "sofa" translates to "someplace where you sit"; Wilson, 2001, p. 177). Cajete (1999, p. 78) brought forth another example, noting that there is no word for education, science, or art in most Indigenous languages. "Coming to know" is the best translation for education in most Indigenous traditions, an expression that marks the relationality between the person and knowledge. In this paradigm, an idea is not important on its own; rather, it is one's relationship with that idea that makes the idea valuable. Wilson (2001) also noted that ideas cannot be owned or discovered; instead they become meaningful through mutual relationships. Kimmerer (2013) emphasized that, when a language dies, much more than words are lost; a perspective through which to see the world has disappeared. As language plays such a crucial role in Indigenous knowledges, many Indigenous faculty members have dedicated their careers to teaching Indigenous languages in academia: "*This is an important piece, that we transmit knowledge [...] from one generation to the next. We have people, Indigenous people, who come to our university and are trying to keep our culture alive through language. So, they offer language courses*" (interview, 12 December 2018). Anishinaabemowin (the language of the Anishinaabe people) is taught at Lakehead University and the University of Manitoba. Cree language is taught at the University of Saskatchewan and the University of Alberta. Inuktitut (the language of the Inuit) is offered at the University of Ottawa and Memorial University. Haudenosaunee languages such as Mohawn, Oneida, and Onondaga are taught at McMaster University and Western University, and Michif (spoken by Métis peoples) is taught at the University of Regina, among others.

The symbol of a gift is often used in Indigenous worldviews to establish and recognize reciprocal relationships. Through gift giving arises an acknowledged collective and individual responsibility towards various forms of life (Kuokkanen, 2007a). This philosophy helps to secure our survival as a society, as reciprocity and giving back are used to create conditions where all living beings can coexist. Kimmerer (2013) noted that gifts are not meant for keeping. The meaning of a gift is in its movement – passing it along and trusting that what is being put out to the universe will always come back. The author also recalled that all gifts are multiplied in relationships and that our work as individuals is to discover what we can give. Beck and Pidgeon (2020) noted that the principle of reciprocity goes beyond "give-and-take." It is about respecting different knowledges and experiences and understanding that each person involved in relationships has something to contribute and something to learn. Kovach (2009) pointed out that there is a sense of commitment to the people in many Indigenous societies. Inherent in this commitment is an understanding of the reciprocity of life and accountability to one another.

Indigenous knowledges, grounded in relationships, must be tended to and renewed (Kovach, 2009), particularly in higher education settings. Building stronger and lasting relationships is grounded in values of taking time, showing love, learning about the other, and respecting different experiences. Relationships are based on trust and built via active engagement with localized knowledge. Indigenous advocacy work has therefore focused on creating awareness of these aspects of Indigenous ways of knowing. This approach directly juxtaposes with the ideas of meritocracy and individual competition that often drive the pursuit of knowledge in universities. Brayboy (2005) noted that Indigenous students often attend higher education at the request of their communities. University credentials are pursued for the larger purpose of gaining skills that may be useful for their communities to flourish. If those relationships are not respected, students find themselves struggling as Eurocentric universities push the ideas of individualism and competition to succeed, which clash with Indigenous values of reciprocity.

Holistic Approach to Knowledges

Indigenous knowledges are considered (w)holistic, as they include not only empirical knowledge that is based on individual experiences and perceptions but also knowledge that expands beyond humankind and draws from animals, insects, land, and spirit (Absolon, 2010; Kovach, 2021). As Kovach (2021, p. 69) observed, "knowledge is cognitive, embodied, instinctual, and spiritual." There is an interrelatedness between these aspects of knowledge that form a whole, healthy person (Archibald, 2008; Pidgeon, 2016). Cajete (2004) argued for fluidity in knowledge, which creates a holistic dimension to knowing whereby truth is not a fixed point but rather an ever-evolving point in balance, perpetually created and perpetually new. People exist in an interconnected system that is constantly being influenced by the wider forces expressed through and by them at the individual and collective levels. The idea of interconnectedness expands to the various disciplinary fields known in the western knowledge paradigm. Indigenous knowledges tend to challenge the compartmentalized and fragmented nature of western sciences that value data-driven evidence-based approaches to knowledge. Interconnectedness is the foundation of Indigenous knowledges that binds together ecosystems, peoples, and places in a cyclical way.

The symbol of the circle has been used by many Indigenous communities to represent holistic approaches to knowledge. The image of a circle symbolizes wholeness, completeness, and, ultimately, wellness. Archibald (2008, p. 11) referenced a holistic circle, noting that "the never-ending circle forms concentric circles to show both the synergistic influence of and our responsibility toward the generations of ancestors, the generations of today, and the generations yet to come." Each Indigenous group has developed its own cultural content and meaning for the holistic circle symbol. For example, Sacred Circle teachings are used as a spiritual belief by Dakota Nations, the Blackfoot Confederacy, and the Cree, Saulteaux, and Assiniboine Nations in Canada (Regnier, 1994). The Sacred Circle symbolizes the idea of harmony and the belief that life occurs within a series of circular movements, building gradual relationships with the land and its broader environment. The use of the Medicine Wheel, which serves as a symbol and a tool to describe a holistic approach to life, is used among the Algonquin, Ojibway, and Cree Nations with some differences between these Nations. As described by Lavallée (2007, 2009), the Medicine Wheel is a circle that is divided into four quadrants, or segments, which are separate but interconnected. The symbolizing colours of black, white, yellow, and red represent the four races – all being equal yet interrelated. The Medicine Wheel also balances between the four spheres of humanity – the mental, physical, emotional, and spiritual. The core essence of the Medicine Wheel is its interdependency and unity, which create an equilibrium within a holistic, interconnected, and nested system (Bopp et al., 2004). Lavallée (2009) pointed out that, while it may seem a simple concept to capture, the teachings associated with the Medicine Wheel may take an entire lifetime to comprehend.

The core values grounding Indigenous (w)holistic approaches to knowledge are found in the 4R framework: *responsibility, respect, reciprocity,* and *relevance* (Archibald & Bowman, 1995; Kirkness & Barnhardt, 1991; Pidgeon, 2016). These values can help guide the work in higher education towards more balanced and equitable approaches to Indigenous knowledges. *Responsibility* leads to understanding the self in relation to others who carry different cultural perspectives and experiences (Beck & Pidgeon, 2020). It speaks to the responsibility of universities to educate themselves about alternative knowledge frameworks, so that Indigenous students will feel welcome there. Responsibility also suggests the opportunity to support participation and self-governance over the everyday activities and affairs of Indigenous peoples in the higher education sector. *Respect* denotes a system that honours different ways of knowing and the principle of the interconnectedness of knowledge and that offers the right for Indigenous peoples to exercise responsibility over their own lives (Kirkness & Barnhardt, 1991). Respect towards Indigenous knowledges is the foundation for building relationships with Indigenous communities in higher education. *Reciprocity* marks the two-way process of teaching, learning, and institutional decision making. This perspective enhances the importance of the collective and the value of co-creating knowledge collaboratively, which leads to decisions that are relevant and respectful towards various perspectives and experiences. As Kimmerer (2013) noted, through reciprocity a gift is replenished, and all of our flourishing is mutual. *Relevance* is driven by the idea that higher education in Canada should be meaningful to all. Every student, staff, and faculty member should be able to see themselves in policies, programs, and services and should be able to learn and co-create new knowledge. Pidgeon (2019) added a fifth R to this framework – *reverence*. Reverence is seen as a grounding value in Indigenous epistemology whereby the Earth, the cosmos, and the individual form interconnected components within Indigenous knowledges. Pidgeon (2019) noted that reverence is not articulated as an R because it connects to the spiritual dimension, and sacred knowledge doesn't always belong to the academy. The principle of reverence further highlights the interconnected relationship between individuals and the physical and spiritual realms and expands the notions of epistemology, ontology, and axiology in Indigenous knowledges, which are inherently connected to the other Rs.

Kovach (2021, p. 68) summarized the key aspects of Indigenous epistemologies or ways of knowing as follows:

- Multiple sources of knowledge, more commonly recognized as *holism*;
- A tangible and intangible animate world that is process-oriented and cyclical, such as that expressed in verb-oriented languages (e.g., with-*ing* endings), which comprise many Indigenous languages; and
- A web of interdependent, contextual *relationships* over time, such as relationships with place, family, and community.

Eurocentric education and political systems and their assimilation processes have severely eroded and damaged Indigenous knowledges

(Battiste, 2016). Established societal structures continue to erase the link between Indigenous knowledges and the places these knowledges emerge from. The tendency to overlook Canadian colonial histories and misinterpret contemporary colonial realities has had detrimental effects on Indigenous peoples, removing the specific and unique relationships peoples have with their lands and place-based knowledges (St. Denis, 2011). These dynamics are grounded in settler colonial ideology and materialize through the politics of knowledge.

Knowledge Politics

The recognition of Indigenous knowledges in higher education is not simply an academic matter but an issue involving knowledge politics. Scholars have long pointed to the inherent power dynamics and politics involved in assigning value to knowledge systems (Battiste & Youngblood, 2000; Foucault, 1980, 1983; Weiler, 2001). The way knowledge is created and communicated, and who owns it and under what circumstances, are all decisions made by the people with power and formal authority. Knowledge is never neutral, and its validity in higher education settings should be viewed in the context of the normative power that groups hold. The dominant cultural group asserts its inherent cultural values, assumptions, and societal norms over others. In Canadian higher education, the dominant body of knowledge has been scientific knowledge stemming from western knowledge frameworks, which has been viewed as a universal body of thought (Dei, 2000). Indigenous epistemologies and ways of making sense of the world have been perceived as inferior. This has resulted in the alienation of Indigenous knowledges and a sense that they are irrelevant. Over decades, Indigenous scholars have documented the systemic and epistemological injustices that Indigenous knowledges and peoples have had to confront in higher education (see Battiste, 2000; Battiste et al., 2002; Kuokkanen, 2007a). Ahenakew (2016, p. 327) argued that the denial of non-western ways of knowing has been ingrained in higher education, with more recent institutional efforts offering only conditional forms of integration that continue to support dominant ways of thinking. Kuokkanen (2007a) pointed out how prevailing indifference, epistemic ignorance, and a lack of interest in knowledge that is different from western knowledge have dismissed and systemically excluded Indigenous faculty in academia. This critical work has exposed how educational institutions have perpetuated the systems that have made Indigenous knowledges invisible, disjointed, and on the verge of becoming lost altogether. With the significant contributions of Indigenous scholars, Indigenous knowledges have been gradually revitalized, reimagined, and strengthened to slowly gain their rightful place in higher education.

Hierarchies of knowledge matter, as they position people differently in higher education with different career opportunities. It matters how knowledge is recognized for the purposes of faculty appointments, yearly assessments (i.e., annual progress reports), tenure, and promotion, as well as administrative leadership opportunities. In the realm of academic research, original, single-author publications are highly valued. This approach fails to acknowledge the intellectual contributions of ideas and theories that have been created collectively, informally, and sometimes incidentally, as may often be the case with Indigenous knowledges. Research funding and institutional support tend to be linked to projects that continue to uphold the mainstream academic knowledge in which quality is assessed by colleagues through a standardized peer-review process. However, activities such as standardization, categorization, various groupings, and taxonomies are not helpful in thinking about Indigenous knowledges, as their core pillar lies in diversity and contextuality. In a similar vein, student scholarships are typically given to those who are enrolled full-time and dedicating their time to working on mainstream research projects with faculty, positioning themselves better for future career opportunities. To challenge these power hierarchies based on one's different cultural experience is a difficult task. As Corntassel (2012) noted, by focusing on "everyday" acts of resurgence, the disruption of physical, social, and political colonial boundaries can be slowly achieved.

Language plays an important role in asserting and maintaining hierarchies of knowledge. Some words are more helpful than others in weakening established power relations. The words "Indigenous perspectives," "Indigenous ways of knowing," "Indigenous epistemologies," "Indigenous knowledge systems," and "Indigenous lived experiences" are perceived as more balanced references to Indigenous knowledges. In contrast, the concepts of "traditional knowledge" or "folk knowledge" can come across as limiting, as these words tend to refer to the idea of passing down a relatively old and fixed body of information, essentially unchanged, from one generation to another (Battiste, 2002). Indigenous knowledges, like any other knowledge pool, are vibrant, dynamic, and changing. The term "Indigenous cultural knowledge" is often used and viewed as paramount to Indigenous identity and as the foundation of self-determination (Alfred & Corntassel, 2005; Vowel, 2016). This reference works if Indigenous knowledges are treated wholistically and with proper nuance. According to Brayboy (2005, p. 434), Indigenous cultural knowledge contains an understanding of what it means to be a member of a particular tribal Nation; it includes particular traditions, issues, and ways of being and knowing that make an individual a member of a community. Culture is rooted in lands as well as ancestors who lived on those lands before current community members (Brayboy, 2005). The term "Indigenous cultural knowledge" becomes problematic when associated with non-Indigenous perspectives of culture, particularly within the discourse of multiculturalism. The political narrative of multiculturalism in Canada is often projected through pedagogy and curriculum in (higher) education spaces and works as a form of colonialism that minimizes and erases Indigenous rights to land and sovereignty (see Sabzalian, 2019; St. Denis, 2011). For Indigenous peoples, Indigenous cultures can best be protected by claiming Indigenous nationhood (Sabzalian, 2019; St. Denis, 2011). Partly for those reasons, Battiste and Youngblood (2000, p. 35) argued that they reject the Eurocentric concept of culture for Indigenous knowledge, heritage, and consciousness as overly limiting. They argued that the Eurocentric meaning of the word "culture" is too narrow a concept to denote a whole worldview, and thus this word can result in fragmented understandings of Indigenous ways of knowing that leave the colonial structures embedded in education intact. Similarly, Kuokkanen (2007a, pp. 58–9) problematized the word "culture" and suggested using the phrase "Indigenous epistemes" in the sense of worldview or discursive practice, but only if the phrase is accompanied by a careful investigation of higher education institutions' responsibility to address various exclusionary practices towards other ways of knowing. Another commonly used phrase in education, used regularly in policy documents in association with Indigenous youth, is the concept of the "achievement gap." This phrase reinforces the dominance of western intellectual knowledge as the gold standard against which everyone else should be measured. It approaches Indigenous students from a deficit perspective and thus perpetuates the authority and power of established knowledge hierarchies without critically examining the shortfalls of the system itself. According to Ladson-Billings (2006), there is a need to move away from the discourse of "achievement gap" to "educational debt," which focuses on the limitations of the system, comprised of historical, economic, sociopolitical, and moral components that have worked against disadvantaged groups. Deficit perspectives on Indigenous knowledges are not helpful. They are part of a neoliberal ideology in which the primary discourse centres on assigning blame to individuals rather than recognizing the shortcomings of societal structures that have created inequities for various groups. Pidgeon (2016, 2008) emphasized that Indigenous student success should be assessed differently and go beyond university graduation rates. Indigenous success is connected to a broader effort by Indigenous peoples to keep their cultural integrity. The achievement and success of Indigenous peoples can be realized by having institutions of learning be respectful of the epistemologies, ecologies, and geographies of Indigenous peoples (Pidgeon, 2008). Such a wholistic view, she argued, must incorporate the physical, emotional, spiritual/cultural, and cognitive needs of the individual, family, and community (tribal/local/global) (Pidgeon, 2008). Broadening our understandings of achievement and success, while incorporating language that doesn't hold up imperial standards, is necessary for creating more equitable spaces in higher education for Indigenous students.

Limitations of Universities in Engaging with Indigenous Knowledges

There are several limitations that stem from knowledge politics that create barriers for universities to engage with Indigenous knowledges. The colonial ideology that academia is grounded in is the most pertinent. Ongoing processes of knowledge oppositionality, misappropriation of Indigenous knowledges, othering of Indigenous methodologies, and dismissing Indigenous theorizing continue to work against Indigenous knowledges and have created a deficit-based binary view that dismisses Indigenous knowledges. Indigenous knowledges are often conceptualized in opposition to Eurocentric knowledge as "science" versus "non-science" (Nakata, 2007, p. 9). This privileging of empiricism over contextualized wholicism has pushed Indigenous knowledges to the sidelines (Kovach, 2021) and created simplistic one-dimensional understandings of Indigenous knowledges. Furthermore, reinterpretation of Indigenous knowledges as "not scientific" has taught Indigenous peoples to mistrust not only their own Indigenous knowledges and Elders' wisdom but also their own instincts (Battiste, 2016). These practices have caused more harm to Indigenous knowledges. The contextuality and diversity embodied in Indigenous knowledge paradigms make it difficult to translate Indigenous knowledges into the western paradigm, which is grounded in the values of individualism, meritocracy, and empirical assessment. The spiritual and community-centred nature of Indigenous knowledges does not fit the western paradigm. This multi-dimensionality of Indigenous knowledges makes it difficult for the mainstream academy to rationalize or contain their essence and parameters, which can potentially lead to misappropriation of the knowledges. This multi-dimensionality continues to present challenges for higher education in accepting the fact that there is no one singular Indigenous knowledge, way of knowing, or way of learning. Accepting that Indigenous epistemologies, methodologies, and theories are equal to, yet distinct from, western knowledges is an important step to counterbalance the hierarchies emerging from knowledge politics. Most importantly, this richness emerging from diverse ways of knowing provides an enormous opportunity for Canadian universities to protect and foster Indigenous knowledges, if done respectfully.

The inclusion of Indigenous knowledges in higher education requires a significant shift in knowledge politics, a challenge to the existing power dynamics, and a recognition of the ongoing impacts of colonialism. Attempting to include Indigenous knowledges and ways of understanding in curriculum is a contentious topic that needs to be approached with carefulness and caution. Nakata (2007) pointed out that making Indigenous knowledges more inclusive within dominant educational spaces will likely result in extraction of elements of Indigenous knowledges, which will lead to simplifying the knowledges. Knowledges will get separated from their holders, and this will result in gradually renewed and transformed versions of these knowledges that are translated into English. Barriers for Indigenous students and scholars to access higher education further add to this potential of misappropriating Indigenous knowledges. While not ideal, the solution Nakata offered is teaching students critical skills and building their language and tools to describe and analyse what they engage in when they are involved in difficult intersections between Indigenous, decolonial, and western approaches to knowledges (Nakata, 2007). It is essential that these conversations are grounded in the critical understandings of hierarchies created by knowledge politics. Therefore, attempts to teach Indigenous knowledges in contemporary higher education settings will always have limitations in transferring such complex knowledge systems into a structure that functions to marginalize Indigenous communities. If done without care, this can lead to commodification of Indigenous knowledges as they are repackaged conveniently for mainstream audiences and the deeper cultural and spiritual meanings of these knowledges are simplified. Addressing the realities of knowledge politics that work to marginalize Indigenous knowledges is paramount in critical decolonial work and required for systematic change in higher education. It is important that Indigenous knowledge systems are not merely added to the existing curriculum as a token gesture, but rather that they are integrated in a way that challenges the underlying knowledge politics and involves and empowers Indigenous communities.

Empowering Indigenous Knowledges

Empowerment of Indigenous knowledges in universities is an important step towards decolonial approaches. One of my study participants noted: *"Universities are where we come to learn. It should be open to Indigenous knowledges because, it's beautiful. It is self-affirming, and it helps people grow"* (interview, 12 December 2018). Scholars agree that Indigenous knowledges should be examined in the broader context of Indigenous empowerment (Battiste, 2002; Herbert, 2010; Stonechild, 2006). Empowerment is understood as engaging in interactions with knowledges that are meaningful, respectful, and ethical, that grow capacity, and that serve as effective change agents for Indigenous communities at large (Herbert, 2010). Cajete (2004) believed that individual empowerment and agency come from one's cultural origin and the belief that human beings are active and creative participants in the world. Battiste (2005) emphasized how, in academic contexts, Indigenous scholars should work purposefully towards activating Indigenous knowledges, methodologies, experiences, and teachings to support self-determination that leads to the empowerment of peoples and knowledges that have been excluded for centuries. Wilson (2013) stated that Indigenous knowledges are meaningless and even harmful if their holders and practitioners are not simultaneously empowered and supported in their efforts to not only survive but also thrive. Wilson (2013) also asserted the importance of reflecting on the colonial past because the recovery of Indigenous knowledges is deeply intertwined with the process of decolonization. It is only through a conscious critical assessment that understanding of the impact of the historical processes of colonization can emerge and can lead to a meaningful change towards empowering Indigenous knowledges. As Pidgeon (2016) recalled, the achievement of Indigenous students in higher education should be assessed based on their experiences of feeling empowered, as this will strengthen Indigenous perspectives, experiences, and epistemologies at large.

There is a wealth of knowledge emerging both locally (Turtle Island or North America) as well as globally with a focus on Indigenous empowerment. In addition to foundational scholarship by authors such as Battiste (2000), Cajete (2000), and Smith (1999), just to name a few, there are a number of journals and journal special issues dedicated to Indigenous knowledges that promote, celebrate, and empower work emerging from Indigenous experiences. Some of these journals that collect a rich and growing body of scholarship by Indigenous authors include *Native Studies Review*; *Wicazo Sa Review*; the *Journal of Indigenous Research*; *AlterNative*; *Decolonization: Indigeneity, Education & Society*; and the *Canadian*

Journal of Native Education. These journals are guided by a broader mission of recovering and strengthening Indigenous knowledges as part of resistance to colonial structures in academia. This work has helped to build stronger partnerships among researchers and enhance cross-disciplinary conversations that benefit both academia and society. A special issue from 2004 of *American Indian Quarterly* has served as an anti-colonial project by making a significant contribution to the literature describing Indigenous knowledges and publishing critical work of authors across Turtle Island (see Wilson, 2004). The volume addresses contemporary societal problems guided by Indigenous knowledges and offers solutions in areas from erosion of biodiversity and ecological sustainability to well-being and new pedagogical approaches grounded in Indigenous cultures. A special issue of *KULA: Knowledge Creation, Dissemination, and Preservation Studies* has featured research on Indigenous knowledges emerging from the lands of Canada (see Hancock et al., 2021). Globally, Mātauranga Māori is an Indigenous knowledge system that incorporates Māori philosophical thought, worldview, and practice (Marsden & Henare, 1992). This knowledge system has been informing contemporary ecological research in Aotearoa New Zealand. Special issues of the *New Zealand Journal of Ecology* (see McAllister et al., 2019) and the *New Zealand Journal of Marine and Freshwater Research* (see Clapcott et al., 2018) are some examples of Mātauranga as a knowledge framework informing the ecology, marine, and freshwater research in New Zealand. A special issue of *AlterNative* from 2014 has explored the theme of Indigenous knowledges impacting the environment from an Australian perspective (see Hutchings, 2014). These are but a few selected examples that demonstrate the increasing emergence of Indigenous knowledges that is leading to empowerment and collaboration on shared societal problems. As a result of such scholarly work by Indigenous individuals, there is an increased momentum towards valuing Indigenous knowledges that carries through higher education, creating broader awareness and stronger understanding of the importance of Indigenous knowledges in contemporary academic contexts.

Conclusion

As demonstrated in this chapter, Indigenous knowledges in their diversity and interdependency present a unique challenge to the Canadian higher education system, pushing the boundaries of what counts as valid knowledge. There is a critical need to examine the processes grounded in the politics of knowledge to reassess how knowledges are supported, validated, and legitimized in higher education contexts.

This includes examining the historical exclusion and ongoing impacts of colonialism. The growing presence of Indigenous knowledges has pressured universities to pause, listen, and reconsider the core foundations of mainstream knowledge paradigms and to reassess the value of western knowledges. In the most recent years, there has been an emerging inquiry by governments, international organizations, universities, scholars, and policy makers into Indigenous knowledges. Less is spoken about the limitations of non-Indigenous institutions in engaging with Indigenous ways of knowing. As Indigenous knowledges are often rooted in a specific community and land, there needs to be a high level of caution exercised when incorporating Indigenous knowledges in academia. It is best done by people from the community to make sure the work centres on Indigenous voices and perspectives and avoids misappropriation and simplification of complex meanings. It also includes working with Elders to ensure that their knowledge systems are represented appropriately in academic curriculum and research. It is important that the processes of addressing Indigenous knowledges in higher education are guided by decolonizing approaches that aim to shift the present dynamics of knowledge politics. Improving access and recognizing the efforts of Indigenous scholars and educators help to create space where Indigenous empowerment can emerge to the benefit of Indigenous communities. This involves fostering ongoing dialogue, collaboration, and learning between Indigenous and non-Indigenous people in order to ensure that Indigenous knowledges are taught and shared in a way that is culturally relevant, ethical, and respectful.

Theorizing Institutional Change from a Decolonial Perspective

Every summer I go up north and we harvest medicine, we harvest roots. So, literally we push our boat into a shallow part of the lake or river, and then, you kind of bend and pull. We pick the roots, the root system. Lots of roots, as they really get stuck to the ground. And this is when you recognize that's what the system is. /... / I think a lot of what we end up doing is shapeshifting the academy. So, I think I've become really an expert at shapeshifting. You know, a trickster.

(Interview, 9 March 2018)

This chapter introduces the theoretical perspective that helps to situate and explain the institutional change in higher education that has resulted from the emergence of Indigenous knowledges. The theoretical insights presented in this chapter are influenced by my positionality and training as a non-Indigenous researcher with epistemological groundings in the western theoretical and methodological paradigm. I recognize the limitations of western theories, as they continue to uphold and prioritize colonial knowledge hierarchies over Indigenous knowledge frameworks. I am also acutely aware of the limitations my non-Indigenous identity creates when I engage with Indigenous knowledges and methodologies without having the necessary cultural connections to these knowledges. I try to resolve this dilemma by recognizing the shortcomings of western theorizations and engaging with critical decolonial perspectives that centre on a consciousness of oppression and social inequity. In this process, I am reminded of the importance of respect, relevance, reciprocity, and responsibility (Kirkness & Barnhard, 1991) in work involving Indigenous contexts. Western theoretical frameworks have been critiqued for perpetuating neutral reductionist and one-dimensional narratives of knowing (Lather, 1991). They tend to produce universalist approaches to knowledge that help to conceal social injustices while overlooking the diverse experiences of marginalized groups (Calderón, 2011; Capper, 2018; Grosfoguel, 2013). Calderón (2011) called out the flattened epistemology present in Eurocentric knowledges that is totalizing and precludes critical interventions derived from an organic knowledge emerging from an Indigenous paradigm. Capper (2018) identified critical epistemic unconsciousness particularly within the field of educational administration, which is often grounded in organizational theory that tends to be linear and does not carefully consider a diverse range of experiences. Such an approach is problematic, as it continues to perpetuate limited understandings of equity-oriented perspectives during the training of the next generation of administrators and school leaders. Capper (2018) advocated for a multiple-paradigm approach as a potential way forward. Understanding a range of epistemologies can help school leaders and scholars determine the epistemological underpinnings of various educational practices and identify the limits and possibilities those practices may create (Capper, 2018). I appreciate and accept this criticism. I also believe that it is important not to fall into absolute rejection of the western forms of knowledge, which can then become a hindrance to learning. We need to be cautious about not reinforcing the "politics of resentment" that unintentionally binds together the colonizer and colonized (Chen, 2010, p. 72). So, to counterbalance the reproduction of one-dimensional hierarchical knowledge, I use insights from institutional theory with a critical decolonial lens that considers existing power hierarchies and emphasizes individual and collective agency in theorizing institutional change. A critical decolonial lens is important for examining the established power dynamics, making those hierarchies transparent, and creating critically informed opportunities for institutional change (Grande, 2015). A critical decolonial lens also has the potential to draw attention to the interconnectedness of knowledges, which is a value grounding Indigenous ways of knowing, while opening up opportunities for learning across diverse knowledge systems. The overall goal of this work is to build equity-oriented policy and practice in higher education. In this chapter, I present a framework that is intentional in viewing institutional change through a critical lens guided by Indigenous knowledges and centred in the processes of decolonial learning.

My personal dilemma of navigating between diverse knowledge frameworks is representative of the larger epistemological conflict that Canadian universities are grappling with. This conflict unfolds around accepting, as a starting point, that settler colonialism keeps generating harmful violent experiences for Indigenous peoples. Universities are grounded in European imperialism and perpetuate Eurocentric epistemologies in their theories, methodologies, and pedagogies through curriculum, policy, and governance structures. In their efforts to address change, their colonial structures are usually kept intact. It is difficult to remove oneself from the deeply rooted epistemology that forms one's personal or institutional essence. Nevertheless, confronting these structures is a necessary step in decolonial learning. In the introductory quote to this chapter, an Indigenous faculty member described the root system as a metaphor for the colonialism that has a firm grip on universities, noting the laborious work that must be done when working towards systemic change. This work resembles pulling the roots of a plant that is strongly grounded in its established environment. The removal of a plant may lead to the creation of a different ecosystem. This process takes time, as growth is dependent on various environmental factors as well as nourishment from the soil. The takeaway from this story is that institutional change is a complex, intertwined process without a quick linear path to or one version of systemic change. The outcome is impacted by the whole ecosystem – forces push from within, and forces press from the outside, but one's own agency is also imperative to shaping the outcome. Indigenous faculty members commented that this change towards prioritizing Indigenous knowledges in Canadian higher education is unfolding, yet it has been a slow process. This chapter begins by providing insights from institutional theory on societal norms, how they emerge and get established, and where there are opportunities for change. Examining the concept of decolonization in relation to learning allows the proposal of a framework that can help generate criticality towards one's biases and collectively established norms, creating a foundation for meaningful engagement with institutional change.

Norm Perspective on Institutional Change

Settler colonialism is a criticized, yet strongly established, ideology in many parts of the world, grounded in dominance and control. Norm literature within institutional theory is a useful starting point for examining how powerful norms are created and how they become established and accepted as patterns guiding social behaviour. Finnemore and Sikkink (1998, p. 891) defined a norm as "a standard or appropriate behavior for actors within a given identity." In other words, a social norm is what people in a group believe to be normal and what they perceive to be a typical or appropriate behaviour (Tankard & Paluck, 2016). Individuals learn about norms and adopt the shared beliefs, values, and behaviours of their social group through social interactions and internalizations (Finnemore & Sikkink, 1998). Norms are conveyed through interactions with family and close friends, learning from media, and experiencing accepted behaviours in schools and workplaces. Our learning is guided by the legacy of the past and thus by socio-cultural contexts deeply rooted in power hierarchies and collective experiences. The success of a norm rests not just in what it says, but in who accepts it and who benefits from it. In norm-building practice, it is the majority that shapes the narrative and determines what is accepted or excluded as undesirable behaviour (DiMaggio & Powell, 1983; Horne & Mollborn, 2020). Once norms are established, they are reinforced through a variety of mechanisms such as social pressure, rewards or punishments that reinforce or discourage certain behaviours, and calls to follow formal rules and policies. In order to establish a norm, there are four main components that must be present: 1) *shared identity* (a group to which the norm applies); 2) *propriety* (the basis on which norms are deemed appropriate or inappropriate); 3) *behaviour* (required action); and 4) *collective expectations* (group beliefs about proper behaviour) (Finnemore & Hollis, 2016). Settler colonialism became an accepted norm when shared identity was established through Eurocentric socio-political order and thought. Propriety was created through claiming ownership of lands and other assets. Normalized behaviour still follows Eurocentric cultural traditions with a collective expectation that everyone will assimilate to the behaviours of the cultural majority. The benefits of settler colonialism have been directed towards the majority cultural groups (white settlers) with limited power for others to create counter-narratives. Nevertheless, norm literature argues that norms are not static and norm perception is a dynamic process in which there will always be pressures to change old norms and create new ones (Finnemore & Hollis, 2016). Higher education institutions are a key space where social interactions are encouraged and learning is supported. In essence, universities play a critical role in the norm-changing process by creating a space where accepted norms can be contested and challenged, eventually shaping larger societal behaviours.

Critical scholarship has problematized settler colonial norms particularly from Indigenous perspectives (see the work of Brayboy, 2005; Brunette-Debassige, 2021; Grande, 2018; Tuck & Yang, 2018). Indigenous faculty have dedicated their efforts to work towards creating normative change through challenging behaviours and values dominant in university structures, including policies and services, academic programs, and overall institutional culture. As a result, the established and shared normative behaviours have gradually started to change.

Shared identity has now been established among Indigenous communities but also with other equity-seeking groups. The term BIPOC (Black, Indigenous, People of Colour) is used as an umbrella term that creates alliances and forms a new platform for challenging oppressive societal structures, encouraging collaboration over shared goals. *Propriety* based on criticizing and questioning the oppressive behaviour of the cultural majority towards Indigenous groups has called out the violence, erasure, and othering of Indigenous knowledges. The *behaviour* that is required to address these issues has been identified as returning land to Indigenous peoples and grounding change within the processes of Indigenization and decolonization. There is a *collective expectation* that inequitable behaviours by various societal groups including governments, non-governmental organizations, and the public should be altered. The argument around diversity and equity presses on collective responsibility and, thus, speaks to the majority of non-Indigenous peoples about their obligation to support the efforts of Indigenous groups towards self-determination as an equity issue grounded in the Canadian constitution.

In addition to norm change from within, there is a range of external pressures that are forcing universities to change. Institutional theory proposes that institutions change when the legitimacy of their current normative practices is called into question (Meyer & Rowan, 2006; Olsen, 2007; Scott, 2005; Thornton, 2004). The voices of Indigenous communities have become an important pressure point for higher education institutions, challenging institutional legitimacy. Oliver (1992) has identified three categories of pressure that can erode an established organizational structure and lead to institutional change. These are *political, functional,* and *social* pressures. *Political* pressures may occur through increased involvement of the government directly or indirectly through the introduction or adoption of new legal frameworks or policy approaches. Examples of this would be adopting the UNDRIP framework, or commissioning work, such as that mandated by the Truth and Reconciliation Commission, that calls into question the roles and responsibilities of educational institutions, including universities. Under political pressures, the logic of confidence and institutional coherence begins to break down, as previously shared norms and legitimate behaviours become superseded by the pursuit of organizational survival (Oliver, 1992). The level of organizational resistance is linked to the level of dependence that the organization has on other organizations that make demands upon it. For example, as universities are directly dependent on governments' funding and general public support, they have little reason to resist the political pressures coming from government-mandated TRC recommendations. Nevertheless, political demands made by only one Indigenous individual without broader support from the organization may end without any visible consequences. Thus, political pressures serve as an important collective factor explaining shifts in the normative behaviours of universities.

Functional pressures may arise from demographic changes or performance-driven demands associated with universities' competition for various resources. Functional pressures exist when economic criteria of efficiency and effectiveness begin to conflict with or intrude on institutional definitions of success. As a result, organizational members may start questioning the intrinsic worth and legitimacy of a higher education degree and the functional relevance of universities to society in general. An example of a functional pressure would be the detection of low access and enrolment rates among Indigenous students in higher education institutions. This can be regarded as a lost opportunity from the perspective of revenue, as Indigenous youth are an increasing demographic group in Canadian society. To mitigate the pressure, higher education institutions are forced to make various program adjustments with focused recruitment strategies. Furthermore, in order to adapt to functional pressures, universities have become more open to inclusive leadership practices by creating new positions for Indigenous peoples at the senior level (e.g., vice presidents Indigenous, associate deans Indigenous). Functional pressures are associated with the practicalities required for organizational continuation.

Finally, institutional change may also occur through *social* pressures associated with differentiation of groups within an organization. Global social movements such as Black Lives Matter, Missing and Murdered Indigenous Women and Girls, and Idle No More have had an impact, according to my research participant:

> *movements around awareness related to gender violence and racial violence have increased their popularity as their information has gotten out to the public discourse. /... / I think that that has also, perhaps, maybe forced politicians to maybe change.* (Interview, 4 December 2018)

Increase in the representation of equity-seeking individuals will bring different interpretive frameworks and social definitions of accepted behaviours to the organization. As a result, these new beliefs act to diminish consensus and problematize taken-for-granted attitudes and practices (Oliver, 1992). These various, often unpredictable, environmental pressures may create interdependencies between actors and a need to collaborate to maintain the legitimacy of the organization. For example, globalization and increased economic competition have created conditions whereby network-based horizontal modes of governance in higher education are emerging (Austin & Jones, 2015; Chou & Ravinet, 2017; Zapp & Ramirez, 2019). This dynamic may also explain the increased involvement of Indigenous groups in university governance and overall decision making.

Responding pragmatically, without decolonial learning, to environmental pressures such as the political, functional, and social pressures described above has led to a policy–practice disconnect in universities. A plethora of research has described how racism and discrimination against Black and minority ethnic students causes stress, discomfort, and anxiety, making these students leave university and face unemployment (e.g., Bhopal & Pitkin, 2020; Iverson, 2005; Ladson-Billings & Tate, 1995). Likewise, Indigenous students in Canadian higher education battle trauma, addictions, and mental health issues stemming from limited recognition of their cultural identity (Gallop & Bastien, 2016; Gaudry & Lorenz, 2018; Pidgeon 2008). Scholars have argued that EDI policy initiatives have a tokenistic nature and do not address issues around the discriminatory institutional culture in academia (Doharty et al., 2021). Instead of engaging in systemic normative shift, university policies have been characterized by a "terror of performativity" where administrators comply with a set of equity targets to demonstrate productivity but do not address the root causes of these inequities (Ball, 2003, p. 215). This policy–practice disconnect can be explained by the fact that insincerely adopted norms are less likely to be openly contested. After all, the whole point of going through the motions of adopting a different norm is to gain benefits from the appearance of accepting the norm. Yet, what is needed for normative change is confrontation of the deeply rooted historical legacies that are represented in institutional structures and that shape individual deep core beliefs and value systems (Sabatier, 1986). Learning how to move beyond the discourse of purely "managing" diversity through performance indicators (Klein, 2016, p. 147) and how to create communities where diverse perspectives are truly valued has become a pressing administrative problem of immediate urgency. There is agreement that approaching change from a learning perspective has the potential to gradually shape normative beliefs (Nutley et al., 2007; Weiss & Bucuvalas, 1980). Critical scholars have emphasized the importance of the decolonial thinking that must occur in order to change systems of institutional hierarchy and established power dynamics in academia (Bhopal & Pitkin, 2020).

Decolonization as an Emerging Norm

The work around decolonization has gained increased attention and acceptance in higher education, which suggests the emergence of a new social norm in the making. Decolonization challenges the ongoing impacts of colonialism and seeks to restore Indigenous ways of knowing, being, and doing. According to Shahjahan et al. (2022), decolonization has evolved from theory into a socio-political movement that is forcing universities to reform their oppressive power relations and to shift institutional norms. Shahjahan et al. (2022, p. 83) defined decolonization as a process devoted to "undoing colonial processes and logic." Styres (2017) understood decolonization as an unsettling process of unravelling the tangled colonial relations of power and privilege in universities. This process focuses on two logics: first, unveiling the mechanisms of coloniality and, second, working towards building a world where many alternative perspectives can coexist (Mignolo, 2011). Decolonization requires the acceptance that (a) colonization is an ongoing structure and ideology prevalent in settler colonial contexts and that (b) decolonization is not merely a theory but a praxis-centred methodological approach intended to destabilize the dominance of Euro-western supremacy through transformative action (Smith, 1999). Decolonization offers a critical lens that helps to engage non-Indigenous peoples in learning and acting to change power imbalances. Decolonization has become a platform that has the potential to gradually become the new institutional norm among Canadian higher education institutions. It is predominantly reflected in policy documents but has slowly become inserted into institutional operations as well (see Stein et al., 2021).

Decolonization in the context of Canadian higher education is closely tied to the processes of Indigenization. Decolonizing and Indigenizing are intertwined, as both processes focus on issues around power, land, and the right of Indigenous peoples to self-determination. Yet, they are not the same. The meanings of these concepts change depending on the positionality and power dynamics people bring to these processes (Grafton & Melançon, 2020). Kovach (2009, p. 42) has pointed out that decolonization perspectives and Indigenization epistemologies emerge from different paradigms. Decolonizing analysis is born out of the critical theory found within the transformative paradigm of the western tradition (Mertens, 2005). Decolonization centres its discourse within the western literature of ongoing colonialism and the dispossession of lands, whereas the Indigenous paradigm is grounded in Indigenous knowledges and methodologies. While a decolonizing perspective remains necessary and can be included as a theoretical position within research, it is not the epistemological centre of an Indigenous methodological approach to research. Indigenous theory emerges from an Indigenous paradigm – Indigenous epistemologies, methodologies, and knowledge frameworks (Smith, 2013; Tuck & McKenzie, 2015) – through the work of Indigenous authors. One of my research participants noted: *"To me, decolonizing and Indigenizing go hand in hand, but decolonizing will be deconstructing the colonial elements that are embedded into the education system. /... / Indigenizing will be bringing Indigenous perspectives and pedagogy into education"* (interview, 14 February 2018). Authors agree that decolonization from an Indigenous perspective is understood as a process that aims to raise the collective voice of Indigenous peoples and redefine Indigenous knowledges against colonial systems of domination, oppression, knowledge dispossession, and erasure in the academy (Battiste et al., 2002; Kuokkanen, 2007b; Simpson, 2014). Decolonization requires recognizing and respecting the inherent sovereignty of Indigenous peoples and their right to self-determination.

Another concept that further muddies the conceptual waters is reconciliation. Reconciliation is considered an important goal in many institutional policy documents, prompted largely by the work of the Truth and Reconciliation Commission (TRC). The TRC defined reconciliation as a process of "establishing and maintaining a mutual respectful relationship between Indigenous and non-Indigenous peoples" (TRC, 2015, p. 1). Bopp et al. (2017) noted that reconciliation is about healing relationships between non-Indigenous and Indigenous peoples, which is important in mending the relationship between the colonizer and the colonized. Yet, there has been a significant amount of critique expressed by Indigenous scholars regarding the reconciliation efforts unfolding in academia. Reconciliation without dismantling the colonial structures that are prevalent in higher education institutions is seen as problematic (Gaudry & Lorenz, 2018). Approaches to reconciliation have been characterized as tokenistic "moves to innocence" (Tuck & Yang, 2012), aimed at relieving the settlers' guilty feelings and releasing them from responsibility without requiring them to give up land, power, or privilege. Daigle (2019, p. 4) described reconciliation in post-secondary contexts as a "settler colonial spectacle" that capitalizes on Indigenous trauma through discourses of reconciling past violent relationships yet harms Indigenous peoples further.

The processes of unveiling the colonial logic in higher education are largely centred on contesting the dominant knowledge epistemologies featuring unequal knowledge hierarchies that universities continue to uphold in teaching and learning (Battiste, 2013b; Brunette-Debassige,

2021). A decolonial lens pushes against mainstream scholarship and theories and champions examining and understanding the world from a different perspective. Indigenous scholars in particular have developed important theoretical approaches that allow them to interrogate the world through an Indigenous lens instead of using a western lens to examine the Indigenous world. These perspectives allow scholars to reveal and critically examine the Eurocentric premises that typically ground the mainstream theoretical approaches in higher education. An excellent example of such theorization is that by Brayboy (2005), who has crafted a Tribal Critical Race Theory (TribalCrit) that helps to examine the experiences of Indigenous peoples in the United States through an Indigenous lens. The theory starts with the basic premise that colonization is endemic to US society. The following are the tenets of the theory (from Brayboy, 2005, pp. 429–30):

1. US policies towards Indigenous peoples are rooted in imperialism, colonization, white supremacy, and a desire for material gain.
2. Indigenous peoples occupy a liminal space that accounts for both the political and the racialized nature of their identities.
3. Indigenous peoples have a desire to obtain and forge tribal sovereignty, tribal autonomy, self-determination, and self-identification.
4. The concepts of culture, knowledge, and power take on new meaning when examined through an Indigenous lens.
5. Governmental policies and educational policies towards Indigenous peoples closely follow each other towards a problematic goal of assimilation.
6. Tribal philosophies, beliefs, customs, traditions, and visions for the future are central to understanding the lived realities of Indigenous peoples; they also illustrate the differences and adaptability among individuals and groups.
7. Stories are not separate from theory; they make up theory and are, therefore, real and legitimate sources of data and ways of being.
8. Theory and practice are connected in deep and explicit ways such that scholars must work towards social change.

This framework honours the counter-stories of Indigenous groups as a legitimate knowledge source and suggests a critical perspective for addressing colonialism in higher education.

Several scholars such as Tuck and Yang (2014), Grande (2018), and Brunette-Debassige (2021) have advocated for *Indigenous refusal* as an analytical lens that helps to enact decolonial institutional change from

Indigenous perspectives. Indigenous refusal is seen as an active voice and alternative practice to recognition of and alignment with accepted Eurocentric hegemonies. Indigenous refusal is seen as a useful part of decolonial qualitative research that is both critical of the ongoing settler colonial ideology and interrogative of the subjective colonial power dynamics present within academic environments (Tuck & Yang, 2014). Grande (2018) called for Indigenous refusal of the academy by rejecting the (false) promise of inclusion and other inducements of the settler state while positively asserting Indigenous sovereignty and peoplehood. Mignolo (2011) took up refusal in relation to knowledge formation, asserting that Indigenous knowledges themselves are a form of refusal – a space of epistemic disobedience that is purposefully "delinked" from western, liberal, capitalist understandings of knowledge as a product. Brunette-Debassige (2021) used the concept of Indigenous refusal to help emphasize Indigenous women administrators' agency in their leadership positions, where they are often forced to speak uncomfortable truths and challenge Euro-western hegemonic norms as intermediaries between knowledge paradigms. She described practices such as rejecting normative administrative activities that contribute to Indigenous oppression, disputing hegemonic leadership practices, and refusing to be neutral or less political in their leadership approaches despite the criticism they often receive from non-Indigenous colleagues. Conversations about moving forward with a critical decolonial lens have emphasized the importance of collective agency both in knowledge production and in impacting institutional decision-making structures (Battiste, 2013a; Donald, 2009; Saini & Begum, 2020).

An important stream of the literature has focused on variations of institutional practice regarding decolonial change. For example, Andreotti de Oliveira et al. (2015) described soft-reform and radical-reform spaces, whereby the latter recognizes and condemns the epistemological dominance that grounds hegemonic colonial practices and the former doesn't. The soft-reform space is present in institutional inclusion efforts that intentionally avoid open conflict and dismiss any alternative approaches as violent, unproductive, and uncivil. Majority groups presume that difference can and should be neatly incorporated on the terms of those doing the including with a predefined consensus at the end of this process, but as authors have argued, this is not enough (Andreotti de Oliveira et al., 2015). Similarly, Gaudry and Lorenz (2018, pp. 218–19) have argued that there are currently three distinct visions, located on a continuum, for an academic engagement with Indigenization – *Indigenous inclusion, reconciliation Indigenization,* and *decolonial Indigenization.* The first, *Indigenous inclusion,* focuses on including more

Indigenous people in the existing system. It is done through recruitment and increases in representation numbers. Indigenous inclusion is problematic, as it tends to view Indigenous learners from a perspective of representation as a group that requires special assistance and accommodation. The responsibility for change remains largely with Indigenous peoples. Second, *reconciliation Indigenization* is a vision that locates Indigenization on common ground between Indigenous and Canadian ideals. It creates a new, broader consensus on debates such as what counts as knowledge, how Indigenous knowledges and western knowledge should be reconciled, and what types of relationships academic institutions should have with Indigenous communities. This approach attempts to engage in decolonization processes, challenging the idea that only western knowledge is valid. It calls for altering the university's structure, educating Canadian faculty, staff, and students to change how they think about and act towards Indigenous peoples and Indigenous knowledges. The main concern with this approach is the extent to which its aspirational rhetoric and slogan-like enthusiasm can translate into actual practice. Third, *decolonial Indigenization* envisions a complete overhaul of the academy by balancing power relations between Indigenous peoples and Canadians and transforming the academy into something dynamic and new. It requires the return of control to Indigenous peoples, communities, and programs to better govern themselves in higher education. Decolonial Indigenization has the potential to transform Canadian higher education from a system of continued colonization and assimilation to one of Indigenous empowerment. We are primarily seeing higher education institutions engaging in the first two approaches. Decolonial Indigenization currently remains a distant vision, mainly advocated by members of the Indigenous community. As demonstrated, institutional approaches to decolonization tend to differ in terms of the level of engagement in their approaches to addressing settler colonialism. Drawing attention to more radical options helps in the norm-building process, as critical framings help to identify the problem and allow consideration of the values underlying those institutional approaches.

Decolonization is not a simple or easy process. It is rather messy, with conflicting views over what it means for different people and different universities. Such divergence speaks to the idea that decolonization is not yet a fully developed norm but is an actively built concept, practice, and social movement. Lee (2023) pointed out the tendency for decolonization movements to descend into nationalism, nativism, and romanticization. He noted that efforts to decolonize can mask deep inequalities that can be inherent also in Indigenous epistemology on a global scale. He called for examining epistemology *as practice* rather than as an abstract matter confined to texts, theories, and discourses. It is important not to assume that certain types of geography (Global North) or identity (white westerners) are inherently incompatible with intellectual or practical engagement with decolonization. Furthermore, racial or cultural identity alone does not automatically trigger decolonial thinking. Institutional change should align with intellectual synthesis and knowledge exchange rather than contestation or hierarchy building.

Decolonial Learning

Universities are learning institutions; learning forms the essence of their operation. Learning in the western paradigm is defined as a change in cognition or behaviour that stems from direct or indirect experience (Argote & Miron-Spektor, 2011). Institutional learning is driven by individuals and their social interactions, and consists of visible and invisible norms, or the accepted behaviours, values, and practices of people working in the organization (Kezar & Eckel, 2002).

Higgins (2007) pointed out that institutional culture looks different depending on who is looking at it and with what purposes in mind, a point that explains the conflict around settler colonialism in universities. Learning, in the Indigenous paradigm, is a relational, interconnected, and wholistic practice. In Indigenous knowledge systems, learning is not solely focused on the acquisition of information or knowledge, but rather encompasses the development of the whole person, including their physical, emotional, intellectual, and spiritual well-being. This approach to learning emphasizes the importance of experiential and hands-on learning, as well as the transmission of knowledge through storytelling, ceremony, and other cultural practices.

Decolonial learning brings both paradigms together. Decolonial learning is a relational process involving inner reflections over the socio-cultural contexts that have shaped one's norms, values, and beliefs and the realization of how those may have contributed to ongoing structures of colonialism that are oppressive to others. In higher education contexts, decolonial learning also means challenging the narratives of privileged knowledge spaces, including privileged theories and methodologies. A way forward on this path is to centre efforts on learning – seeking knowledge, cultivating one's motivation to engage in difficult conversations, and building one's efficacy in believing that everyone can contribute to meaningful change. Bopp et al. (2017) argued that the task of leadership at every level of the organization is to create and sustain a culture of learning that is inclusive and welcoming to everyone, as everyone needs to act in order to bring about meaningful change. It is important to avoid pushing people away or refusing to walk together, something that may already be occurring. One of my interview participants commented:

> *A polarization has happened. We have some very strong Indigenous academics who are quite angry and are basically saying get out of the way ... let us do it. But we all live on the same boat, planet Earth. Our challenge is how do we move that forward together?/... / I think we need to open up and have some honest, brave conversations about how we can find a solution. And learning is about knowing your story, knowing my story, knowing our history.* (Interview, 9 March 2018)

The first step for non-Indigenous peoples towards decolonial learning is confronting whiteness and one's privilege. Critical scholars have noted that whiteness serves as a political construct of power that asserts the superiority of norms that benefit one cultural group over others (Gusa, 2010; Higgins, 2007). In order for the organization to engage in sustainable structural and systematic change, the institutional culture of whiteness needs to be confronted, problematized, and unpacked through sustained, purposeful, and continuous efforts. Challenging whiteness means challenging a sense of ownership and entitlement that has emerged through historically established normative values (Gusa, 2010). It includes reflecting on one's positionality individually, as well as collectively, and thinking deeply about the impacts of the knowledge that dominates higher education spaces. Deep cognitive frames, such as the normative perception of whiteness, can only be changed gradually by a deep norm-altering level of learning. This takes place over time and translates into organizational change gradually through changing deep core values and then more formal institutional policies and regulations. Conscious, deliberate attempts to examine, question, and learn about one's privilege must become a standard practice in higher education contexts.

In order for core values to change, deeper, meaningful learning processes must take place. Argyris and Schön (1997) differentiated between two types of learning: single-loop learning and double-loop learning. The first results in temporary change in an organization; the second generates irreversible, transformative change. In *single-loop learning*, the focus is on re-establishing stability and normality in the organization by enacting corrections and eliminating errors (for example, uncritical engagement in the reconciliation process). Solutions that come from single-loop learning focus on the external manifestations of the problem and leave internal values, norms, and beliefs intact – hence, the label "single-loop" (e.g., seeing Indigenous inclusion as merely an issue of increased numbers in representation). *Double-loop learning* focuses attention on the root causes of a problem and the changes that need to be made in the attitudes, values, beliefs, and practices of individuals to bring about enduring results (Bauman, 2002). The difference between single-loop and double-loop learning is that, in the former, change is at a surface level, whereas in the latter, change occurs in underlying principles (Coburn, 2003). With single-loop learning, the acquired knowledge is for the short term and intended to facilitate routine, day-to-day problem solving. Double-loop learning, on the other hand, is intended to ensure the long-term future of the organization by analysing core issues and making policy judgments. It is double-loop learning that is required for decolonial learning. Haig-Brown (2010), a non-Indigenous researcher working with Indigenous communities, has situated her work within the concept of *deep learning*. She views deep learning as emerging after years of living and working in Indigenous contexts. Deep learning, in her view, is a more meaningful and transformative form of learning that goes beyond surface-level information collection and involves challenging one's own core assumptions and beliefs. Deep learning is closely linked to decolonization, as this process requires a level of openness and vulnerability on the part of a learner.

In organizational contexts, it is important to identify the mechanisms and practices that can facilitate deeper levels of learning. Boyce (2003) noted that practices that involve continuous inquiry and dialogue and utilize an action-based learning approach are essential. Action learning is a process in which individuals learn by actively engaging with and reflecting on real-world problems. It involves a group of individuals working collaboratively to solve a specific problem or challenge, while also developing their own individual knowledge, skills, and understanding. Action learning can help with widening awareness of the assumptions held by oneself and others, personal systems of inquiry, and improving the quality and effectiveness of the language used in an organization. It is crucial to embed changes into institutional structures by directly linking them to strong leadership and integrating them into policies. Only with strong administrative support can long-lasting structural changes be achieved.

Theoretical Framework for Decolonial Institutional Change

The theoretical framework presented below (see Figure 1) summarizes the key components that must be considered for decolonial institutional

Figure 1. Theoretical Framework for Decolonial Institutional Change

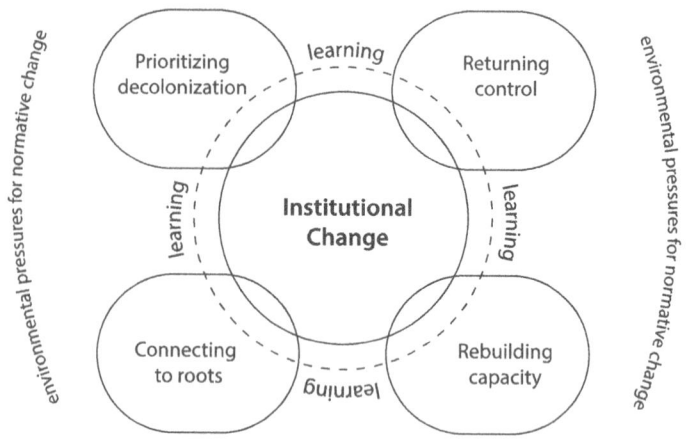

change to take place. The framework summarizes the critical literature that has emerged from Indigenous scholarship (e.g., Bopp et al., 2017; Gaudry & Lorenz, 2018; Gunstone, 2013; Pete, 2016; Povey et al., 2022) as well as from the insights shared by my research participants. Table 3 unpacks the framework further by suggesting some of the action items that higher education institutions may consider in their work towards structural institutional change. This framework is primarily meant as a conceptual guide for educational institutions that are considering ways in which they can best think about change in their institutions. There are four core pillars that guide institutional change informed by Indigenous knowledges: 1) prioritizing decolonization; 2) returning control; 3) rebuilding capacity; and 4) connecting to one's roots, including land. These pillars are interconnected through the processes of learning that lead to shifts in normative beliefs and translate into changed individual and collective behaviours. Such learning needs to focus on conversations around settler colonialism and its direct and indirect mechanisms. Only when individuals engage purposefully in learning activities can norms and behaviours change. Institutional change is also affected by larger environmental factors that contain political, functional, and social pressures. The environmental dynamic underscores the importance and relevance of the advocacy work carried out by Indigenous communities from within and without higher education institutions. Their work has had direct impact on the priorities, directions, and scope of institutional change. Below I comment further on the four core pillars of this theoretical framework.

Table 3. Core Principles and Examples of Proactive Institutional Approaches to Decolonial Institutional Change

Core principles	Examples of proactive institutional approaches
Prioritizing decolonization	Institutional culture of learning: – acceptance of the harm of colonialism, seeing one's role in it – confronting the culture of whiteness – continuous inquiry and dialogue through university-wide critical engagement – meaningful, reflective acknowledgment of land – removal of various artifacts of colonialism – respectful engagement with Elders – reimagining the concept of excellence and innovation Policy: – anti-racism strategies – employment equity policies – unconscious bias workshops – smudging policies
Returning control	Governance: – senior-level Indigenous leadership positions – established spots on senates and boards of governors for Indigenous leaders – Indigenous ethics boards Policy: – policies for increasing Indigenous decision-making power (e.g., in senates, boards of governors, Indigenous advisory councils) – formally recognizing the contributions of community-based knowledge keepers (e.g., honoraria, committee memberships)
Rebuilding capacity	Hiring: – setting hiring priorities for Indigenous faculty and staff (e.g., cluster hires) Funding: – widening access for Indigenous peoples (e.g., student recruitment, scholarships, faculty research grants) Research: – recognizing and valuing Indigenous knowledges and methodologies (in tenure processes, by providing physical spaces) Program development: – introducing curriculum that incorporates Indigenous perspectives (e.g., programs, courses)
Connecting to land	Research and teaching: – valuing knowledge that emerges from land, Indigenous communities, spiritual and personal experiences Policy: – recognizing and returning Indigenous lands (e.g., territorial acknowledgments, Treaty recognitions) – moving sites of research and learning off campus, including thesis defences – policies for smudging – policies for recognizing community engagement in tenure and promotion

Prioritizing Decolonization

The first pillar of the framework is prioritizing decolonization within non-Indigenous institutional structures. This involves confronting the culture of whiteness and assessing one's privilege and the ongoing structural mechanisms that perpetuate colonial ideology. My research participants shared that decolonization is a non-negotiable in the processes of institutional change, highlighting the work that non-Indigenous people need to take on:

> *Decolonizing is a big part of our journey here. / ... / I can decolonize, okay, but I shouldn't do it by myself. You should also do it. All of my students should do it. Everybody in this faculty should do it.* (Interview, 9 March 2018)

As noted, decolonization is a complex and multilayered process without one clear path. Nevertheless, decolonization should be a practice cross-cutting all activities in higher education institutions, including policy work, governance decisions, research endeavours, innovation initiatives, programming, pedagogical methods, and teaching practice. It is most visibly translated into institutional culture and climate. It can be purposefully cultivated through meaningful, yet difficult, conversations and collective action. Without addressing colonialism in its direct and indirect formats across organizational structures and disciplinary areas, the opportunities for sustainable change are limited.

Returning Control

Self-determination has been at the core of Indigenous advocacy work. While this advocacy work has yielded some advances, more needs to be done at the institutional level. Returning control to Indigenous peoples within university governance structures, policy development, land use, and programmatic developments helps to break down the established power hierarchies in universities. It also supports the aspirations to self-determination and independence of Indigenous communities. There is a need to actively shape the narrative using strength-based, empowering perspectives, as this is related to returning control to Indigenous peoples. One of my research participants described a situation in the child welfare sector where there were doubts expressed whether Indigenous peoples are capable of governing themselves:

> *When I was still working in child welfare, the system was changing in regards to power. All of a sudden, the control for child welfare was shifting to Indigenous*

people. And issues of racism and othering rose to the top. You know – "Can we trust these Indigenous people to actually take care of these kids? They can't even take care of their own families." / ... / I think it's absolutely imperative that we find a space to have these ... I don't call them safe conversations, I call them brave. There is this overriding narrative that if we [non-Indigenous peoples] have more control, we will do things better. That's not necessarily been the case. (Interview, 3 December 2018)

Returning control is giving up power and shifting decision making over to Indigenous communities, individuals, and organizations while ensuring that Indigenous peoples have a meaningful voice in decisions that affect them.

Rebuilding Capacity

The third pillar of the framework is rebuilding capacity for Indigenous knowledges, including languages and cultural traditions. It is important to provide spaces where this knowledge can be taught to Indigenous youth. Universities can support this process through their hiring decisions, choice of appointments to leadership positions, support for Indigenous research projects, and provision of student scholarships that help to build and strengthen Indigenous knowledges. It is important to stretch capacity-building activities beyond representation numbers and to provide necessary supports after a person has entered the university (e.g., mentoring, financial supports, supporting community-building work). The following quote from one of my research participants is illustrative of the idea of rebuilding capacity:

This is an important piece that we transmit knowledge, right, from one generation to the next. And, it is important being a steward of the land, to hold Canada accountable for the Treaties that were signed. We're losing that ability for these young people to hold Canada accountable because they're no longer learning what it means to be a steward of the land in the Treaties that were signed by their ancestors. So, there's a disconnect happening there, and it has implications for our Treaty relationships. And I wanted to build that capacity among my people. (Interview, 12 December 2018)

It is essential that this aspect of rebuilding knowledge becomes central to institutional change in higher education so that there is a next generation of youth that is in a position to embody the cultural knowledge that can empower Indigenous communities. This is essential to Indigenous peoples' cultural survival and efforts of self-determination.

Connecting to Roots

Prioritizing respectful relationships with one's roots and particularly with land is central to the diversity of Indigenous knowledges. Land is an important knowledge source from which Indigenous peoples get guidance. It is crucial not to lose this connection to wholistic knowledges that have been accumulated over centuries and that emerge from particular lands, places, and communities. The connection to land really means the connection to one's roots. Higher education institutions play a key role in strengthening such connections whereby Indigenous knowledges can function in parallel with the western paradigm as equal and respected. Returning to land and building connections with nature can serve also as a crucial remedy against the mental health problems that our society increasingly is grappling with. One of my research participants shared her connection to land:

> *I never understood my fascination with rocks. / ... / But, it's the earth speaking to us. And, here, this is an old knowledge, you know. This is Earth, millions of years old. This is old knowledge. And, we're all impacted by it.* (Interview, 18 December 2018)

Boyce's (2003) research demonstrated that the challenge of successful change is less about planning and implementing and more about developing and sustaining new ways of seeing, deciding, and acting. Successful decolonial learning is about learning enough collectively so that ingrained institutional norms, practices, and behaviours may change. Sustaining change in higher education is dependent upon sustaining the conditions of deep decolonial learning through policy and practice. There is no one linear path on this journey. It requires consistent and continuous efforts from university leaders and all members of the organization. Indigenous individuals, through their critical scholarship and advocacy, have led these processes. Now it is time for non-Indigenous peoples to take an active role in them as well. It is collaborative work that leads to mutual learning and a changed path that will be walked together.

Conclusion

This chapter has provided a decolonial perspective on institutional change vis-à-vis Indigenous knowledges in Canadian higher education. It has drawn attention to the norm literature, explaining how norms emerge and change. Decolonial learning is a pathway forward, grounded in collaborative efforts that engage both Indigenous peoples and non-Indigenous peoples in relational reflections over diverse perspectives, epistemologies, and lived experiences. This chapter aligns with Battiste's (2013a) remark that decolonization is not about rejecting all theory or research grounded in western knowledge, but it is about creating a new space where Indigenous peoples' knowledge, identity, and future are calculated into the global and contemporary equation to create a new, visionary future. Donald (2009) similarly reflected that, if colonialism is indeed a shared condition, then decolonization needs to be a shared endeavour. This is achieved when Indigenous peoples and non-Indigenous peoples face each other across historic divides, deconstruct their shared past, and engage critically with the realization that their present and future are tied together. Centring our work on critical decolonial approaches, building capacity, returning control, and connecting to one's roots provides a conceptual representation of the institutional change unfolding across higher education in Canada.

Governance and Policy

I'm of a firm opinion, unless you see it in a policy and a direction, you know, a blue-print, somewhere, people can easily ignore and say I don't have to do it.

(Interview, 9 March 2018)

Indigenous post-secondary education is not considered a distinct, autonomous part of the Canadian higher education system. As such, Indigenous peoples are largely dependent on policies and programming developed by mainstream universities that operate within western knowledge frameworks. Furthermore, access to higher education is often dependent on the financial support available. While the K–12 schooling of First Nations students is financially supported by the federal government, neither the provincial nor the federal government has assumed direct responsibility for funding Indigenous students in the higher education sector. Various decisions involving admissions, programming, financial support, appointments to leadership positions, and hiring faculty and staff are all made by the individual university or college (Jones, 2002). As a result, the focus, attention, and support provided to Indigenous students and educators is inconsistent and varies greatly across higher education institutions. Often the university still tends to behave as what Kuokkanen (2007a, p. 130) referred to as the "guest-master," who is not necessarily hostile to the presence of Indigenous knowledges but still works to contain them within the existing colonial structures. Institutional governance structures, including policy development, occur within the western knowledge paradigm. There is consensus that opportunities for Indigenous self-governance in mainstream universities are an essential part of decolonizing higher education systems in Canada (Pidgeon, 2016; Povey et al., 2022). Increasing these opportunities involves strengthening capacity and giving Indigenous peoples control over determining priorities, practices, and policies involving them. Reciprocal relationships with Indigenous communities also entail having community representation in formal positions of power such as boards of governors (Pidgeon, 2014).

Over decades the number of Indigenous individuals in academia has grown, yet studies have pointed to the continued underrepresentation and marginalization of Indigenous peoples among administrators, faculty, staff, and students when compared to non-Indigenous peoples in Canadian universities (Smith, 2019; Universities Canada, 2019). Smith's (2019) study specifically pointed to the notable absence of Indigenous peoples in leadership roles across Canadian universities. Only 1.2% of senior administrators identified as Indigenous women, whereas the number of Indigenous men and non-binary Indigenous individuals was so low that it was unreported (Smith, 2019). Lavallée (2020b) argued that Indigenous individuals, women in particular, have increasingly started to take on leadership roles in Canadian higher education institutions, but this has not been a smooth process. Brunette-Debassige's (2021) doctoral work highlighted how Indigenous women administrators continue to struggle in their leadership work, actively resisting the colonial academy, while their opinions often get overlooked. Povey et al.'s (2022) study pointed to the fiscal constraints and funding cuts that Indigenous leaders have to navigate that lead to unsustainable models of activities. There is consensus that leading the structural systemic change in universities is often left on the shoulders of the few Indigenous leaders. Overburdening Indigenous people and continuous denial of their agency in educational governance and decision making is a serious barrier for institutional change. Nevertheless, while change has been slow and various challenges remain, there has been increasing attention among Canadian higher education institutions to modifying existing governance and policy structures.

Changes in Governance and Decision Making

Institutional governance structures have remained relatively constant in the Canadian higher education system, with the majority of institutions operating in a traditional bicameral system of boards and senates. The responsibility for administrative and fiscal matters is assigned to a corporate board of governance, and the responsibility for academic matters in most universities is assigned to a senate or an equivalent body (e.g., general faculties council, *commission des études*) (Eastman et al., 2022; Pennock et al., 2015). Institutional governance structures also encompass a wide range of administrative positions, including the senior leadership roles of president, vice-presidents, provosts, deans, associate deans, department heads, and program directors in addition to staff, faculty, and student organizations. Indigenous scholars have noted that this governance model is deeply rooted in colonial ideology of knowledge hierarchies and perpetuates western values of meritocracy, individualism, and competition (Debassige & Brunette Debassige, 2018). Indigenous governance practices are less compartmentalized; they generally prioritize community involvement, consensus-building, and respect for the diversity of Indigenous knowledges. Elders and other Indigenous knowledge keepers are often part of Indigenous governance models (Pidgeon, 2016).

Board of Governors. Governing boards in Canadian universities continue largely to represent the dominant cultural group. While an Indigenous presence among the representatives of university governing boards has become more common, having an Indigenous person serve as the chancellor of a board is rare and draws public attention. For example, when Shirley Cheechoo, a Cree filmmaker, served as a chancellor of Brock University from 2015 to 2020, she was the first woman and the first Indigenous Canadian to hold this position. Santee Smith, a Mohawk artist, was installed as chancellor of McMaster University in 2019. In media outlets, these nominations are often portrayed as historical occurrences. For example, in June 2020, the University of British Columbia reported that "the Board of Governors appointed the Honourable Steven Lewis Point to become the university's 19th Chancellor. He will be the first Indigenous person to hold the position" (University News, 2020). In 2021, Brandon University announced that Senator Mary Jane McCallum was appointed as its new chancellor and that she was the first Indigenous chancellor in the university's history and the first woman to be appointed to the role (Brandon University, 2021). These occasions may easily remain one-time occurrences that draw public attention to institutional diversity efforts unless they are approached in a more systemic manner. Therefore, ongoing work must focus on introducing policy mechanisms for securing continuity in Indigenous representation among university governance structures. Trent University has proceeded to set diversity requirements for its governing board: no less than 40% from each gender, 30% of the board must be from Central Ontario, and one governor must identify as disabled, racialized, or Indigenous (CAUT, 2018a). Setting certain quotas may help to focus more attention on the composition of decision-making bodies, yet a question arises around the institutional supports available for Indigenous persons to be able to have continuous access to and a meaningful impact on policy decisions.

University presidents. The senior executive officer at most Canadian universities is the "president and vice-chancellor," appointed by the Board of Governors. An Indigenous individual carrying out the role of a university president is still unusual (with the exception of First Nations University of Canada), but some instances have been occurring lately. Dr. Deborah Saucier, a Métis woman, became president and vice-chancellor of Vancouver Island University in 2019. In 2020, Ojibway Mike DeGagne was appointed as the first Indigenous president of Yukon University. These appointments are important in terms of empowering Indigenous voice through the vision these university presidents promote. They have made reconciliation initiatives, Indigenous programming, and Indigenous student supports clear priorities. These top leadership positions allow the exercise of power and direct authority to implement Indigenization goals while drawing more attention to decolonizing the systems and structures within Canadian higher education institutions.

University senates. The representation of Indigenous faculty in the composition of university senates has been an area without much scholarly attention. Senate spots are typically allocated through faculty council elections, and the work is counted as service to the university. Thus, appointments of Indigenous faculty to senates are typically short-term and occur without targeted efforts to increase visibility among Indigenous faculty in Senate composition. However, there are a few examples where institutions have implemented important policy changes for Senate representation. For example, at the University of Manitoba, a proposal was approved in 2021 whereby the ongoing addition of five Indigenous members to the Senate by faculty and school councils was approved. These five senators would serve in addition to any other Indigenous senators who might be elected by faculty or school councils or appointed based on their administrative positions (University of Manitoba, 2021). This shift indicates a move towards increasing the strategic presence and voice of Indigenous representatives in the university's governance structure.

Institutional advisory boards. A long-standing development in higher education governance is the formation and appointment of Indigenous advisors, advisory boards, presidential task forces, and/or reconciliation committees. Some have been in existence for decades; others have been established more recently. For example, the Aboriginal Council of Queen's University was established in 1992. The Council provides advice and assessment on Indigenous matters to the Board and the Senate. McMaster University introduced the Indigenous Education Council in 2013, with the primary goal of advocating for the advancement of

Indigenous education at the university. The Dean's Advisory Council on Indigenous Education at the Ontario Institute of Studies in Education was established in January 2017. In 2019, the University of Toronto appointed two Indigenous individuals to serve in the roles of academic advisors on Indigenous curriculum as well as on Indigenous research. The University of British Columbia has established a President's Aboriginal Advisory Committee (Vancouver) and Okanagan Aboriginal Advisory Council. Their board of governance also established an Indigenous Engagement Committee in 2019 to monitor progress towards goals set in their Indigenous strategic plan. These advisory committees have been heavily involved in the work of developing institutional strategic plans, offering their expertise and knowledge to university programming (Brunette-Debassige, 2021; Pete, 2016). Many of these committees have developed clear goals for decolonization and Indigenization in their universities. However, while Indigenous advisory committees have become quite common among post-secondary institutions in Canada, their capacity for impact is linked to the fact that they operate in an advisory role and do not necessarily have formal authority to control decisions. Therefore, it is important to recognize the importance of their work but also to pay attention to the changes needed in their mandates in order for them to have a meaningful impact on organizational change.

Senior leadership positions. According to Universities Canada (2019), Indigenous people constituted 2.9% of senior university leaders, which is lower than their representation in the general academic population (5%). The creation of new Indigenous vice-president positions within Canadian higher education institutions has become an emerging trend. Provost and vice-president Indigenous positions have been created across many universities and colleges, including the University of Alberta, the University of Calgary, the University of Manitoba, the University of Saskatchewan, and Western University. Western University and the University of Manitoba have also created associate vice-president Indigenous positions. These are all senior leadership appointments that increase the voice and presence of Indigenous communities. Most of these appointments stem from recommendations that have been the result of lengthy committee work engaging Elders from the community as well as Indigenous faculty, staff, and students. The reports have challenged the current organizational structure of universities (see University of Manitoba, 2019, pp. 16–17), leading to distinct changes in university governance with stronger Indigenous presence at senior levels. For example, at the University of Manitoba, the vice-president Indigenous is now positioned at the same level as other university vice-presidents (e.g., academic, research, and administration). However, in many cases, the power hierarchies have remained intact, and Indigenous leaders with their significant portfolios are often expected to report to higher-ups, typically non-Indigenous vice-presidents.

Developments have occurred at the unit level, where newly created administrative positions include associate dean or assistant dean positions related to Indigenous activities. Some examples include an associate dean Indigenous education position in faculties of education (e.g., Simon Fraser University, the University of British Columbia, the University of Manitoba, Humber College), assistant or associate deans Indigenous in medicine and health-related faculties (e.g., Cumming School of Medicine at the University of Calgary, Rady Faculty of Health Science at the University of Manitoba, McMaster University), associate vice-principal Indigenous initiatives and reconciliation (Queen's University), and vice-dean Indigenous in the College of Arts and Science (University of Saskatchewan). These unit-level positions help to carry out Indigenous work within specific disciplines, which is crucial from the perspectives of programming and curricular change. Positions in smaller units, such as program directors, heads of centres, and department heads, mostly in Indigenous-focused programs, are also opening up to Indigenous individuals. One example here is Dr. David Fortin, who was appointed as the director of McEwen School of Architecture at Laurentian University in 2018 and has been noted as the first Indigenous director of an architecture school in Canada (Laurentian University, 2021). Furthermore, there has been an important uptake among Indigenous students of opportunities to have a voice in institutional decision making. In addition to Indigenous student associations, there have been new discipline-specific developments such as Indigenous law students' associations (e.g., the University of Ottawa, the University of Toronto, Lakehead University), Indigenous business students' societies (e.g., the University of Saskatchewan, the University of Manitoba), and others. These are examples of how Indigenous youth are becoming organized and are making sure that their voices get included in university governance.

Changes in Strategic Planning

Institutional strategic plans are an important formal mechanism for facilitating organizational change. Strategic plans provide a better understanding of institutional priorities, values, and aspirations and lay out a path to get there. Strategic plans are important documents, as they are used to direct activities, allocate resources, and assess organizational performance. They also filter down to the activities and planning processes of faculties and departments, influencing programmatic decisions and individual research agendas. As noted in the quote at the beginning of this chapter, policy documents matter, as they hold people formally accountable for action. According to Louie (2019), it is imperative to have formal policies in place, as these help to protect the rights of Indigenous academics to undertake their roles in the higher education system. The development of institutional strategic plans typically involves input from the broader campus community, aiming to create ownership of and commitment to the goals identified. There is an important distinction between institutional academic plans and Indigenous strategies. Academic plans provide a broader academic direction across a university, while Indigenous strategies speak specifically to Indigenous activities. While academic plans may contain Indigenous priorities, these documents tend to be much broader in scope and nature. It is important to reiterate that, in most cases, the development of Indigenous strategic plans has resulted from the concentrated efforts and work of Indigenous communities, while the process of developing an academic plan has fewer Indigenous participants and opportunities for Indigenous peoples' impact. A wave of new Indigenous strategic plans emerged after the release of the Truth and Reconciliation Commission's *Calls to Action* (2015) document among Canadian research-intensive universities (see Table 4). However, while for many universities having a formal Indigenous strategy is a new development, there are several universities that engaged in these processes long before. One of the earliest was Berger/Kirkness's (1984) *Report of the President's Ad Hoc Committee on British Columbia Native Indian People and Communities at the University of British Columbia* (UBC, n.d.). Similarly, *A Framework for Planning* was introduced in 1998 at the University of Saskatchewan, which identified four priority goals intended to improve the educational opportunities of Indigenous peoples (University of Saskatchewan, 1998). In addition, a few universities have developed distinct anti-racism policies that help to tackle the ongoing issue around racism in universities (e.g., UBC, York University). These documents speak to a shift in institutional norms and values.

There is a difference in how academic plans and Indigenous strategic plans reflect the importance of decolonization in institutional change. References to truth and/or reconciliation are a frequent theme in academic plans, while decolonization is hardly mentioned. Decolonization is a central theme in Indigenous strategies. Only four universities, with relatively recent academic plans, have mentioned decolonization as an important consideration in their institutional strategic documents – the

Table 4. List of the Institutional Plans and Indigenous Strategies of 15 Canadian Research-Intensive Universities

Province	University	Documents
Alberta	University of Alberta	1. *Institutional Strategic Plan: For the Public Good* (2016–21) 2. *University of Alberta Indigenous Strategic Plan: Braiding Past, Present and Future* (2022)
	University of Calgary	1. *Institutional Strategic Plan and Strategic Vision Eyes High* (2017–22) 2. *Indigenous Strategy: ii' taa'poh'to'p: A place to Rejuvenate and Re-Energize during a Journey: Together in a Good Way: A Journey of Transformation and Renewal* (2017)
British Columbia	University of British Columbia	1. *Strategic Plan: Shaping UBC's Next Century* (2018–28) 2. *UBC Indigenous Strategic Plan* (2020)
Manitoba	University of Manitoba	1. *Strategic Plan: Taking Our Place* (2015–20) 2. *Interim Strategic Plan: Our Shared Future: Building on Our Strategic Plan* (2021) 3. *University of Manitoba Indigenous Senior Leadership Report and Recommendations to the Provost and Vice-President (Academic)* (2019)
Nova Scotia	Dalhousie University	1. *Dalhousie University's Strategic Plan: Third Century Promise – or Si'st Kasqimtlnaqnipunqekl Teli L'wi'tmasimk* (2021–6)
Ontario	McMaster University	1. *Strategic Plan* (2016–21) 2. *Indigenous Strategic Directions* (2021)
	Queen's University	1. *Strategic Framework* (2021–) 2. *Yakwanastahente'ha Aankenjigemi: Extending the Rafters: Truth and Reconciliation Commission Task Force Implementation Report: Year Five* (2022)
	University of Ottawa	1. *Strategic Plan: Destination 2020: Discover the Future* (–2020) 2. *Indigenous Action Plan* (2020)
	University of Toronto	1. *Strategic Research Plan: Excellence, Innovation, Leadership* (2018–23) 2. *University of Toronto: Answering the Call Wecheehetowin: Final Report of the Steering Committee for the University of Toronto: Response to the Truth and Reconciliation Commission of Canada* (2017)

(Continued)

Table 4. (*Continued*)

Province	University	Documents
	University of Waterloo	1. *Strategic Plan: Connecting Imagination with Impact* (2020–5)
	Western University	1. *Western University Strategic Plan: Towards Western at 150* (2020) 2. *Indigenous Strategic Plan* (2016)
Quebec	Laval University	1. *Strategic Plan: Dare, Inspire, Achieve, Building the Future Together* (2017–22) 2. *En Action Avec Les Premiers Peuples Plan D'Action* (2020)
	McGill University	1. *Strategic Academic Plan* (2017–22) 2. *Provost's Task Force on Indigenous Studies and Indigenous Education: Final Report* (2017)
	Université de Montréal	1. *Strategic Plan: Planification Stratégique* (2016–21) 2. *Plan d'action en matière d'équité, de diversité et d'inclusion pour le programme des chaires de recherche du Canada* (2018)
Saskatchewan	University of Saskatchewan	1. *University Plan 2025: Strategic Framework and Narrative* (2018–25) 2. *Indigenous Strategy: ohpahotan. oohpaahotaan: Let's Fly Up Together* (2021)

University of Manitoba (2015), Queen's University (2023), the University of Saskatchewan (2018), and the University of Toronto (2018). While the University of Manitoba and the University of Saskatchewan have shown continuous commitment specifically towards Indigenous communities, the other two universities see decolonization as part of their broader social justice agenda. Reconciliation as a commitment to Indigenous peoples is at the forefront in many academic plans, but only a few universities have articulated a specific action plan in relation to this priority. The exceptions are the prairie province universities (the University of Alberta, the University of Saskatchewan, and the University of Manitoba), which accommodate more Indigenous students. The University of Alberta's strategic plan is an example of a pragmatic approach to institutional Indigenization, as it noted the importance of recruiting and supporting Indigenous peoples for the purposes of training skilled labour. Such approaches can be seen as a response to political and functional pressures, where value-based shift is not clearly visible. The University of Saskatchewan has taken a more ideological approach. Its academic plan for 2025 noted that "the world needs a university in which Indigenous concepts, methodologies, pedagogies, languages, and philosophies are respectfully woven into the tapestry of learning, research, scholarship" (University of Saskatchewan, 2018, p. 13).

Indigenous strategies are typically framed in a more critical manner, centring on self-determination with an emphasis on structural, systemic change in higher education. The theme of colonialism is frequently mentioned in most Indigenous strategies, highlighting decolonization as a path forward. One example of such an approach is found in the University of British Columbia's (UBC) Indigenous strategy, which described the university's central role in perpetuating the legacy of colonialism by training "many of the policy makers and administrators who operated the residential school system" and "accepting the silence surrounding it" (UBC, 2020, p. 8). This perspective suggests a normative change whereby the university is expressing its commitment to shifting values. The University of Alberta's Indigenous strategy listed decolonization as its guiding value, encouraging universities to approach structural changes from a decolonial lens. McMaster's Indigenous document further stated that "it is understood that the colonial structures and systems must be disrupted or dismantled" (McMaster University, 2020, p. iii). Western University's (2016) first-ever Indigenous strategic plan was grounded in the narrative of reconciliation but highlighted institutional roles and responsibilities in supporting Indigenous research, education, and campus life. The document applied a critical lens by calling for working through the systemic, social, and ideological issues that inhibit the university from becoming a culturally safe and responsive space for Indigenous peoples (Western University, 2016). This articulation of colonialism in policy documents demonstrates how advocacy work around colonial legacy gets incorporated into policy documents, where it starts to shape the dominant narrative and impact values, norms, and, eventually, collective behaviour.

Indigenous strategic plans read as a reclamation by Indigenous people of power and control over Indigenous knowledges, emphasizing the centrality of community-led knowledge within university structures. For example, the University of Saskatchewan's Indigenous strategy explicitly stated that "This strategy uplifts Indigenous voices. / ... / This strategy is a gift to non-Indigenous people. / ... / The gifting of this strategy does not signal the end of struggle; it signals awakening, resurgence, and renewal" (University of Saskatchewan, 2020, p. 3). The idea of gifting characterizes a process of relationship building in Indigenous worldviews by giving, receiving, and paying back (Kuokkanen, 2007a). Gifting as an act of building relationships contributes to the processes of self-determination and self-governance of Indigenous peoples in higher education. Most Indigenous strategic plans have included the names of traditional knowledge keepers, language teachers, translators, and community members who contributed their insights to the development of these documents. This is a way to highlight community connections and the importance of collaborative efforts in the processes of decolonization.

Funding is an important consideration in implementing Indigenous strategies. A proactive example has been provided by the University of Ottawa. The University of Ottawa's Indigenous Action Plan listed not only specific activities but also specified funding allocated to those initiatives. The university worked with an operating budget of $3.6 million to support Indigenous activities over a five-year period (Fulcrum News, 2020). The document featured a comprehensive plan listing specific action items with budget lines and stakeholder responsibilities. The straightforward nature of this plan has a promising outlook for policy implementation.

Changes in Hiring and Employment Policies

Hiring Indigenous faculty has become a competitive race among Canadian universities. New institutional hiring and employment efforts have played an important role in providing increased access for Indigenous individuals to mainstream higher education. This change, which has resulted from new policy efforts, was noticed by a research participant, who pointed out that *"Policy is a big giant … It has led to hiring practices changing. It has led to greater support from such places as the Provost Office for Indigenous initiatives"* (interview, 9 March 2018). According to a survey conducted by Universities Canada (2019), 60% of Canadian higher education institutions are taking steps to increase Indigenous faculty representation in their organizations. Institutions have set specific recruitment goals and are working towards recognizing Indigenous community-based knowledge as an important aspect of tenure and promotion. Cluster hiring of Indigenous faculty has become a notable approach among universities. For example, McGill University (2017, p. 40) committed to hiring 15 Indigenous professors over the next three years and stipulated that there would be targets for further hiring, to be set on a periodic basis. Similarly, Memorial University of Newfoundland committed to hiring up to five tenure-track or tenured appointments for First Nation, Métis, Inuit, and Indigenous candidates

(Memorial University, 2020a). The University of Saskatchewan committed to hiring 30 Indigenous scholars (Gaudry & Lorenz, 2018). The Werklund School of Education at the University of Calgary, in one faculty alone, hired six Indigenous assistant professors between 2012 and 2015 (Louie, 2019). Moreover, in the same institution, the Faculty of Arts hired seven Indigenous academics in a cluster hire in 2017 (Louie, 2019). While cluster hires may speak to institutional performativity, this approach provides important opportunities to create Indigenous support networks, increase mentorship opportunities, and lower emotional stress and share service demands among Indigenous colleagues. Having several Indigenous faculty members represented in a faculty creates a critical mass that can advocate for implementing strategic priorities with changes in curriculum and programming.

In addition to cluster hiring practices, universities are using the language of preferential or targeted hiring. Several universities (e.g., McGill University, Queen's University, the University of Ottawa, the University of Alberta, the University of Calgary) have included a preferential hiring clause in their hiring policies for both staff and faculty. Targeted hiring language is aimed at attracting only people who self-identify as Indigenous. However, the broadness of this language has been critiqued. A simplistic assumption is made that Indigenous identity is automatically accompanied by Indigenous knowledges, which overlooks the fact that people who identify as Indigenous may not ever have had any lived experiences with their Indigenous heritage or community. Furthermore, Deer (2020, p. 111) pointed out that the broad use of the word "Indigenous" in the Canadian context opens the potential for the recruitment of those who identify as Indigenous but are not Indigenous to the territories of Turtle Island, and thus are not capable of asserting the territorial, ancestral, or linguistic identities or Indigenous knowledges that have become valued in the academy. While new employment positions help to create a critical mass of Indigenous faculty, administrators, and staff on campus, and thus increase the likelihood of prioritizing Indigenous initiatives and decolonizing efforts overall, there is a lack of institutional supports beyond hiring practices. An Indigenous faculty member shared their experience:

> They're giving us the opportunity and say, well, here it is – we're leaving this open to you. We've hired you; let's see what you can do. (Interview, 22 November 2018)

Louie (2019) has made a strong argument describing how faculties are expecting Indigenous individuals to contribute their knowledges yet are providing limited supports for faculty members to spend time in their communities, on the land, or taking part in ceremonies, which are all integral to furthering their expertise in Indigenous culture, language, and knowledges. Brunette-Debassige (2021) raised issues about staff hiring. Despite the recent Indigenous hiring efforts mentioned above, the systemic lack of focus on hiring Indigenous staff members has contributed to making the labour of this group invisible. Indigenous staff members are often hired to work with non-Indigenous faculty to help them implement Indigenous content in their teaching, raising questions about how this approach may benefit Indigenous communities. A decolonizing approach to hiring practices would mean engaging community in the hiring processes, including Indigenous knowledge keepers and elders. This could mean conducting interviews or evaluations in Indigenous languages or involving traditional Indigenous protocols in the selection process. Another decolonizing approach to hiring is not to fit Indigenous faculty members within the established disciplinary framework but to allow Indigenous academics themselves to indicate how they could contribute to the faculty beyond disciplinary boundaries. Assessment for tenure and promotion should include Indigenous committee members and prioritize work in the community and on the land.

The federal government has played a role in shaping institutional hiring and employment policies in Canada. Canada's federal Employment Equity Act from 1995 addressed the removal of barriers that have a discriminatory impact on people, including Indigenous individuals. Most higher education institutions have developed their own employment policies or guidelines to support diversity in hiring. Several of these policies date back to the 1980s and 1990s (e.g., the University of Calgary, the University of Manitoba, McMaster University, the University of Toronto, the University of Waterloo). The Université de Montréal adopted employment equality policies for women back in 1988, before any government requirement, and has expanded it to include visible minorities, Aboriginal people, and people with disabilities (Université de Montréal, 2018). More recent statements on employment equity have emerged in relation to institutional equity, diversity, and inclusion efforts. Dalhousie's Employment Equity Policy was approved in 2017 (Dalhousie University, 2017). According to this policy, Dalhousie wishes to institute active measures to eliminate discrimination and to reverse the historic under-representation of Indigenous peoples (especially Mi'kmaq), members of racialized minority groups (especially historic African Nova Scotians), persons with disabilities, women, and persons belonging to sexual orientation and/or gender identity (SOGI) minority groups within its workforce (Dalhousie University, 2017).

Following this policy adoption, Dalhousie University created a precedent in 2018 when it restricted its search for a new senior leadership position (vice-provost student affairs) to racially visible or Indigenous candidates (CBCNews, 2018a). This was the first time a higher education institution in Canada pursued employment equity by excluding candidates from the privileged dominant cultural group, which created a wider public debate. Many higher education institutions have newly implemented unconscious bias training involving interactive workshops, online modules, or other types of learning activities. Unconscious bias training can cover a range of topics, including racial and gender bias, disability bias, and age bias, among others. The purpose of such training practices is to raise awareness of individual bias that creates barriers for diversity and to take steps to reduce its impact on decision making and interactions with others.

The federal government's Canada Research Chairs (CRC) program has further played a role in prioritizing employment equity for Indigenous peoples. In accordance with CRC's Equity, Diversity and Inclusion policy, universities are being asked to track their hiring according to four federally designated equity categories – women, racialized/visible minorities, persons with disabilities, and Indigenous persons. Tracking hires according to these categories allows for the universities to have a targeted approach to Indigenous employment. As of June 2019, there were 39 (2.1%) CRCs held by Indigenous faculty out of 1,836 CRCs across tiers. Thirty-four Indigenous individuals were hired as Tier 2 CRCs (emerging researchers, future leaders), and five were hired as Tier 1 CRCs (established world-class researchers) (CRC, n.d.-a). While this number may seem very small, the percentage was even smaller in 2009 – 0.4%. A core weakness in the CRC performance reports is that they focus primarily on the numbers of researchers hired and do not really get to the supports researchers need, once hired. The hiring of Indigenous researchers increases institutional opportunities to gain access to attractive funding provided through the CRC program. For example, by appointing a Tier 1 CRC, an institution receives $200,000 annually for seven years (CRC, n.d.-b), from which money is allocated to an individual researcher for their research activities.

This financial incentive, paired with institutional efforts to hire Indigenous faculty, has created dilemmas for Indigenous faculty. Often Indigenous individuals are recruited early, when they are still in their PhD program, as the pool of qualified individuals is small. Recruitment agencies have become involved in this competition to further pressure

Indigenous people to apply for faculty positions early. A faculty member commented:

> *So, there's one agency in particular that contacted me a couple of times, at least, over the duration of my trying to get through my PhD dissertation because a certain university was looking for an Indigenous candidate, and especially one that could speak French as well. [Yeah] / ... / It seems that universities are looking more and more.* (Interview, 23 November 2018)

Being hired when they are still graduate students places Indigenous faculty members in a vulnerable position, as they are expected to complete a dissertation in addition to fulfilling other faculty responsibilities. Nevertheless, overall, the emphasis on and increase in hiring Indigenous individuals was viewed supportively by the Indigenous faculty members interviewed. One Indigenous faculty member summarized this development as follows: *"These hires we have with Indigenous focus, to me, that's different because it's the institution putting their money where their mouth is. That is a good thing"* (interview, 9 March 2018).

With increasing opportunities for Indigenous peoples ranging from tenure-track faculty positions to research grants and student scholarships, cases of Indigenous identity fraud have emerged across Canadian universities. The issue is complex and associated with ambiguity, stemming from the colonial histories and current institutional practices, requiring deeper-level commitment and attention from the universities. Foremost, there are contested meanings of what constitutes Indigenous identity. Combinations of genealogy/ancestry, formal status, and community affiliation are often used as legitimacy criteria (McKay, 2021). However, formal band/tribal membership does not necessarily equal cultural standing, holding Indigenous knowledges, or community acknowledgment. Individuals may belong to several communities or there may be no community affiliation at all. Indigenous collective identities are frequently reshaped as the Canadian state negotiates treaties, land claim agreements, and self-government agreements, giving rise to new political units and legal identities (Teillet, 2022). When facing such ambiguity, navigating discourses of authentic Indigeneity may be particularly challenging. As noted by Teillet (2022), universities have relied primarily on an honour system of self-identification, especially for faculty positions.

Universities have left solving Indigenous identity fraud cases with the Indigenous communities, whereby the issue is framed as an Indigenous problem and Indigenous responsibility. Henry & Tait (2023) convincingly pointed out that the problem should be approached from the perspective that it is the non-Indigenous peoples that are falsely claiming Indigenous identity. The authors argued that the cases should be treated as an issue of academic misconduct and dishonesty by the university. Otherwise, all Indigenous people at the universities will fall under surveillance, experiencing microaggressions and suspicion for being Indigenous, losing their rights and privacy in the process (Henry & Tait, 2023).

Reporting an Indigenous identity fraud is an extremely laborious and emotionally taxing process that brings up an issue of safety for the person reporting the case. Caroline Tait in Henry & Tait (2023) shared her painful experiences with institutional bureaucracy when investigating and filing an identity fraud case at the University of Saskatchewan. As noted by Teillet (2022), universities tend to support excellence in performance rather than reveal the fraud cases. The overall recommendation is to have in place consistent policies across the country, grounded in a collegial process that includes significant Indigenous faculty representation when assessing cases of academic dishonesty associated with Indigenous identity fraud (Teillet, 2022, Henry & Tait, 2023). There also should be an agreement on what the consequences for Indigenous identity fraud should be, which currently differ by institution. The process of developing such policies requires significant resources from the university.

Several universities are engaged in developing principles, policies, and practices to address Indigenous identity fraud, but there is no unified approach yet on how these cases should be handled. Teillet (2022) argued that self-identification, a common approach to determine Indigenous identity, has been shown not to be enough; formal verification of ancestral connection and community acceptance is now often required. Several universities, including the University of Saskatchewan (2022) and Queen's University (First Peoples Group, 2022), have developed policies related to proof of Indigenous identification. McMaster University and the University of Laval are requiring formal ancestry documentation or proof of status for admission to spots reserved for Indigenous applicants. Proactively addressing the issue of Indigenous identity fraud is of utmost importance to higher education institutions on the path towards decolonization, as this will ensure that resources and positions allocated for Indigenous individuals are used appropriately.

Changes in Admission Policies

Stonechild (2006) noted that policies for First Nations students, including efforts to enhance access to higher education, have evolved significantly over the years, with the biggest strides made in increased participation rates. Post-secondary education has become more accessible for Indigenous students, in part due to new institutional admissions policies, access or bridging programs, and more inclusive procedures when assessing prior learning. As part of decolonization efforts, universities are aiming to assess candidates holistically, considering their lived experience and extensive Indigenous community service as well as their academic records, including prior course credits in Indigenous topics. Universities have introduced educational equity committees or EDI-focused admissions committees to assess applications from equity-seeking individuals, including Indigenous applicants. Preston (2016) reported that the University of British Columbia assesses the educational history, work experience, cultural knowledge, educational goals, and other achievements of prospective Indigenous students in its admission process. The University of Winnipeg has an Indigenous Language Proficiency Requirement, which recognizes Indigenous languages as equivalent to other languages for admission purposes. Four institutions (the University of Alberta, the University of Manitoba, McGill University, and Queen's University) among U15 Canadian research-intensive universities have stated specific performance indicators related to Indigenous student admission and recruitment (Tamtik & Guenter, 2019). A core strategic goal of the University of Saskatchewan was to have Indigenous students represent 15% of the university's total enrolment by 2020 (University of Saskatchewan Council, 2012). Some faculties have introduced a special admissions consideration category for Indigenous applicants (e.g., the University of Manitoba's Faculty of Psychology), where Indigenous applicants need to identify themselves and will then be assessed in a different pool. The University of Manitoba's Faculty of Education has developed a diversity admission policy for their teacher education program with the largest enrolment target for candidates identifying as Indigenous (14%) compared to 7% for other categories (UM Today, 2016). The policy, which came into effect in September 2017, allows administrators to make every effort to offer 45% of all available positions in teacher education based on applicants' voluntary self-identification in one (or more) of four diversity categories. Over the three years since the new policy was applied, an average of 9.6% of the students were Indigenous people from Canada, which was still short of the set enrolment target (CBCNews, 2020). Nevertheless, changing admission policies is one approach that helps to provide better access for Indigenous youth to higher education.

Changes in Academic Programming

The changes in institutional priorities have led to increased focus on innovative academic programming, providing more relevant and meaningful coursework to Indigenous students. Over the years, there have been new regulations implemented for degree and diploma programs, as well as (mandatory) coursework requirements related to Indigenous topics. Since 1969, Indigenous Studies programs have multiplied across the university sector in Canada (Andersen & O'Brien, 2017). Brunette-Debassige (2021) noted that by 2015 nearly half of all Canadian universities offered an Indigenous Studies undergraduate program, and at least three universities have raised these programs to department or disciplinary status (the University of Alberta, Trent University, the University of Winnipeg). There are some universities that have introduced policies and regulations requiring students to take an Indigenous course. The purpose of such a mandatory course requirement is to create a wider awareness of Indigenous topics, which may help with normative change. For example, the University of Winnipeg has developed a list of courses that may be used to fulfil a course requirement from a relatively small set of academic disciplines (Friesen Lepp, 2018). In February 2018, the senate of Trent University approved the introduction of a new university degree regulation requiring all undergraduate students to complete at least one course with approved Indigenous content (Trent University, n.d.). Lakehead University made a commitment that, by the beginning of the 2016/17 academic year, all academic units would have introduced at least one 0.5 Full Course Equivalent course containing at least 50% (equivalent to 18 hours) of Indigenous knowledge and/or Aboriginal content (Lakehead University, n.d.) in their undergraduate programs. The University of Manitoba Senate passed a motion to modify graduation requirements for the Bachelor of Arts degrees in the Faculty of Arts to include an Indigenous content requirement (University of Manitoba, 2020).

Deer (2020) suggested that the provision of Indigenous programs has been historically more likely to occur in Indigenous/Native Studies departments, faculties of education, and some health sciences faculties. In other fields, such as science, engineering, and architecture, the development of Indigenous academic programming may still be a new endeavour. In some cases, Indigenous programming has been the result of explicit professional relevance (e.g., the exploration of the social determinants of health for Indigenous populations in faculties of medicine), while in other cases, programming exists because of a government mandate (e.g., a provincial government that makes it necessary for new school teachers to have had some course work dedicated to Indigenous Studies) (Deer, 2020). Henry et al. (2017b) argued that despite programmatic policy change, Indigenous Studies undergraduate programs continue to face constraints while operating within dominant Euro-western academic, disciplinary, and budgetary structures. Deer (2020) also pointed out that initiatives to develop new Indigenous academic courses and programs frequently require extensive study, consultation with Indigenous communities, and negotiation. This perspective further highlights the importance of Indigenous communities, their expertise, and their contributed work to programmatic changes in Canadian universities.

Faculty Perspectives on Impacting Change

This overview of documented changes in governance and policy does not sufficiently capture the lived experiences of Indigenous individuals working towards facilitating such change. According to Indigenous research participants, the work of meaningful change in institutional governance, including policy change, has been a long and complex process, often met with resistance. Several Indigenous participants agreed that there has been a noticeable change in higher education governance towards commitment to Indigenous perspectives. The following quote by an experienced faculty member from the social sciences illustrates this idea: "*I'm enjoying the level of interest, and dedication to change that I see in [academic] institutions. /… / When I started here in 1994, it was not like this*" (interview, 10 April 2019). This quote demonstrates how Indigenous knowledges and activities are gradually becoming a priority in the policy and practice of Canadian higher education institutions. Many participants shared their personal experiences of advocating for policy change but highlighted how their work has regularly been contested and resisted by the dominant cultural group. Experience of resistance to attempts to change established structures was a prevalent theme in many interviews. The following comment reflects how non-Indigenous decision makers have used the "committee culture" to minimize opportunities for Indigenous peoples to make change. The ways in which Indigenous committees have been titled and positioned within the organizational hierarchy can contribute to either the advancement or hindrance of the individual agendas of people in power. An Indigenous faculty member shared her story about how a committee title was used to diminish the efforts of its work:

> We made a committee that was composed of all representatives from all of the Indigenous education authorities in [location], plus the Métis, plus urban Natives, plus Aboriginal organizations. This was initially supposed to be a Steering Committee, not an Advisory Committee. / … / They [college leaders] came and said, well, you're not doing this! We were basically told to our faces – you guys are an Advisory Committee only. You have no power to direct policy or dictate anything to anybody. So, after that happened, our name was kind of mud. (Interview, 14 February 2018)

Another example of barriers created by lack of institutional support is evident in the following reflection. An Indigenous faculty member shared an occasion when decisions by senior university leadership ruined efforts to organize people around an Indigenous matter:

> We have gotten the trust of a lot of very key people in this province and, they [university leaders] did it again. They said, "Okay, do this, do this," so we made this committee. We had a gigantic meeting that was going to take place at Thunderbird Lodge. We were going to have a ceremonial aspect to it, but at the last minute, they refused to fund it. And they refused to give us the space to do anything on campus. So, they made it seem as though they wanted us to succeed, but, in fact, they put obstacle after obstacle in front of us, so that we would not. Leaders of the university. So, I'm talking about the vice-presidents. I don't think the president was involved in this. But, I think, his de facto people in charge were the vice-presidents. There were two of them in particular. (Interview, 14 February 2018)

Similar barriers have been met by newly appointed Indigenous leaders. One example that created significant media attention took place at the University of Manitoba in 2018 when the recently appointed vice-president Indigenous engagement, Dr. Lynn Lavallée, resigned after serving in the position for a year. Dr. Lavallée shared that, instead of being able to develop new Indigenous initiatives, she found herself repeatedly forced to justify to non-Indigenous senior administrators why Indigenous initiatives are important (CBCNews, 2018b). The University of Manitoba is not the only university within the Canadian higher education sector that has faced public confrontations with structural racism. Similarly, Angelique EagleWoman resigned from her position as dean of the Law School at Lakehead University, citing systemic racism and discrimination at the school (Yang, 2018). Sandra Muse Isaacs resigned her position as a professor at Saint Mary's University in Halifax, citing the school's failure to make progress against the legacy of colonialism (Bundale, 2018). In April of 2018, elder Marilyn Buffalo was dismissed one month before a two-year contract extension with the University of Alberta (CBCNews, 2018b), raising strong critiques from the community for disrespect in the treatment of Indigenous Elders. As a result of public outcry pointing to institutional failure in the path towards reconciliation, universities and colleges have slowly started to examine and address the broader campus climate in confronting systemic and structural issues. At the University of Manitoba, this process culminated in an in-depth report analysing the situation within the senior leadership and making clear recommendations for change, several of which have already been implemented (University of Manitoba, 2019). This example demonstrates how the critical work done by individual Indigenous faculty members, despite significant emotional burdens, individual failures, and personal sacrifices, has created a slow change in institutional practices and accepted behaviours.

Decolonizing the structures of Canadian higher education institutions is a long process involving learning that may lead to change in deeply rooted norms and values. It is a comprehensive, multi-layered process that cannot be addressed by a single report or a presidential committee. Pidgeon (2016) pointed out that Indigenizing the academy cannot be achieved through one strategy – it is a cumulative and complex living movement that aims to see post-secondary institutions empowering Indigenous peoples' cultural integrity through respectful relationships in their policies, programs, and services. For example, one Indigenous participant reflected:

> *The university is fumbling around to a certain extent. They're like any large institution. Give me a, you know, policy or a two-day workshop that's going to fix all of this. [Chuckles] [Hmm, hmm] This is long, hard, slogging work about how we work together. And, you know, it just takes time … and we're not going to convince everybody because some people are rooted in their anger for whatever reason.* (Interview, 3 December 2018)

The focus needs to be at the individual level, accompanied by support from the leadership, so that each individual can contribute and play their part in the process. The theme of working together for change was expressed in the interviews several times. A participant applauded institutional efforts at their faculty to push for change. In their view, the attempts to work towards decolonizing institutions had been genuine, and there were promising prospects for working together for broader change:

> *There's a lot of good intentions. I believe it. I believe there's good intention here. Like, [name of the dean] told me that they hired a bunch of Indigenous scholars, and they're going to hire more, 8, or 10, or 11, or something like that, in total, across the campus. And that, in the future, we would work together to see what we could do to make things better.* (Interview, 14 February 2018)

While there was generally a sentiment of support and acknowledgment of institutional effort in the interviews, there were some faculty members who were more cautious. The institutional grand narratives around empowering people or making strides in achieving diversity targets sounded hollow to some and created doubts about the institutional willingness to cooperate. The way in which institutions frame these narratives has tended to minimize the decades-long efforts of Indigenous peoples working towards change. These narratives position institutions, as opposed to Indigenous individuals, as the catalysts for change, overlooking Indigenous people's time, expertise, and advocacy work. An Indigenous faculty member commented:

> *I think part of the hiring of us [Indigenous faculty] is to hopefully see that there might be opportunities for them [non-Indigenous individuals] to show that they are good organizations, right?* (Interview, 22 November 2018)

Another Indigenous faculty member shared how she, in her administrative position, was able to work with the dean of the faculty to make sure diverse voices were represented in decision-making processes. She particularly mentioned work aimed at disrupting the norms and values (status quo) that are taken for granted by non-Indigenous people. She reflected:

> *When I was director of the program, a lot of times I'd be at meetings where I'm the only woman there and definitely the only Aboriginal person, and feeling the difference of that, how do people perceive you. /... / When [name of a dean] was our dean, at one point, we went to talk to diverse groups. We physically went to meet with the groups and say, look, send your people to us. [Chuckles] And that was a sight. /... / Because if we don't do that, it would never happen. Because we have to disrupt the flow, you know, the status quo, in different ways. And, we need it with people who think about it principally, and logistically, and willingly to put themselves to work alongside us and not always try to be up ahead on the agenda.* (Interview, 14 February 2018)

An ongoing challenge for members of Indigenous communities is how to move these university change efforts beyond policy statements and strategic priorities towards greater levels of actual institutional reform (Pete, 2016). While much has been achieved, as illustrated in this chapter, the institutional change in policy and governance from decolonizing perspectives is still a work in progress with many structural barriers to overcome.

Conclusion

This chapter described the institutional governance and policy developments that have occurred in the higher education sector in Canada. It documented changes in governance structures, strategic planning processes, hiring and admission policies, and academic programming.

While much has been achieved, there are further opportunities for decolonial change to empower Indigenous peoples and give them control of their own education. In particular, further support in capacity-building is needed for Indigenous leaders to be able to enact required changes in academia and contribute to their communities. By bringing forward the voices of interview participants, the chapter highlighted the ways in which institutional structures tend to be grounded in advocacy work from within. This change has been subtle, and those championing this work have often encountered personal failures. Nevertheless, there is evidence that speaks directly to how Indigenous communities have been able to impact collective norms and values within universities. While some progress has been made, significant barriers remain for non-Indigenous peoples to address. There is a need for continued work from decolonial perspectives to ensure that Indigenous post-secondary education can fulfil its potential through meaningful governance structures and policy change.

Institutional Climate

Policy is one thing. And then you hit the ground and you're ... all of a sudden ... you've got hostility coming towards you and you're not really sure why, you know.
(Interview, 3 December 2018)

Institutional climate is an elusive, yet crucial, aspect of any higher education system. It is elusive because institutional climate is not easily detectable, as it is composed of an intricate web of social relations constructed by members of an organization (Hurtado et al., 2008). Institutional climate is closely connected to norms, as climate reflects the shared values, beliefs, and behaviours that shape organizations, including universities. Norms are unwritten expectations for collective behaviour that shape institutional climates. Institutional climate unfolds in individual and collective attitudes, perceptions, behaviours, and expectations in regard to race, gender, ethnicity, sexual orientation, and abilities but also in regard to knowledge systems (Hurtado et al., 1998; Schneider et al., 2017). It is difficult to address or measure institutional climate, as it is mostly about the feeling one gets when on campus, in the classroom, or interacting with others. When norms in a university are equitable and inclusive, all members of the community feel welcomed and respected. Yet, often individuals' perceptions of the collective norms may be at odds with the actual collective norms universities perpetuate. This disconnect has been a persistent theme for Indigenous knowledges. Formal university policies may create the perception of a strong institutional commitment to Indigenization and decolonization, while the normative collective practices continue to ignore the experiences of Indigenous peoples and, in fact, may further perpetuate structural inequities (Tuck & Yang, 2012). Working towards change in an institutional climate involves examining existing perceptions and norms, confronting individual attitudes, and tackling formed behaviours. This can be done through the lens of decolonial learning where systemic barriers, attitudes, and behaviours get confronted and critically examined. Without this work, institutional efforts largely remain at the surface level with ongoing struggles to overcome racism, discrimination, and resistance to the inclusion of Indigenous perspectives in administrative practices and curriculum (Pidgeon, 2014). Aspirational language used in institutional policy documents regarding Indigenous initiatives is still the prevalent norm. When it comes to Indigenous knowledges, there is little commitment to deeper-level decolonial change (Gaudry & Lorenz, 2018). According to Pidgeon (2016), successful institutional transformation towards valuing Indigenous knowledges is a complex and layered process that should centre on the lived experiences of Indigenous communities. Universities have shifted their institutional climates only when Indigenous students have experienced empowerment in their self-determination and strengthened their cultural integrity during their academic journey (Pidgeon, 2016).

Hurtado et al. (1998) proposed an analytic framework for unpacking the complexity of institutional climate. These authors suggested specific components that are useful for examining institutional climate, focusing on 1) a campus's historical legacy of including or excluding various racial or ethnic groups; 2) its structural diversity (i.e., the numerical and proportional representation of diverse groups on campus); 3) its psychological climate (i.e., individual perceptions, attitudes, and beliefs about diversity); and 4) its behavioural climate (i.e., collective norms, how different racial and ethnic groups interact on campus). This framework guides this chapter in examining the changes occurring in the institutional climate in universities in relation to Indigenous knowledges.

Addressing Historical Legacy

The legacy of colonialism continues to impact Indigenous peoples' experiences with higher education. Deficit-based stereotypes and racialized acts of discrimination that are ingrained in our society and carried forward by higher education institutions support patterns of domination, exclusion, and marginalization of Indigenous peoples (Henry et al., 2017a). Indigenous researchers have continuously called upon educational institutions to address the harm done to Indigenous communities, heritage, and languages and to engage in meaningful decolonization practices (Battiste, 2018; Fontaine, 2017; Pidgeon,

2019). As a result, post-secondary institutions have started to publicly acknowledge the colonial legacies and their roles in perpetuating those legacies. While often critiqued for their performative nature and incapacity to go beyond awareness-building (see Asher et al., 2018; Vowel, 2017), these formal statements play an important role in sending signals about shifting attitudes and collective norms across the institution. An aspect of the colonial legacy that sends a direct message about the values institutions uphold is the various artifacts exhibited on campus. Statues, paintings, framed portraits, and buildings with donor names can be painful reminders of the historical legacies to Indigenous peoples and serve as a mechanism of systemic oppression. Taking down the statue of Egerton Ryerson in front of Ryerson University (now Toronto Metropolitan University) is one of the examples where the history of colonialism and treatment of Indigenous peoples has been publicly confronted. Ryerson, a superintendent of schools in Upper Canada, was tasked by the federal government with preparing a proposal for implementing industrial schools for Indigenous children that started the residential school era (Crocker, 2022) and is, thus, considered one of the architects of Canada's residential school system. It was the voices of Indigenous groups and their advocacy work that created pressures on the university administration to take action. Following a lengthy process with the involvement of university Elder Joanne Dallaire and many other members of the Indigenous community, the name change of the university was approved in 2022 (Rancic, 2022). This example speaks to the wider grassroots movements gaining momentum across Canada and confronting historical legacies in universities. Such work, grounded in learning and followed by action, sends a signal about the shifting values in institutional norms, impacting institutional climate.

Territorial Land Acknowledgments

The Truth and Reconciliation report called for educational institutions to reflect on their colonial foundations. Within this context, territorial land acknowledgments have scaled up in scope, becoming a standard practice at any public event. Acknowledging territory identifies the Indigenous peoples of the area and, in a symbolic way, recognizes the colonial legacy of the institution in place and time (Pidgeon, 2016). It is both cultural and political practice that is fundamentally tied to Indigenous nationhood (Wark, 2021, Wilkes et al., 2017). Wilkes et al. (2017) explained that, at their core, land acknowledgments recognize and appreciate Indigenous people's right to self-determination and autonomous existence. The nature of land acknowledgments varies, depending on the existence of formally signed treaties and particular geographical and institutional contexts. A comprehensive overview of various land acknowledgments developed and used by Canadian colleges and universities has been provided in a report titled *Guide to Acknowledging First Peoples & Traditional Territory* by the Canadian Association of University Teachers (see CAUT, 2017). Wilkes's et al. (2017) study analysing land acknowledgments used by Canadian universities demonstrated that the nature and scope of land acknowledgments are fluid and change over time. There is a shared sentiment that, while acknowledging territory is essential in building relationships with local Indigenous communities, it is only a small part of cultivating strong relationships with Indigenous peoples.

When territorial acknowledgments were first presented in non-Indigenous contexts, they were somewhat shocking statements, reminding people of Indigenous presence and the colonial history (âpihtawikosisân, 2016). With increasing recital of territorial land acknowledgments, the initial purpose and meaning of these practices has started to change. Wark (2021) noted that land acknowledgments have become performative exercises, absorbing Indigenous peoples and rewriting the colonial history. Instead of working towards returning Indigenous lands and revitalizing Indigenous languages and ways of living, these recitals have become hollow, strictly symbolic gestures among non-Indigenous peoples with limited criticality and historical knowledge (King, 2018; Wark, 2021). Asher et al. (2018) stated that, while territorial acknowledgments help to work against the daily erasure of Indigenous peoples, they often perform as a protective layer for non-Indigenous peoples against taking meaningful action. Tuck and Yang (2012, p. 10), more critical, pointed out that these statements work as "settlers' move to innocence" – attempts that aim to relieve feelings of guilt and responsibility without giving up land or power or privilege. Sabzalian (2019) recalled that acknowledging Indigenous homelands, peoples, and nations is an important practice if the person doing the acknowledgment engages with the deeper meaning of these statements and builds their responsibility for and involvement in issues that concern local Indigenous peoples. An example of a critical personal engagement with a territorial land acknowledgment was presented by Janzen (2019) when she reflected on her relationship with Indigenous lands on Treaty 1 Territory. A decolonial approach to land acknowledgment involves recognizing and centring the statement on Indigenous sovereignty over their traditional lands, while reflecting on one's contributions towards this goal.

The lengthy process of developing and introducing territorial land acknowledgments is often framed as an accomplishment of institutional efforts to collaborate with Indigenous communities. Wilkes et al. (2017, p. 92) challenged this perspective and argued that the current practices adopted by universities were driven mainly by the actions of three groups: 1) faculty and students in Indigenous Studies departments and centres, who recognized visiting guests and speakers from other nations and territories as well as the territory and nation that they were on; 2) activist movements such as Idle No More; and 3) the influence of large-scale political events and dialogues such as the 1996 Royal Commission on Aboriginal Peoples and the work of the Truth and Reconciliation Commission. Similarly, Onkwehonwe Rising (2020) has argued that this institutional change has been achieved through the tireless work of Indigenous women by calling attention "in particular [to] the many brilliant and strong Indigenous Sisters who have struggled and pushed for this practice to become accepted as an ingrained activity."

It is, therefore, essential to recognize that the practices of land acknowledgment have been driven by the advocacy and educational work of Indigenous peoples and only accepted by post-secondary institutions, where they may serve alternative purposes. Applying a decolonial lens in this process means that non-Indigenous peoples must take meaningful action disrupting the colonial patterns of oppression and accept their role in the loss of Indigenous land and culture. A good starting point for gaining further knowledge on this topic is the "Whose Land" tool,[1] developed by Indigenous peoples, both in an app and a website format, that helps its users to learn about the lands and how to properly acknowledge them.

Cultural Practices and Ceremonies

Hosting Indigenous cultural practices and spiritual ceremonies, such as smudging and pipe ceremonies, sharing circles, and feasts, is another development that has gained acceptance across Canadian higher education institutions. These ceremonies are important to Indigenous communities, as they help to strengthen connections with Indigenous roots and foster a supportive institutional climate. Introducing cultural practices into mainstream university operations has not been an easy process. The presence of Indigenous cultural practices in universities

---

1 See https://www.whose.land/en/.

has taken tireless work by Indigenous faculty and community members who have dedicated a significant amount of time to sharing their knowledge of Indigenous heritage and traditions and educating university managers and administrators about how to ethically include cultural practices and ceremonies in institutional policies.

A Universities Canada (2013) survey reported that 78% of Canadian post-secondary education institutions have incorporated powwows, feasts, smudging, or other Indigenous cultural practices into their celebratory activities. Powwows that feature Indigenous languages, cuisine, drumming, songs, and dance, typically held at students' graduation or welcoming ceremonies, are becoming common in post-secondary contexts. If carried out properly, involving Indigenous peoples and knowledge holders, these celebrations can have a powerful impact in creating a supportive institutional climate for Indigenous peoples. An Indigenous faculty member reflected on the profound importance cultural traditions have in their life, attesting how music brings strength to their existence:

> *Indigenous music, whether it's drum music or powwow music or sacred music or any of those things, if we're making it ourselves or if we're listening to it ourselves or if we're producing instruments or we're having Indigenous people come in /... / it's the biggest filler of the soul.* (Interview, 14 February 2018)

Many institutions have developed smudging policies. While these policies may often be rigid (asserting smudging to be a potential fire hazard), developing these procedures with Indigenous communities pushes the boundaries of a system and forces people to reflect on the deeper meaning of smudging and prayer. While they are an important part of Indigenous cultural heritage and a significant way to honour Indigenous cultures, performing these cultural practices without the knowledge of the sacred teachings is a form of cultural appropriation. The following concern was expressed by an Indigenous faculty member:

> *There's people who are taking aspects of Indigenous education and just running with it. Smudging is a big one. Smudging is probably the biggest cultural appropriation because it's the easiest thing to do, right. So, people are lighting sage or whatever they're lighting and as if that's all there is to it. But there's so much more to it. So many people don't bother to get those teachings.* (Interview, 14 February 2018)

Ceremonial practices are embedded in Indigenous cultures; they include belonging to a clan and a family and knowing the deeper meaning of a ceremony. It is crucial that higher education institutions help to safeguard and further support exercising these practices in an ethical way by providing space and allowing flexibility for keeping such traditions alive.

While some gains have been achieved, there is still considerable resistance present among universities and their established bureaucracies to accommodating various cultural practices. Sasakamoose and Pete (2015) provided a rich description of their experiences and efforts to confront administrators in their university in order to change institutional policies related to smudging, feast ceremonies, and the involvement and compensation of Elders. Episkenew (2013) shared, among other examples of cultural misalignments, how she, as a university administrator, received direction and a firm execution plan for a meeting from superiors who overlooked the importance of building relationships and co-creating knowledge, as was customary in her Métis culture. Lavallée (2009) described how, in order to include an Elder as part of a dissertation committee with voting rights, she was required to develop a formal curriculum vitae for the Elder, capturing their 70 years of accomplishments, in order for them to be formally recognized as an associate faculty member of the university. Such examples provide vivid evidence of the daily struggles and systemic barriers faced by Indigenous peoples in mainstream universities while trying to make room for Indigenous perspectives and cultural traditions that go against the Eurocentric ways of university operations.

Elders on Campus

Elders and knowledge keepers are the pillars of Indigenous communities, as they carry deep cultural knowledge and teachings with them. An Indigenous faculty member powerfully summarized the importance of Elders: *"Every time an Elder dies, we lose a library, basically"* (interview, 12 December 2018). Because Elders occupy an important leadership role in Indigenous communities, they have an instrumental role in shaping overall campus climate as well. Having Elders and knowledge keepers invited to campus has become a vital part of creating a supportive institutional climate for Indigenous knowledges. Many universities have developed relationships with one or a group of Elders from local communities to provide support to students, staff, faculty, and administration in Indigenous ways of knowing and being. Elders-in-residence programs are becoming common across Canadian universities (e.g., the University of Victoria, Queen's University, the University of Toronto, the University of Manitoba). These are permanent positions for Indigenous knowledge keepers who provide cultural and spiritual guidance, lead cultural teaching sessions, speak in classrooms, carry out ceremonies and events on campus, and are also available for individual mental, spiritual, emotional, and physical guidance. It is important to recognize the diversity among Elders. The teachings resonating in one community or institution may not necessarily connect to others. The importance of Elders is not always well understood or respected in formal administrative practices (Sasakamoose & Pete, 2015), indicating that more learning needs to occur at the individual level for perceptions and norms about Elders to change.

Physical Spaces

Most higher education institutions in Canada are operating on the stolen lands of Indigenous peoples (Smith & Smith, 2018), where institutions decide whether or not to allocate physical space to Indigenous groups or for Indigenous activities. Universities Canada (2013) reported that, in 2010, over 30 meeting rooms or student lounges were made available for Indigenous students in universities across the country. By 2012, the number of those spaces had almost doubled (Universities Canada, 2013), which indicates a move towards Indigenous peoples reclaiming and asserting their right to physical presence on campus. Increasingly, higher education institutions have started to provide funds for buildings that celebrate and house Indigenous knowledges, research, and teachings. Migizii Agamik or "Bold Eagle Lodge" at the University of Manitoba was built in 2008 with a budget of 5 million dollars. Indigenous students can use it as a computer lab, student lounge, or gathering space. The building was designed by architects including Indigenous graduates of the University of Manitoba and incorporates many of the traditional teachings of Indigenous peoples of the area. For example, seven tamarack trees forming the pillars of the building represent the Seven Sacred Laws of Anishinaabe culture. The Circle Room, symbolizing the cycles of nature, is used for ceremonies, meetings, and classes that require a sacred, collaborative space (Indigenous Connect, n.d.). Another example from Quebec features the Pavillon des Premiers-Peuples (the First Peoples Pavilion) at the Université du Québec en Abitibi-Témiscamingue. The building, with a budget of 5 million dollars, offers a place of exchange and research with Indigenous partners and supports scientific research and knowledge dissemination activities (Radio Canada, 2017). First Nations House of Learning on the campus of the University of British Columbia, a 4.2-million-dollar project, is a place for Indigenous gatherings and programming for Indigenous students, faculty, and staff on campus (UBC, n.d.). Verna Kirkness, a Cree scholar and lifelong advocate for Indigenous languages, cultures, and education, was the key visionary advocating for this space. The building is currently being extended with another 3.6 million dollars to include counselling services, larger meeting rooms, and room to house more staff (Warkentin, 2021).

Another development in providing dedicated physical space to Indigenous communities is giving back small pieces of land for establishing Indigenous gardens. Indigenous teaching gardens or medicine gardens have opened at the University of British Columbia, the University of Prince Edward Island, the University of Alberta, Western University, and the University of Manitoba. These gardens incorporate Indigenous knowledges and are used as sites to celebrate traditional food practices and educate about cultural approaches to healing and relationship building that create cultural connections to land (Datta, 2019). Peach et al. (2020) argued that, while they are vitally important to the Indigenous community, the sustainability and use of these spaces is dependent on the ability of Indigenous peoples to exercise self-determination in these spaces and not be constrained by the university administration. Smith and Smith (2018) further pointed out that Indigenous landscapes, plants, and gardens have been given an opportunity to be revitalized but often with permission and within defined parameters of administrators who are making sure not to upset the status quo of the university.

These are just a few examples of spaces and places dedicated to Indigenous heritage that have been established on various campuses across Canada. A former Indigenous student shared their observations of the change in locating physical space for Indigenous student organizations:

> I think there's growing support out there. For instance, you know, the Aboriginal Student Centre used to be tucked away on the fifth floor of the University Centre. It was like two offices, and where the students would study was like one room, no windows. And that was for all Indigenous students to go to. So, it was very small. Now, they have their own building, so now they [Indigenous students] actually have quite a big support system and space. (Interview, 12 October 2018)

This comment further attests to the fact that there has been a move towards prioritizing the importance of cultural teachings in Indigenous students' university experiences. This quote underscores that it is important to consider where those spaces are located on campus and to examine whether those rooms are easily found, widely accessible, and create a welcoming, homelike atmosphere. Because the power imbalance continues to exist, it is important to support the cultural learning experiences of Indigenous students without minimizing the validity of Indigenous perspectives through physical spaces.

Structural Composition/Representation

Structural diversity, which accounts for numerical and proportional representation of Indigenous faculty, staff, and students, provides another mechanism for influencing institutional climate. Research supports the idea that increasing the structural diversity of an institution is helpful for improving the learning experience for diverse student groups (Hurtado et al., 1998). Institutional norms change via students' increased social interactions with others on campus. Connecting with others who have similar experiences can help to reduce social stigma, minimize tokenistic approaches to individuals belonging to minority groups, and increase the attitude of belonging, which can translate into higher academic achievement or employment success (Hurtado et al., 1998).

The representation of Indigenous faculty across Canadian higher education institutions has been historically very low (see Table 1, p. 000 on representation data). One of my participants noted being the first Indigenous faculty member at their university when they started in the late 1990s: *"I was actually the very first Indigenous scholar that they ever hired at [name of the university]"* (interview, 22 November 2018). As noted in the previous chapter, universities have pursued various approaches to increase the numbers of Indigenous peoples in their institutions. These include cluster hirings, establishing targets or quotas, using preferential language to recruit Indigenous applicants, and implementing mandatory unconscious bias training. While the numbers of Indigenous hires are slowly increasing, they are nowhere near to becoming a critical mass for a larger systematic change. The experience of working in isolation and feeling lonely is common among Indigenous scholars:

> *When you hire here, there and whatever else, you're kind of sprinkling, like, little bits of pepper of Indigenous people in different faculties and different departments and different programs. You're still kind of stuck as an isolate. You feel like a little bit of an uninhabited island.* (Interview, 23 November 2018)

Another faculty member argued that institutional initiatives often stop at hiring, with limited focus on further supports, including mentoring:

> *There's these strategic plans, and I know they talk about Indigenous initiatives. I see that largely as manifesting in hiring and … but, beyond that … ?* (Interview, 23 November 2018)

Overall, structural diversity is an important pillar for normative change, while strengthening the capacity for Indigenous knowledges and returning control to Indigenous communities. Research participants noted that numbers and institutional recruitment targets are not everything. The singular act of increasing the number of Indigenous peoples on a campus will not automatically create a more positive institutional climate. Similarly, increased numbers of Indigenous peoples will not necessarily change perceptions, behaviours, or attitudes within the campus community if no attention is given to opportunities for decolonial critical learning that can then shape the institutional climate.

How It Feels to Work in Academia: Behaviour of Colleagues and Students

The attitudes and beliefs of colleagues, staff, and students form a crucial part of academics' work environment, which is directly connected to work success. While all research participants in this study described their current work environment as mostly supportive, the literature has overwhelmingly reported on racist attitudes influencing the experiences of Indigenous faculty, students, and staff in Canadian higher education institutions (see Bailey, 2016; Henry et al., 2017a). The following observations on changing attitudes at the faculty level were made: "*This faculty has been very, very supportive*" (interview, 12 December 2018); "*I definitely get the sense of the value in the [name of the faculty]*" (interview, 14 February 2018); "*What I can say, with limitations, is that I have found [name of the faculty], they've been supportive, in terms of what I'm trying to do*" (interview, 22 November 2018). Indigenous faculty members shared the view that their success seemed to matter to their faculty-level administration. Instances where additional supports were being made available to them, ranging from added financial incentives to the reduction of their teaching load, made them feel understood and appreciated:

> *I think we have a pretty supportive dean who's trying to understand, in his own way, what this all means. So, it's new for him as well.* (Interview, 22 November 2018)

> *I've seen the investment of people, the commitment to change.* (Interview, 9 March 2018)

One faculty member was a bit more cautious but still recognized the generally supportive environment in their workplace. This faculty member linked this increased attention to Indigenous issues brought forward by the TRC's report:

> So, I think there's a lot of good intention, but [laughs] whether we succeed, whether we succeed or not, I think, is probably going to depend on how long the momentum of the Truth and Reconciliation goes on. (Interview, 14 February 2018)

While the overall working environment was mostly perceived as positive, some participants commented about the attitudes of individual colleagues. Occasions where there was resistance to change or colleagues who were oblivious to the effects of their comments were shared. From the following quote, it is evident how such remarks are not always tolerated and get confronted:

> I mean, there's some people, like … [name of the person] who would probably wish that I was not even here./ … / You look at our colleague, [name of the person], who just blurts out things. /… / I just won't sit back about stuff like that. I'll call on them. / … / I'm playing a trickster here when I do that. (Interview, 9 March 2018)

Participants noted that the increased presence of Indigenous faculty has made some of their colleagues more deeply engaged in learning about Indigenous perspectives and knowledges. They recognized that some colleagues had become very knowledgable and supportive about Indigenous perspectives. Then, there were others who were simply not willing to change. The following was described by a participant:

> They can dismiss what you're saying, right. And I think I've learned to read body language, in some sense, who's listening and who's not, [laughs] or who'd rather have me shut up and not carry on. (Interview, 9 March 2018)

While there was a consensus that people are becoming more informed about Indigenous histories, experiences with racism continue to surface from time to time. All but two Indigenous faculty members shared their personal stories about racism and racist attitudes at their institutions. Racism was not explicitly addressed in the interview questions, but this theme kept appearing in the individual stories. A faculty member summarized: "You've got this deep, deep racism against Indigenous people that continues" (interview, 3 December 2018). Another faculty member pointed out: "There are challenges with racism and discrimination, all these things that happen in academic institutions. I've had it every way" (interview,

22 November 2018). Concerns over attitudes towards Indigenous students in a competitive university program were expressed:

Indigenous students are treated very differently, as if we're somehow less intelligent than other students that come through the program. /… / It's been difficult for some of our students, for them to recognize the levels of racism that we experience day-in and day-out at the [name of the university]. (Interview, 12 December 2018)

Racist attitudes expressed predominantly by non-Indigenous students were mentioned as a daily source of anxiety and stress. Challenging the authority of Indigenous instructors from a position of race created conflict and impacted the overall classroom climate:

I will admit, I'm a bit nervous and I'm a bit worried because of some of the comments that have been made by my colleagues related to their observations around our students, that our non-Indigenous students are quite racist and that there's a lot of racism, very overt racism, in the classroom. (Interview, 4 December 2018)

According to participants, these [racist] classroom situations seemed to occur frequently, ranging from direct confrontations on the part of non-Indigenous students to a more subtle form of resistance through discriminatory or racist ideas presented in students' research papers that Indigenous instructors needed to read and mark. Participants agreed that these situations must be addressed, because, as faculty members, they felt personally responsible for educating students who will become future professionals and will carry those attitudes forward. One Indigenous faculty member reflected:

Our future police officers, the future nurses, the future social workers, and so we need to shape all of that because there is a lot of racism in society, and you see that heightened in the recent cases. I am just experiencing, not from all of the students, the strong resistance, and it is frustrating. (Interview, 14 February 2018)

Yet these occasions add emotional labour to the workload, whereby Indigenous faculty must undertake extra effort to succeed in academic environments that were not designed with their needs and perspectives in mind. Experiencing racism, resistance to change, and daily confrontations creates psychological and physical barriers for Indigenous individuals, influencing their feeling of safety in the workplace. Occurrences from the past, when Indigenous faculty had to confront and educate others after hearing offensive comments during faculty meetings, were also shared in the interviews. Speaking up against racism had led to tensions among colleagues. These occurrences of confrontation cause emotional trauma and may result in fatigue, loss of focus, and becoming distracted from one's professional responsibilities of teaching, service, and research. One faculty member shared that they preferred fake niceness over conflict to protect themselves emotionally. That tactic helped them to stay focused on their professional work:

> *If I have to hear people pretending to be nice to me, I'd rather have that actually than the naked racism or thinly veiled racism or unintended racism that I experienced at [name of the university] the first time, in 2006.* (Interview, 14 February 2018)

As many administrators and decision makers from the dominant cultural group are often being exposed to Indigenous perspectives for the first time, changing their attitudes and perceptions takes time.

The psychological climate on a university campus also includes certain perceptions by some university administrators about the work Indigenous faculty should take on. Often the dominant expectation is that new Indigenous hires should assume major responsibilities for Indigenizing and decolonizing their faculties. Interviewees brought up the assumption that being Indigenous automatically equalled expertise in all things Indigenous in the eyes of some administrators. There were enhanced expectations for Indigenous faculty to lead institutional Indigenous initiatives in addition to their primary work:

> *One of the contentious issues for a lot of Indigenous academics is that, when institutions ask for this kind of thing [Indigenization], or say that we want to do that, a lot of times the work falls on Indigenous academics to do this, you know. They [Indigenous academics] still have to be doing all the stuff you do for tenure and stuff like that.* (Interview, 3 December 2018)

There seemed to be a lack of recognition about the heterogeneity that is an essential part of Indigenous peoples in Canada in regard to Indigenous knowledges, cultural traditions, ceremonies, and languages. A faculty member revealed that the attitudes they had experienced from some of their other Indigenous colleagues had not necessarily all been supportive or in alignment with their own views. This comment suggests that people from an oppressed group can simultaneously be oppressive towards others. Trauma and violence experienced throughout life can have this impact:

> *What I do find is that there is a level of lateral violence that I've experienced from other Indigenous faculty here, yeah / ... / differences of opinion and, not being able*

*to speak about those things in a way that's healthy. / ... / That's the piece that often
is not talked about within Indigenous – because there's a perception, particularly
by non-Indigenous people, that all Indigenous people are traditional, and they're
not.* (Interview, 3 December 2018)

These situations can further ingrain a feeling of isolation within a
university that is not easy to handle. Hurtado et al. (2008) noted that
the way individuals perceive their campus climate is dependent on
their own positionality, representation, and power in the organizational
structure. Overcoming obstacles ingrained in the institutional climate
has required Indigenous faculty to work much harder to thrive in the
academy. In order to adapt and adjust, individuals may often need to
suppress their individual beliefs and values for the purpose of fitting
into a mainstream university. Creating a supportive individual psychological climate plays a crucial role in institutional efforts to decolonize
the workplace and provide opportunities for learning among non-
Indigenous peoples in academia.

How It Feels to Work in Academia: Institutional Behaviour

In addition to developing relationships with one's colleagues and
students, the feeling of being noticed and respected comes from institutional collective behaviour. In higher education institutions, this is
largely driven by the decisions and actions of the institutions' senior
leadership. Across higher education institutions in Canada, there are
many examples where universities have started to shape their behavioural climate through publicly endorsing supportive action towards
Indigenous knowledges. Issuing formal statements, organizing celebratory events, and creating awareness campaigns are part of this
shift. Examples include holding annual Indigenous Awareness Weeks,
celebrating National Indigenous History Month, and commemorating
Missing and Murdered Indigenous Women and Girls. Approaching
these events from a strengths-based perspective is important in shifting
the collective behavioural climate. Examples where Indigenous peoples
are celebrated for their leadership and achievement are many. In February each year, the University of Saskatchewan organizes Indigenous
Achievement Week, when it celebrates the successes and contributions
of Métis, First Nations, and Inuit students, staff, faculty, and alumni. In
May, the University of Manitoba honours Indigenous leaders and their
outstanding achievements. In addition to public events, there are scholarships and awards established to recognize the achievements of Indigenous students. Beginning in 2009, McMaster University has awarded
the Harvey E. Longboat Graduate Scholarship for First Nations,
Inuit, and Métis Students in the amount of $15,000 to recognize and

acknowledge an Indigenous graduate student studying at McMaster (McMaster University, n.d.). The University of Calgary, the University of Toronto, and York University have launched their Provost's Post-doctoral Fellowship Awards for Indigenous and Black scholars with a value of $50,000 (the University of Calgary) and $70,000 (the University of Toronto and York University) per year (University of Calgary News, 2021; University of Toronto, n.d.; York University News, 2021). These are just a few examples of the initiatives Canadian post-secondary insti-tutions are engaged in that are helpful for shaping collective norms. Critics rightfully point out that one celebratory week or a scholarship offer may have a limited check-box-type nature. However, norms are shaped slowly through small steps that, accompanied by other institu-tional supports, may eventually lead to a cumulative normative change. Noticing and continuously celebrating the outstanding achievements and strengths of Indigenous peoples allows new attitudes and percep-tions to emerge.

Several supportive comments were made by Indigenous faculty members in regard to institutions providing resource-based supports for Indigenous activities. Various funding decisions, in particular, were viewed as clear proof of institutional commitment:

> *I think the [name of the university], with the Indigenous Engagement Officer we have, and positions for Indigenous scholars across all faculties, shows strong commitment.* (Interview, 14 February 2018)

> *The university has put aside a good chunk of money, it's about half a million, for any unit within the university that would like to Indigenize or work on Indigeni-zing.* (Interview, 3 December 2018)

There is currently no clear data on how much universities annually spend on Indigenous activities. Project- and program-based funding decisions are a common and relatively easy way of showing institu-tional commitment towards Indigenization and reconciliation. How-ever, these are often short-term measures and can lead to fragmented or projectified approaches in funding Indigenous activities. Many Indig-enous strategies and reports have called for post-secondary institutions to set aside a dedicated operating budget or a continuous independent budget line for Indigenous initiatives (e.g., McGill University, 2017; UBC, 2020). Having a budget line or dedicated percentage of an overall institutional budget for Indigenous activities would help to secure con-tinuity in activities and create a more holistic approach in institutional commitment to Indigenization. It would also send a strong message across the university community about where institutional priorities lie. Furthermore, the budgeting process needs to be transparent, so that it is clear how much has been spent, where the money went, and who benefited from it.

Formal public statements may either enhance or hinder relationships between Indigenous individuals and other groups. Hindrance can occur if public statements are made for show and not followed by action. Limited institutional approaches towards publicly condemning racism without meaningful structural change received criticism from Indigenous faculty. Indigenous faculty members felt that institutional formal statements were not enough. An interview participant reflected:

> I think the university needs to be very active in their denouncement of anti-Indigenous sentiment and racism. I'm not quite sure that the university has taken a strong stance on some of that, some of those issues [of racism]. /... / There was an incident where some perceived act of racism was dismissed by the administration. (Interview, 4 December 2018)

Another participant shared their opinion about the limited approach senior administration took after a racist incident occurred on campus:

> I know the president immediately came out and said we don't stand for racism and stuff like that. /... / I wasn't totally happy with the president's response because I thought, yes, we do need to condemn racism, but an acknowledgment around the need for conversation around this is not enough. /... / And so what I would have liked was the president to have a more nuanced response. /... / This highlights the need to have a conversation about how do we work together to move us forward towards reconciliation. (Interview, 3 December 2018)

This quote above shows that formal statements do not necessarily tackle the attitudes and behaviours at a deep level. Racism has been a permanent problem in higher education institutions for decades. Waves of white administrators "discovering racism" have led to a certain fatigue among Indigenous individuals and sometimes ended with feelings of withdrawal:

> I know there's a lot of dialogue going on here at this institution about racism and all these types of things, but I don't even want to be a part of the conversation anymore because, as far as I'm concerned, I've seen both sides of it, and neither side has been pretty. (Interview, 22 November 2018)

Colonial patterns of exploitation at the organizational level are often unintentionally repeated when Indigenous faculty are overburdened with various administrative and service tasks. An Indigenous faculty member commented:

> Look at me. I'm an untenured professor, and I'm in the role of a director. What better way to sabotage my ability to try to get tenure, right, than to take on an administrative role, when I haven't even reached my tenure? (Interview, 12 December 2018)

A recent faculty hire expressed a similar experience of high expectations that they would take on the role of Indigenizing their institution:

> Hiring doesn't speak anything to the experience when you actually arrive to the university in a new position and what kind of environment it will be. And, then, you know, I think also there might be an open question as to how much the aspirations of universities to Indigenize will fall on the faculty, especially a new faculty that are trying to get their bearings, so, you know, there are all kinds of complications. (Interview, 23 November 2018)

These hidden assumptions and expectations shape experiences in relation to institutional climates when Indigenous faculty are hired with double the commitments expected of other hires. They are also in the spotlight in the organization, where their activities are noticed and closely observed. When it comes to both psychological and behavioural climates, while some important strides have been made, the overall concern expressed in the interviews had to do with the unconscious and hidden expectations of non-Indigenous peoples that reinforce exclusionary attitudes and perceptions. The experiences of Indigenous faculty point to the fact that institutions must start addressing attitudes and behaviours in organizations in more proactive ways, moving from public statements towards monitored action centring on decolonial learning approaches.

Faculty Perspectives on Impacting Institutional Climate

In order to change an institutional climate, work must occur from both directions – strong support from the university's senior administration and everyday work by individuals in their organizational units. As demonstrated by the comments of Indigenous faculty members, challenging and changing institutional climate through individual interactions forms a core aspect of their work in academia. This work is done in classrooms, changing the attitudes of students, and through professional work activities with their colleagues. It involves continuously unpacking individual and collective perceptions and confronting the attitudes of people around them. A faculty member shared the personal difficulties they had gone through, yet they were still hopeful that they could influence change:

> It's like that old saying, you know – "If you're not part of the solution, then you're part of the problem." So, we can't just simply sit back, write, I guess, about things, unless we're really willing to make change. And I haven't always seen that, at least from my experience. (Interview, 4 December 2018)

They hoped that approaching people individually could lead to broader affirmative action and organizational change. This speaks to the importance of creating space for learning to happen through social interactions. The participant commented:

> Sometimes it's just simply that, you know, if people's ears are open and they're receptive to things, you can change people's minds about things. (Interview, 4 December 2018)

Having open conversations about difficult, uncomfortable topics is part of the decolonial learning process. This may lead to confronting individual attitudes towards racism, which takes courage and experience. It is often assumed that Indigenous faculty members are experts at handling conflict emerging from difficult conversations and that this should be their primary responsibility. Early-career Indigenous faculty shared comments about their nervousness over their limited knowledge of how to handle these situations. Faculty members commented:

> I've heard about it [racism in the classroom] now, and it's making me worried /… / I haven't heard, formally, any discussions around how, in the classroom, a professor should handle situations of racism. (Interview, 4 December 2018)

> There are some people who don't know how to have conversations about difficult things, yeah. (Interview, 12 December 2018)

For more established faculty, reaching tenure had helped them to openly start to confront the perceptions of others. With tenure, they had gained formal protection from the institution. They had established authority and were now willing to educate their non-Indigenous colleagues. A faculty member shared their approaches to confronting racist attitudes with students:

So, if they're being racist, I will call them on that, but I don't call them a racist. I look at the action. I try to get them to look at the action. I say, you keep saying this or doing this. When you're going to be a teacher, keep in mind, someone is going to call you on that, and someone is going to challenge you, and you're going to hurt people along the way. Do you really want to hurt people?/... / I talk about gender issues a lot, you know, because there's – that's where I use that as my starting point, then to bring in issues on racism and attitudes towards Indigenous people. (Interview, 9 March 2018)

Indigenous faculty members frequently brought up examples of times when they had had to fight for their cultural traditions and ceremonies to be accepted and accommodated. The next quote demonstrates how an Indigenous faculty member, while still a PhD student, had to take up work to challenge institutional norms in regard to smudging. Their reflection is a testament to how institutional change has been a bottom-up process driven by Indigenous individuals, even if things have not changed immediately:

Of course, there was the need to justify smudging, and my supervisor was very supportive and encouraging with that process. I ran into issues with smudging as part of that process. Moving forward, I had my research circles off-site, so that we didn't run into those issues. And then, with my defence, I wanted an Elder to do the smudging, and I was successful. I feel we are at a point where these things shouldn't be that the student needs to advocate for these things. There should be protocols already in place for them – the student should have these options available to them. (Interview, 14 February 2018)

Several Indigenous faculty members brought up instances when rigid institutional regulations had suppressed the use of Indigenous cultural traditions or pedagogies. They attributed these instances to a lack of cultural exposure on the part of administrators, similar to the experiences described by Sasakamoose and Pete (2015). One issue that emerged was resistance to the compensation process for Elders who were performing ceremonies as part of a land-based learning experience for a class. A faculty member shared:

When I wanted to give money to the Elder for having a Sweat Lodge with my students, I couldn't just do that. I had to take it out of my own pocket. Why? Why should I have to do that? If we really mean Indigenous education, and yet I have to take it out of my personal funds to do it? (Interview, 14 February 2018)

Another participant commented on the continuous struggle to incorporate Indigenous cultural traditions within the framework of rigid academia:

I felt that the whole time when I was doing my PhD, I had the commitment to bring Indigenous elements into mainstream education in a decolonizing journey, but I felt that I have been jumping through hoops every step along the process, for example, trying to have an Elder on my committee and them being recognized as a committee member. (Interview, 14 February 2018)

Nevertheless, faculty members still shared a hopeful perspective, noting that attitudes and perceptions are slowly changing. The following comment illustrates that opinion:

There's just things that people wouldn't get away with now. We're not there, but we're a lot further than we were. I think things are getting better. I know they're getting better. (Interview, 14 February 2018)

While the Indigenous faculty members were hopeful, there was also a worry that small wins achieved through hard and time-consuming work might be easily lost when people retire or leave the university and the institutional memory disappears:

The biggest challenge, I think, is you push forward, people leave, people retire, and then the other generation who's coming up don't know what has happened, and so an institution will retract on and they don't realize it. And so they're pushing for the same issues that you were pushing for, that you already won, and now you have lost it again. (Interview, 22 November 2018)

Changing institutional climate is a long-term process that often takes more than the work of one generation of people in the organization. With small gains, there is always a concern that firmly established norms may fall back into their original state. Therefore, what is needed is a deeper-level decolonial engagement that is mindfully facilitated in the universities. Indigenous faculty have opened up these processes, and now it is up to non-Indigenous peoples to make sure these changes are grounded in deeper structural change that is rooted in shifted values, attitudes, and behaviours.

Conclusion

Indigenization and decolonization efforts in higher education spaces are directly dependent on overall institutional climates, how it feels to work in a university, and what is the relationship among colleagues, students, staff, and administrators. Hurtado et al. (2008) argued that an examination of the institutional climate should be the first step in campus-wide planning for supporting racial diversity. Activities that address historical legacies, increase the structural composition of Indigenous individuals on campus, and examine and change individual and organizational attitudes and hidden perceptions are imperative in this work. Shifting a campus climate should be intentional and strategic. One way to do this is by creating spaces for dialogue and engagement between Indigenous peoples and non-Indigenous peoples, where both groups can learn from each other and work together to address systemic barriers and injustices. This work should happen both inside and outside of the classrooms, meeting rooms, and office spaces. It should be done in collaboration with Indigenous peoples and their histories, knowledges, pedagogies, and practices. Efforts to create a supportive institutional culture need to be intentionally anti-racist at the system level to avoid creating dedicated pockets of Indigenization or anti-racist action on campus without changing the foundational structures on which Canadian universities operate. Addressing institutional climate must be a comprehensive process aimed at transforming the overall feeling that people get when entering a campus or doing their everyday work there. While a lot has been achieved in regard to shaping institutional climate, there needs to be stronger support and targeted action in institutional practices to make sure higher education institutions move from awareness-building to affirmative, dedicated action.

Teaching and Learning Approaches

Universities are where we come to learn. And it should be open to Indigenous knowledge because it's beautiful. / ... / Indigenous knowledges offer a beautiful way to see the world.

(Interview, 12 December 2018)

Finding culturally relevant knowledge in university curricula that fully speaks to Indigenous experiences in Canadian higher education is still an area that needs much attention. Many Indigenous students leave university early without a diploma, as their higher education experience has been traumatic and detached from their lived experiences (Beitman Brener, 2017; Kristoff & Cottrell, 2021). Some of the reasons for this are the lack of Indigenous content in university coursework, very few Indigenous faculty teaching relevant courses, and the overall limited acknowledgment of Indigenous epistemologies in the teaching pedagogies used (Rae Scott, 2020; Restoule et al., 2013). Ragoonaden and Mueller (2017) demonstrated that respectful adoption of Indigenous knowledges into post-secondary coursework increases academic persistence among Indigenous students. Indigenous faculty members working in post-secondary contexts often feel direct responsibility to fill this gap. Bringing Indigenous knowledges and pedagogies into the classroom to support students' learning has become an important mechanism for change. As Indigenous knowledges have not been readily available, sharing knowledges by engaging in teaching approaches that speak to Indigenous perspectives has become a driver for change for Indigenous faculty. Grounding their work in Indigenous pedagogies of teaching helps them to confront the hierarchical nature of knowledge in mainstream academia and to strengthen the position of alternative ways of knowing. Furthermore, emphasizing the contributions that

Indigenous peoples have made in Canada in the teaching process has helped to highlight the beauty of Indigenous knowledges and make use of them as a foundation for learning.

The underlying fundamental feature of Indigenous pedagogies is their work around decolonizing knowledge hierarchies (Morcom, 2017; Scully, 2012; Smith, 2012). Indigenous philosophies and teaching methods offer a different perspective on learning that challenges and disrupts Eurocentric hierarchical knowledge systems, functioning as a form of transformation and change (Cote-Meek & Moeke-Pickering, 2020; Smith & Webber, 2018). Morcom (2017, p. 129) noted that the fundamental principle for decolonizing education is holism, which authentically reflects Indigenous knowing, understanding, doing, and honouring. Indigenous teaching philosophies view the learning process holistically, focusing on interrelationships between the self and the community, the environment, the land, the earth, and the divine (Andreotti et al., 2011; Morcom, 2017). Learning is seen as a personal, subjective, spiritual, and transformative process (Kanu, 2011) that flows across disciplinary boundaries. Therefore, Indigenous pedagogies value a person's ability to learn independently by observing, listening, and participating with a minimum of intervention or instruction (Battiste, 2002). In this approach, typical power relations between a student and a teacher cease to exist, and learning happens without knowledge being compartmentalized by subject area. One of my research participants described their approach to teaching and learning as rounded and not hierarchical:

> *[I am] looking at Eurocentrism, and unpacking those elements, and creating space where all learners are valued, and education is not linear or top-down but circular.* (Interview, 14 February 2018)

Classrooms serve as core sites of decolonizing practice, as this is where the social interaction occurs that shapes individual perspectives, attitudes, and beliefs. In classroom discussions, the dominant norms and individual biases emerge and get examined and unpacked. This is where decolonial deep learning occurs when individual norms and values get impacted and potentially transformed.

Creating Transformative Learning Spaces

There are many examples of how Indigenous faculty members have incorporated their epistemologies and holistic philosophies into their teaching practice. A group of Indigenous scholars from the University of Calgary shared a variety of pedagogical approaches that they have used to decolonize classrooms (see Louie et al., 2017). Storytelling, as opposed to lecturing, is an approach that engages students through relatable experiences. By sharing familiar situations and action-oriented plots, students become engaged and invested in material, which leads to relationship building and learning. Asking students the questions "Who am I?", "Where do I come from?", "Where am I going?", and "What are my responsibilities?" is often a starting point for storytelling among many Indigenous communities that focuses on identification. Situating oneself within one's personal stories and community helps to build relationships between people (Absolon & Willett, 2004). Ottmann, as noted in Louie et al. (2017), described how such an approach from her Anishinaabe tradition provides an opportunity to examine students' diverse positionings and perspectives and allows for the instructor to respond respectfully, yet critically, working relationally to identify experiences of power, privilege, and marginalization. She further reflected on practising this approach, noting that it leads students to reflect on the various connections between individuals and places. Sharing survival stories from Elders as community leaders has been another approach in which storytelling has been used as a pedagogy (Lambert, 2013). Providing context and then using selected photos, images, voices, videos, and music of Elders sharing their life stories can be a powerful approach to making the viewer/listener understand and learn about these histories and about the commitment and courage it takes for once silenced people to reclaim their lives.

Marie Battiste (2013a, p. 10) has described her teaching approaches when educating teacher candidates. She focuses her work around building awareness and critical understanding of the mechanisms through which schools perpetuate social norms around race, power, and privilege. She uses a three-step approach: teaching about anti-racism as a first step, teaching decolonizing theories and strategies as a second step, and teaching Indigenous knowledge systems as a remedy to Eurocentrism as a third step (Battiste, 2013a). When she teaches these steps, teacher candidates develop an understanding of how difference has been constructed and normalized in society and how schools play a key role in perpetuating those narratives, endorsing neutrality, colour blindness, and meritocracy as core values that exclude some students (Battiste, 2013a). Her critical decolonizing approach to teaching actively resists normative assumptions and taken-for-granted perspectives while advocating for transformative change.

Dwayne Donald (2021, p. 55) at the University of Alberta described "kinship-relationality" as a guiding principle in his teaching and learning practice. Focusing on forming kinship connections helps to create relations that tie all forms of life together and, thus, guide and stimulate learning about ourselves and others around us. Donald (2021) advocated for moving away from informational teaching styles that use PowerPoint presentations, as is common in mainstream western pedagogical approaches, and moving towards relational pedagogies. He argued that the holistic complexity of human perception is disregarded when teaching and learning is reduced to a simple telling of information about certain selected topics of interest. He practises a relational style of pedagogy by taking his students on regular river valley walks where he shares his wisdom and knowledge while engaging them in qualitatively different ways of being exposed to new knowledge.

Indigenous Maternal Pedagogy, examined and applied by Jennifer Brant (Brant, 2017), draws from an Indigenous women-centred worldview that helps to establish a nurturing teaching and learning environment in classrooms. Maternal Pedagogy is grounded in the experiences of Indigenous women, promotes cultural identity development for students, and encourages ethical dialogue between Indigenous and non-Indigenous learners (Brant, 2017). This approach fosters agency, advocacy, and activism through shared Indigenous maternal teachings (Brant, 2017). Brant (2017) has argued that such a pedagogical approach creates a safe space where students can be their whole authentic selves and share their realities and lived experiences. The goal is to establish an ethical space where cross-cultural and anti-racist conversations can happen. In this pedagogy, a wholistic, yet actively decolonizing, approach is applied through the lens of female empowerment.

Indigenous pedagogies also include a variety of teaching strategies that are inspired by artistic traditions, such as deep-listening activities, metaphorical representations, performance, and dance. These activities encourage students to exercise creativity and imagination through which a more complex understanding of relationality emerges holistically. The creative aspect of this work can disrupt strongly held assumptions and stereotypes, and overcome potential barriers to deep learning. A research participant shared how she uses visual tools from nature to foster creativity in her graduate class in order to build deeper relationships with students:

> One of the exercises I have them [students] do was to go to the beach and pick 33 rocks. /… / With each of these rocks, usually, I will have the students make a Medicine Wheel. So, this rock here in the middle [shows rocks on the table] represents the mind, heart, body, and spirit. But it also represents your lifetime, your infancy and your childhood years. And, then, the red represents adolescent years.

And then the black is your adult years. And the white is your elder years. /... /
So, you can use this [Medicine Wheel] as a life cycle for people. So, I get them to
explain to me, give me two examples of something that happened to you when you
were an infant or a child that you remember that contributes to who you are today.
So, these would be significant moments in their life that really imprinted on them
and really defines who they are as an individual. /... / This is another way to go in
deeper and to be a little bit vulnerable. (Interview, 12 December 2018)

As is apparent in this example, connection to the land is central and can be cultivated through creative learning activities. Land-and place-based pedagogies are viewed as a mechanism for regenerating Indigenous social, spiritual, and physical connections with land and place (Claxton, 2020; Webber et al., 2021; Wildcat et al., 2014). In practical terms, this pedagogical approach includes moving from the classroom onto the land and learning from the surroundings and, if possible, from knowledge holders in Indigenous communities. An Indigenous faculty member commented on how the graduate program and most courses in their faculty were set up differently to ground learning within Indigenous pedagogies. An Indigenous approach often features going to an Elder for insight and knowledge. In their program, Elders served as formal co-instructors of a course. They commented:

It's a very different way of teaching. I don't teach by myself in my classrooms.
I teach with a Knowledge Holder. And that's innovation. Because they bring in
Indigenous knowledge [to the classroom]. (Interview, 12 December 2018)

Assessments form a core part of university coursework. Indigenous faculty have been developing ways of assessment that honour Indigenous philosophies. Indigenous pedagogies assert collective decision making and relationality, and this philosophy also informs assessment and grading practices. Dustin Louie shared how he practised negotiation with his students when assigning grades (Louie et al., 2017). He provided students with extensive formative feedback on their written assignments, asking them to reflect upon the merits of their submission before the final grade is granted (Louie et al., 2017). The consideration of formative feedback during the negotiation process promotes further critical thinking and deeper-level reflection. That way, both the instructor and a student can participate in decision making and also learn in the process. Co-creation of evaluation principles encourages the establishment of trust and equal positionality in classrooms, which have historically been dominated by a student–teacher hierarchy.

Ragoonaden and Mueller (2017) described culturally responsive programming at the UBC Okanagan campus for first-year Indigenous university students. The authors emphasized the various supports that were necessary for this programmatic change. Grounded in Indigenous knowledges, the introductory course "Introduction to Academic Pedagogy: An Aboriginal Perspective" was offered in collaboration with local and place-based First Nations communities, Aboriginal Access Programs and Services. The presence of peer mentors helped to support the development not only of academic skills but also of relationships, shared experiences, and community building among first-year university students. This approach was also viewed as supporting the social and emotional well-being of students.

These examples highlight how Indigenous teaching methods provide a different path to knowledge, supporting creative, experiential, ethical, and relational ways of learning. Indigenous teaching approaches also help to decolonize and transform learning spaces that have been operating according to the mainstream norms held in Canadian higher education system for decades.

Decolonizing Programming with Indigenous Content

In Canadian higher education settings, Indigenous faculty members typically tend to teach in specialized programs, since departments of Indigenous (or Native) Studies in Canadian universities are scarce (Henry, 2012). Faculties of education have been at the forefront with their programmatic development, building new programs for educating teachers on Indigenous perspectives. As Haig-Brown and Hoskins (2019) noted, Indigenous teacher education programs have proven to be a powerful influence in the resurgence of Indigenous cultures and languages. Similarly, a research participant highlighted the importance of teacher education programs:

> Teachers are producing curriculum that helps their students understand what we have contributed to this country, understand our realities. I think that's really critical. (Interview, 10 April 2019)

Indigenous teacher education programs affiliated with various Canadian universities have been operating since the 1970s (More, 1981). For example, the Indian Teacher Education Program (ITEP) at the University of Saskatchewan has been operating since 1972/3. The program has developed into one of the largest teacher education programs in Canada, offering a hybrid delivery of on-campus and community-based courses. Its four-year Bachelor of Education (BEd) degree enrols over 600 students. Throughout the program's 40-year history, there have been 1,500 Indigenous graduates, and over 200 of these graduates have obtained a master's or PhD degree (Mattern, 2013). More (1981) reported that other universities, such as the University of New Brunswick, McGill University, Lakehead University, Memorial University, Brandon University, the University of Manitoba, the University of Saskatchewan, the University of Alberta, the University of Calgary, Simon Fraser University, and the University of British Columbia, also offered Indigenous teacher education programs and had been highly effective in increasing access, achievement, and graduation rates for Indigenous students (see More, 1981). Many of these teacher training programs still function successfully today in modified formats, while new programs in other subject areas have been added. The Nunavut Arctic College (with five campuses throughout the North) offers a variety of post-secondary programs for Inuit students in business, nursing, social services, and education (Preston, 2016). At the graduate level, the University of Saskatchewan's College of Education is offering an Indigenous Land-Based Education program at the master's level. More recent developments include the Bachelor of Education program offered at the University of New Brunswick that focuses on Wabanaki languages and cultures. Its second cohort was accepted in 2021 (University of New Brunswick, web). The Senate of the University of British Columbia's Vancouver campus approved a new master's program in Indigenous Education in June 2021 (Gamble, 2021). These programs typically operate on a cohort-based model composed primarily of Indigenous students and taught by Indigenous faculty. Cohort-based models for Indigenous programs have proven to be successful, as they help to foster the formation of social relationships among students and contribute to the overall academic achievement and retention of Indigenous learners. An Indigenous faculty member who teaches an Indigenous cohort in social work emphasized how important such connections are to the students:

What we teach in our program is that relationships are key to everything that you do, and relationships are sacred. (Interview, 12 December 2018)

A few exciting developments have occurred in the realm of law degrees. In 2018, the University of Victoria started to offer the world's first Indigenous professional law degree program. It is a joint-degree program where graduates get two professional degrees: Juris Doctor (JD) and Juris Indigenarum Doctor (JID). It allows graduates to practise within Canadian Common Law while immersing them in knowledge of Indigenous legal traditions (UVic News, 2018). Learning in this program occurs outside of the classroom, with mandatory field studies in Indigenous communities across Canada. In 2001 the University of Victoria Faculty of Law started to collaborate with Nunavut Arctic College and the Akitsiraq Law School Society to establish a cohort-based model for Bachelor of Law degrees for Inuit students in Nunavut. In addition to law subjects, a compulsory program in language training (Inuktitut) is offered to better represent clients and assist with interpretations, while students are able to live in the community. As noted by Wright (2002), this program has provided a model for Indigenous legal education in other places locally and internationally (Australia).

With the increased popularity of micro-credentials among Canadian universities and colleges, several institutions have introduced micro-credentials on Indigenous topics such as Indigenous entrepreneurship (University of Northern British Columbia), Indigenous and Canadian government relations (Red River College), and Indigenous policing (Lethbridge College). With micro-credentialling, there is a danger of leaping into quick solutions that provide a formal certificate for employment purposes while further privatizing higher education spaces (see Wheelahan & Moodie, 2022). In the face of pressures to Indigenize Canadian universities, there is an increased need to include relationship building, community involvement, and holistic approaches to Indigenous knowledges when developing micro-credentials on Indigenous topics. These decisions need to be made with high caution so as not to further exploit Indigenous knowledges in a university context without community approval or consent.

While some Indigenous faculty get to teach in Indigenous-focused programs such as those described above, many are left teaching individual courses on Indigenous topics outside of specialized cohorts. Mandatory Indigenous coursework requirements, implemented across Canadian higher education institutions, have created dilemmas for Indigenous faculty. Mandatory Indigenous courses are typically composed of mostly non-Indigenous students, leaving Indigenous faculty with limited opportunity to interact with Indigenous students. A concern was expressed by several people in the interviews who noted their limited prospects for developing new area-specific coursework and teaching Indigenous content to Indigenous students. These opportunities are essential to rebuilding capacity in Indigenous knowledges and connecting to one's roots and, thus, serve as a decolonizing approach to teaching. Instead, many of the Indigenous scholars I interviewed were busy teaching general mandatory courses (e.g., in social studies, kinesiology, criminology) and supporting non-Indigenous students. One faculty member reflected: *"I don't see opportunities for Indigenous students to be able to take courses with me"* (interview, 22 November 2018). Faculty face the dilemma of deciding what work is more important to them – following the faculty-specific expectations of mandatory coursework or asking to teach specialized courses to the small number of Indigenous students who need their guidance the most. Faculty shared reflections on how the former is a lost opportunity for their university and a limited use of their expertise. This perspective aligns with similar findings from the literature that have highlighted structural, pedagogical, and ideological challenges around the mandatory coursework requirement. Concerns have been expressed around limited opportunities to develop Indigenous community-based programs while all the energies of Indigenous faculty are instead steered into educating the dominant cultural group (Brunette-Debassige, 2021; Gaudry & Lorenz, 2018).

Another implication of having to teach large groups of students enrolled in mandatory courses has to do with the significant increase in teaching-related workload, leaving limited time for research. A faculty member commented:

> *So, they're [the university administration] actually interested in the idea of a first-year sociology course that looks at Indigenous issues, and they mentioned that to me. /… / I don't know what my teaching is going to look like for the next few years, and it's actually quite daunting that I might go from being a, you know, a 300-students-per-year prof to a 500-students-per-year prof.* (Interview, 23 November 2018)

> *Teaching is taking so much of my time. I'm actually having trouble keeping up with the traditional requirements of the job, or aspects of the job. / … / This teaching load is very significant for me.* (Interview, 23 November 2018)

One faculty member described their experience teaching an introductory-level mandatory course to non-Indigenous students as challenging. The experience was not very rewarding, as many students struggled with the idea of engaging with coursework around Indigenous issues:

> *I have a class of 240 students, many who don't understand why they have to do any Indigenous content or how the course that I teach is Indigenous content, and it upsets some of them. /… / So, there was some resistance. But over time people kind of get used to it.* (Interview, 22 November 2018)

Another faculty member expressed similar sentiments, recognizing that the coursework had been somewhat helpful in building awareness among students:

We call it [the course], "Law and Indigenous Peoples". /… / So, looking at historical dispossession, looking at the Indian Act, and looking at how the courts have tried to resolve those historical controversies with their jurisprudence on treaties, Aboriginal rights, and Aboriginal title. So, these are things that are, for the most part, completely new to the students and a bit eye-opening for them. So, in that sense, I find that rewarding. (Interview, 23 November 2018)

Higher education institutions can play an important role in supporting the specialized expertise that Indigenous faculty bring. This knowledge could be used to support the success of Indigenous students, who have been struggling with limited Indigenous coursework in universities for decades. However, this is not always done. One Indigenous faculty member described a situation from a few years ago when Indigenous content at a graduate level was taught by non-Indigenous faculty, while Indigenous instructors were asked to teach introductory coursework without any significant Indigenous content:

At the [name of the university] they never took us seriously. /… / We never got, the three of us, never got to teach Indigenous students, except for maybe one or two a term. And that's because there was an Indigenous Teacher's Program separate from the mainstream. So, they mainstreamed us, and it [the specialized program] was run by a non-Indigenous educator with a master's degree. (Interview, 22 November 2018)

This is an example of how programmatic decisions by administrators can have a profound impact that either hinders or enhances the work of Indigenous faculty in transforming and decolonizing the system through their teaching practice.

Perspectives on Impacting Change

Change in teaching practice is a process that, according to Indigenous faculty, has not been revolutionary or ground-breaking. Indigenous faculty consider their pedagogical practice as inherent, natural, and in alignment with their worldview and lived experiences. Research participants confirmed that land- and place-based pedagogies, as well as Indigenous ceremonies, have always been part of their ancestry and their being, and have been their way of sharing knowledge.

In higher education contexts, they have brought their knowledges to the classroom without any excessive efforts or seeking institutional endorsement:

I've been doing smudging in the classroom way before it had become a topic of conversation. I've been doing a lot of sharing circles in the classroom, I've been doing a lot of the pedagogy, way before, so I'm not asking for anybody's permission. I'm using my avenue, my position, my privilege, as a professor to do those things, right? / ... / I'm telling you, as an Indigenous scholar, this is what I do. And this is what I insist upon. And, of course, you know, you get more confident in doing that. (Interview, 9 March 2018)

The politics of knowledge was brought into conversations whereby it was noted how the dominant cultural group is eager to define certain pedagogical approaches and declare them innovative. Institutions tend to publicly showcase any new programmatic initiative associated with Indigenous knowledges in their promotional materials as innovative, exemplary, and ground-breaking. Nevertheless, faculty members agreed that Indigenous pedagogy and teachings have always existed, whether within or outside of the classroom setting. Rather, it is the higher education institutions that have formally started to accept Indigenous knowledges and become more willing to incorporate these approaches into specialized programs or courses.

Participants noticed the shift in universities to focusing more on developing new programs with Indigenous content. However, they were very clear that these shifts have primarily occurred because of the work of Indigenous individuals, advocates, and leaders. Indigenous leaders have used their positions to advocate for change and to make sure the changes are implemented through policy and practice in higher education institutions. One faculty member reflected:

In my experience in the Faculty of Social Work, you know, there were some really strong individuals that were here at one time. [Name of a well-known Indigenous scholar] used to be in our faculty. He was one of the key driving forces in our faculty that helped develop this program that I now teach in. (Interview, 12 December 2018)

Indigenous programs grounded in Indigenous pedagogies are on the rise in Canadian higher education institutions, yet there are difficulties in aligning these programs with existing academic structures and coursework. The following quote shows how Indigenous leaders have been able to advocate for a different approach. In this example, a new program in social work in a university was grounded in Indigenous perspectives, with different arrangements made compared to traditional programs in higher education. The faculty member described how community-based Elders played a crucial part in the program without needing a formal PhD degree or university affiliations. Breaking rigid institutional policies was not an easy accomplishment, yet change was achieved. They described the distinct approach taken in the program for student advising:

> *Our program is new. /… / There is a committee; we call them Advisory Council. In our Advisory Council, there's a different composition between a person who's doing a project or a person who is doing a thesis. /… / If they're doing a project, they can pick a person from the community as advisor and a Knowledge Holder and work with them.* (Interview, 12 December 2018)

Being grounded in Indigenous pedagogy and Indigenous positionality, faculty members shared how, in their teachings, they asked students also to consider their individual positionality and privilege associated with who they were and how they acquired knowledge. By applying a critical lens, students become more mindful of their own biases and individual perspectives, which triggers learning and ultimately may shift individual norms and attitudes. A faculty member reflected:

> *The things that I encourage students to consider in their own work are shifting their paradigms from primarily western-dominant privileged frameworks to be inclusive of Aboriginal and Indigenous frameworks, to recognize the difference and recognize also the overlap. We don't just have two completely separate [worlds]… there are spaces of overlap and things where frameworks come together.* (Interview, 9 March 2018)

A distinct theme emerged in the interviews when two Indigenous faculty members shared how their Indigenous students helped them to become stronger advocates for Indigenous knowledges. This dynamic points to the fact that social interactions between people within an organization play a crucial role in influencing change. Strength comes from working together, developing relationships, and supporting one another in a higher education setting. Indigenous students' seeking for their lost culture has become a significant tool of empowerment and transformation for Indigenous faculty. The following story was shared:

> *So, the [Indigenous] students there, they would come into my music and art class and, very anti-anything that had to do with spirituality. By the end of the course, they were right in there, you know, even making spiritual instruments, sacred*

instruments, like the drum. Or even rattles. Yeah. They would do it, because, and I don't know if I'm right, but I have a belief that many Indigenous people in some way are trying to get back to themselves. We're trying to find who we were again because we've lost our way. We've lost our way. (Interview, 14 February 2018)

A different story was shared by an Indigenous faculty member about gaining perspective and motivation to become an advocate for Indigenous knowledges after interacting with an Indigenous student who expressed doubts about their course content. As a result of this encounter, this faculty member became more mindful and critical towards the material that was presented to their Indigenous students. They reflected:

I remember my very first course in Native Studies. I had – she was an Indigenous student. I came in. I didn't know exactly what I was going to do. I taught Social Studies. I put on a tape and she asked me, you know, if she could come to my office. She said, professor, I don't know if I want to stay here. I just came from [name of the university] and they had no Indigenous content, and I hope this isn't going to be the same here, that I'm not going to get my history. And it challenged me to become a better instructor, a better professor; it challenged me to look deeper at these things. (Interview, 22 November 2021)

The interview participants said that teaching from Indigenous positionality had been helpful in changing the value frameworks of some non-Indigenous students. They saw conversation and open dialogue as an opportunity for shifting norms. This process takes more than teaching one course with Indigenous content. A faculty member described the different standpoints that their students had when taking their course and the change some students experienced during the course:

They [students] are going to pass my class – Indigenous Studies class – but did they open their minds and hearts to see past their own lens of preconceived notions? For some students, they were just not willing to change their perspectives. / ... / A lot of them come in with their journal reflections, and there are some that jump onto anything that is brought up in class /... / It's a handful of students that we are talking about and how much they have grown in the course. Thus, just getting educated more on some of the [Indigenous] topics helps. (Interview, 14 February 2018)

Indigenous faculty tended to be accustomed to some students' resistance to change. Resistance was seen as quite normal, and faculty members did not express having overly high expectations of immediate transformation after they presented Indigenous content. One faculty member shared:

> For someone suddenly to realize that the land that they live on has been stolen, and taken, is not a comfortable feeling. They're going to resist that. (Interview, 9 March 2018)

Nevertheless, one faculty member expressed that it was important not to take resistance personally, as decolonizing work is meant to be uncomfortable. They were trying to rationalize those incidents as teaching moments and not as personal attacks. Coping mechanisms such as rationalization are helpful to avoid burnout: "*I don't take a lot of those things personally, I never have. But I will challenge things more head-on than I would in the past*" (interview, 9 March 2018).

Persistence was seen as important in decolonizing work. As change takes time and is grounded in individual norms, perceptions, and attitudes, perseverance and determination are key in these processes. One faculty member reflected on how they tried to maintain relationships with students, even after uncomfortable conversations in the classroom had taken place and even after a course had ended:

> After that experience [a difficult confrontation in a classroom], when we come back to work, he [a student] kind of avoided me, avoided having hallway conversations, but I'd always call out, hi John. [Laughs.] I do that, right. I see somebody, I always say hi, probably more faster than they would say hi. That's just who I am. (Interview, 9 March 2018)

In the interviews, perspectives on impacting change in teaching were largely associated with decolonizing work in which issues around power and privilege get examined and discussed. Teaching pedagogies in and of themselves were not perceived to be innovative or particularly ground-breaking, but Indigenous pedagogies were seen to help generate different kinds of critical conversations with students. As a result, students' perceptions, attitudes, and norms get confronted and challenged in a setting that is conducive to change. For Indigenous faculty members, it was essential to be able to teach Indigenous students, so that the youth can carry forward Indigenous teachings, cultural traditions, and heritage and have better opportunities to do that with their higher education degrees.

Conclusion

Indigenous knowledges, traditions, and languages are shared through Indigenous teachings. Community and land serve as crucial elements in this process, helping to create authentic and holistic learning experiences for students. There are many complexities involved in topics discussed in Indigenous courses. These courses are not simply about content – Indigenous history, language, and worldview. They are also about identity, power, privilege, and prevalent colonial ideologies. This is essential work that happens from within the juxtaposition of colonial practices and an emerging acceptance and understanding of different knowledge systems. Critical decolonizing approaches to teaching practices require significant emotional labour and often take a toll on Indigenous faculty's physical and mental well-being.

Indigenous faculty's work, through bringing Indigenous teachings to universities and colleges, has had an impact on programming and curricula. There has been an increase in establishing new programmatic offerings and initiating curricular changes. However, scholars have noted that the current landscape of the Canadian higher education system often features "pockets of presence" (Pidgeon et al., 2014, p. 1) of Indigenous knowledges. While there is more diversity occurring across programs, according to Henry (2012), most of the programmatic development appears in help-oriented areas such as social work, education, and law. Henry (2012) also pointed out that developing or creating a program does demonstrate a university's commitment to Indigenous Studies to a certain degree, but programs are associated with insecurity because of the ease with which they can be discontinued. Establishing a department of Indigenous Studies shows much greater commitment.

Building capacity among Indigenous peoples for facilitating such organizational transformations is essential, as Indigenous cultural teachings continue to be threatened in Canada. Higher education institutions can play an important role in protecting, safeguarding, and advancing Indigenous cultural knowledges. A key approach there is providing opportunities for Indigenous faculty to interact with Indigenous students in the coursework they teach. Fostering Indigenous knowledges through teaching provides a crucial mechanism for youth to be exposed to some of these teachings they have not experienced before, creating deeper connections to the land and allowing them to learn about languages and spiritual practices that embody Indigenous cultural traditions. Furthermore, teaching in higher education settings provides an important venue for change that challenges the unequal knowledge systems that universities currently operate within. Using a variety of teaching pedagogies, distinct knowledge sources, and holistic teaching approaches supports the push for broader decolonial change. While many challenges remain, a solid foundation has been established to ground further cross-institutional efforts to strengthen the position of Indigenous knowledges in Canadian higher education institutions through teaching pedagogies and programmatic developments.

Research

Research, to me, is when you're creating something that reflects Indigenous peoples' worldviews and values. Then you're doing research from Indigenous perspectives. Whether or not it's recognized in society formally is irrelevant.

(Interview, 10 April 2019)

Research activity forms the essence of universities. The pursuit of new knowledge and critical reflection on existing knowledge constitutes the foundation, mission, and purpose of higher education institutions. Furthering knowledge through research helps to solve societal problems as well as contribute to a country's economic growth. Research production is a key indicator in evaluating faculty in the tenure and promotion process, comparing and ranking post-secondary institutions, allocating finances, and making assumptions about overall institutional contribution to society. What knowledge is valued, what kind of research is being conducted, and what kind of ideas are being pursued in research projects are questions associated with politics of knowledge. As Indigenous peoples have had limited access to higher education institutions, the current organizational norms do not always support or represent the research needs or directions of Indigenous communities. The concept of research in itself does not align well with Indigenous ways of furthering knowledge. As stated by former Chief Norman Bone, Keeseekoowenin First Nation: "As Indigenous Peoples we have always done research, always searched for understanding, ways of being and knowing the world around us in order to survive, we just didn't call it research" (University of Manitoba, 2014, p. 4). Valuing research that is grounded in Indigenous perspectives and that is critical, applied, and community-oriented forms the essence of decolonizing research practice in universities (Battiste, 2000; Henry & Tator, 2012; Kuokkanen, 2007a).

The relationship between Indigenous peoples and research has been highly problematic. Indigenous communities have had painful experiences with various projects carried out on them, to the extent that research has become one of the dirtiest words for Indigenous peoples (Smith, 1999). Research projects conducted in Indigenous communities have not always been ethical, meaningful, or useful to the individual or community being researched, leaving community members with a deficit-based narrative and feeling broken (Tuck & Yang, 2014). Research practices used by non-Indigenous scholars have caused substantial loss to Indigenous knowledges, heritage, and languages. As a result, Indigenous communities have become extremely cautious about research projects associated with them. Battiste and Youngblood (2000) proposed that the core premise of any research involving Indigenous peoples is that Indigenous peoples should control their own knowledge and do their own research. If others should choose to enter into collaborative relationships with Indigenous peoples, the research should directly empower and benefit Indigenous communities and heritages rather than the researchers themselves, Canadian institutions, or society (Battiste & Youngblood, 2000). The purpose of this statement is to protect communities from any further extraction of resources, knowledges, ideas, expressions, and teachings and from any kind of commodification of knowledge. Wilson (2003, 2008) argued that research from Indigenous perspectives should be viewed as a ceremony in which Indigenous scholars build relationships with individuals and communities and remain accountable through the new knowledge that is produced from these relationships.

Over the past decades, the position of Indigenous research in Canadian higher education institutions has been gradually strengthening, moving away from the margins towards an area of institutional priority. Institutional Indigenous strategic plans attest to that development (e.g., UBC, 2020; University of Ottawa, 2020; Western University, 2016). Powerfully critical research carried out by Indigenous scholars, thinkers, and researchers has led to creating a significant pathway for Indigenous knowledges in academia. This work has facilitated norm-changing conversations and has started to normalize the position of Indigenous knowledges in higher education institutions. Indigenous researchers have become influential voices in research around decolonization, connecting colonialism and systemic inequities in areas such as homelessness, health, access to education, and beyond. Kuokkanen (2007a) pointed out that Indigenous research has become recognized as unique for several reasons – it is grounded in participation by the communities being researched; it acknowledges traditional genealogical and other organizing structures; it is relevant to the communities being studied; and it focuses on culturally appropriate methodologies and codes of conduct. Most importantly, this research is activist in the sense that it is committed to capacity building and addressing the damage done by colonialism (Kuokkanen, 2007). Indigenous research methods that are more in line with traditional knowledges and processes have started to shift conversations about the ways in which research should be conducted.

Knowledge created by Indigenous researchers has provided an attractive alternative way of thinking about complex societal problems such as environmental sustainability, climate change, and the diverse social or economic needs of peoples across the globe (Wuttunee, 2004). Partly for these reasons, the Canadian federal government has become increasingly focused on encouraging the contributions of Indigenous research, stating that "social sciences and humanities research undertaken by and with Indigenous peoples and their knowledge systems is a key investment in this future" (SSHRC, n.d.-a). Support through government-level policy documents has followed. For example, in May 2015, the Social Sciences and Humanities Research Council (SSHRC) developed an Indigenous Research Statement of Principles that lays out values guiding research by and with Indigenous peoples (SSHRC, n.d.-b). The principles include a revised definition of Indigenous research that highlights the social aspect of knowledge construction where co-creation of knowledge occurs across disciplines and among individuals with diverse cultural identities. In that document, Indigenous research is described as:

> Research in any field or discipline that is conducted by, grounded in or engaged with First Nations, Inuit, Métis or other Indigenous nations, communities, societies or individuals, and their wisdom, cultures, experiences or knowledge systems, as expressed in their dynamic forms, past and present. Indigenous research can embrace the intellectual, physical, emotional and/or spiritual dimensions of knowledge in creative and interconnected relationships with people, places and the natural environment. (SSHRC, n.d.-b)

In 2019, a strategic research plan, *Setting new directions to support Indigenous research and research training in Canada 2019–2022*, was released by the federal Tri-Council research agencies in collaboration with Indigenous communities (see SSHRC, 2019). This strategic plan sets a direction for new ways of doing research, highlighting the greater need for Indigenous peoples themselves to lead and set research priorities. This document is a first attempt to facilitate coordinated cross-Canadian efforts for Indigenous research. It also articulates a national vision for the work conducted in Canadian universities. This national direction has been complemented by work on new research ethics standards across organizations and institutions, aimed at reconceptualizing research through decolonizing and Indigenizing perspectives.

Changes in Research Ethics

The manner in which research projects involving Indigenous communities are carried out is a key aspect in examining change in institutional research practices. As Eurocentric methods of research have been highly exploitative and confined within oppressive structures, and have featured conflicting standards and values (Battiste, 2013a; Stonechild, 2006), research ethics guidelines have been at the forefront of organizational change. This change has been led by Indigenous individuals. The right of Indigenous communities to own, control, access, and possess information about their peoples is fundamentally tied to self-determination and to the preservation and development of Indigenous cultures. Indigenous leaders, organizations, and community groups have become active lobby groups and gatekeepers, specifying which research projects are worthy of funding, time, and resources (Ball & Janyst, 2008). Both institutional and federal funding bodies have increasingly included Indigenous peoples in proposal review and selection committees, where their choices and concerns play an important role in decision making.

The idea of safeguarding Indigenous knowledges and traditional cultural expression is grounded in the United Nations Declaration of Rights of Indigenous Peoples (UNDRIP, 2007), which states that "Indigenous peoples have the right to maintain, control, protect and develop their cultural heritage, traditional knowledge and traditional cultural expressions" (UNDRIP, 2007, p. 22). In Canada, the Royal Commission on Aboriginal Peoples, guided by the advice of Indigenous researchers, formulated a set of Ethical Guidelines for Research in 1993 (see RCAP, 1993). The document requires that serious consideration be given to the benefit of research for the communities involved (Battiste, 2007). Protective guidelines have also been developed by Indigenous communities themselves. For example, the First Nations principles of Ownership, Control, Access, and Possession (OCAP®), publicized by the First Nations Information Governance Centre, assert that First Nations have control over data collection processes and that they own the collected information and control how it can be used (FNIGC, 2014). Battiste (2007) described the work of Mi'kmaw Ethics Watch in receiving and assessing research protocols in the community. Other Indigenous groups have taken on similar work. For example, Inuit Tapiriit Kanatami has developed the National Inuit Strategy on Research (NISR), calling for governments and research institutions to engage ethically in research projects involving Inuit (Inuit Tapiriit Kanatami, 2018). The strategy identifies areas that could use a strengthened research base to benefit Inuit. These examples demonstrate ground-up policy work aiming to resist the reproduction of colonial relationships as previously carried out in research.

Various policy frameworks and institutional guidelines for ethical academic research involving Indigenous communities have been developed in higher education settings as well. As noted, Indigenous knowledges are protected federally through the Canadian Tri-Council research ethics guidelines. In the *Canadian Federal Tri-Council Policy Statement on Ethical Conduct for Research Involving Humans* (TCPS), Chapter 9 focuses explicitly on "Research Involving the First Nations, Inuit and Métis Peoples of Canada" (TCPS2, 2018). This chapter lists requirements that need to be followed by any research project that engages Indigenous individuals, but particularly research funded by Tri-Council grants, to prevent further colonial practices occurring. Many universities and colleges have developed their own research guidelines of ethical practices for research with Indigenous communities. Examples include *Protocols & Principles for Conducting Research in an Indigenous Context* by the University of Victoria (2003); *Recommendations for Ethical Research with Indigenous Peoples – Draft* by the University of Saskatchewan (2008), the *Framework for Research Engagement with First Nation, Metis, and Inuit Peoples* by the University of Manitoba (2014), the *Research Impacting Indigenous Groups Policy* by Memorial University (2020b), and *Research Guidelines with Indigenous Peoples* by Sheridan College (2020). In addition, the Dalhousie Faculty Association has negotiated a broadened definition of scholarship to recognize non-traditional and Indigenous forms of scholarship and knowledge (CAUT, 2019).

Hayward et al. (2021) conducted a review of various research ethics boards, protocols, frameworks, and guidelines associated with Indigenous projects used across Canada. Their findings pointed to three main types of documents that are currently in place: 1) documents that balance individual and collective rights; 2) documents that uphold culturally grounded ethical principles; and 3) self-determined research processes, methods, and knowledge translation (Hayward et al., 2021). The authors concluded that Indigenous-developed frameworks demonstrate that, for research to be transformative, meaningful, and reciprocal to a community, it must uphold Indigenous ethical principles

(Hayward et al., 2021). Regardless of the particular type of documentation used in a research project, it must acknowledge that Indigenous communities and peoples know best what is needed for bettering their lives. As a result, universities must aim to work collaboratively with Indigenous communities in the spirit of partnership, aligning research practice with the purpose of Indigenous self-governance.

Decolonizing Research Methodologies and Measuring Impact

The contributions of Indigenous faculty go beyond establishing community-centred research protocols. The work of changing the essence of research practice itself is part of a much larger development associated with self-determination and decolonization in higher education. While there is no single agenda for Indigenous research, Indigenous scholars have increasingly drawn attention to the political nature of the research process, challenging the nature and epistemology of research conducted in universities and emphasizing the need to decolonize research practice in higher education. Linda Tuhiwai Smith (1999, 2018a) has stated that decolonizing research means having a critical understanding of the underlying assumptions, motivations, and values that inform research practices. Traditional knowledge production methods commonly used by non-Indigenous researchers are part of a history of colonization that precludes Indigenous engagement and collaboration (Stonechild, 2006). Decolonizing research methodologies should start by interrogating the power relationships found within the Indigenous-settler dynamic between individuals but also in our higher education organizations.

As part of decolonizing and Indigenizing research efforts, Indigenous scholars in Canada have been increasingly engaged in theoretical work on Indigenous research methodologies as a form of resistance to the dominance of western knowledge and research paradigms that deny alternative ways of knowing (Battiste, 2000; Battiste et al., 2002; Donald, 2009; Kovach, 2009; Youngblood Henderson, 2002). For example, the work of Kovach (2010) critically challenged the politics of knowledge production while advocating for a rightful place for Indigenous methodologies and tribal epistemologies within academia. Wilson (2008, pp. 6–7) encouraged the use of Indigenous methodologies, stating that Indigenous methodology is about relational accountability or fulfilling one's role in relationships with the world. The shared aspects of relationality can be fulfilled through the choice of research topics, methods of data collection, and forms of analysis and presentation of information (Wilson, 2008, p. 69). Donald (2009) used the term "Indigenous Métissage" to describe decolonizing approaches associated with ethical relationality in research. His approach supported collaboration – not denying difference but seeking to understand how particular historical and cultural contexts have shaped the way a person understands and experiences living in the world. This approach requires time to build the personal relationships that allow Indigenous peoples to become active participants in the research process and claim power and ownership of the process (Donald, 2012; Lowan-Trudeau, 2012).

Knowledge produced through research projects is motivated by different rationales from creating wealth or making new innovative discoveries. Indigenous research is mostly motivated by creating a positive impact on one's community, while actively working towards overturning the hundreds of years of colonization and institutional hostility to Indigenous knowledges and practices. Tuhiwai Smith (2018a) argued that the big political agenda of Indigenous research is to create a paradigm shift and a transformation that tackle colonialism and create new power relations that support Indigenous well-being and self-determination. At the individual level of a researcher, however, the agenda is perhaps more modest – even a small contribution to any of the following tasks is significant: to make a positive difference in the lives of Indigenous peoples; to improve health, social, and economic outcomes; to regenerate languages and cultures; to remove institutional barriers to Indigenous participation; and to restore Indigenous knowledges and values as a way of living and being (Smith, 2018a, p. 33). Undeniably, most Indigenous research methodologies are designed to impact the community, but they also aim to centre the co-production of knowledge and the strengthening of existing spaces for Indigenous knowledges, cultures, and peoples to thrive in. As Tuhiwai Smith (2018a, p. 33) noted, while individual researchers seek "discovery," a more accurate framing of research work comes from Māori knowledge that sees research as a "recovery" of knowledge.

A different starting point for research raises issues of how to measure the impact of Indigenous research. There is a need to reappraise the ways in which research is being assessed and measured and what standards are currently being used in higher education institutions. Part of institutional efforts to decolonize research practices should aim at creating organizational environments that support the unique nature of research work conducted by Indigenous faculty members. Decolonizing assessments should account for significant amounts of time spent in the community, away from traditional classroom environments. The demonstrated impacts of such research may not translate into a stream of research publications or citation records but into the well-being of the community, strengthened knowledge, rebuilt capacity, and further connections to one's roots. Developing institutionally different standards for measuring research impact has become an important aspect of decolonizing research in higher education.

Institutional Research Supports

The most prominent mechanism for supporting Indigenous research projects is the availability of funding. Comments of Indigenous faculty members suggested that there are increasing amounts of funds, both from federal and institutional sources, available for research. A faculty member reflected:

> I know there's certainly support at the federal level with SSHRC, for Indigenous research, which I'm hoping to apply for next year. And, as I said, there has been some good support, I think, at the university level for internal grants as well. (Interview, 4 December 2018)

Others concurred: "*I think there are grants here that I never saw, you know, when I was at the [name of the institution]*" (interview, 22 November 2018); "*I've seen, in the last few years, nothing but good things occur*" (interview, 9 March 2018). A SSHRC report has stated that, between 2007 and 2016, $345.9 million were awarded by the SSHRC granting council to research related to Indigenous peoples, which accounted for about 10% of overall research funding (SSHRC, 2018). There was a clear agreement among participants about the attractiveness of the federal Tri-Council research grants. However, provincial funding support for Indigenous research across different provinces such as Ontario, Manitoba, British Columbia, and Quebec was referred to as insignificant because of the limited amounts available, quick deadlines, and fragmented priorities. There was a sense that a faculty member's time is better invested in finding larger, more reputable grants:

> Provincial research funding comes out yearly, and then people wait until really late to find out what it [the area of priority] will be. The advice I've gotten from my colleagues is that it is so impoverished now, that it's almost not worth the effort to apply for. (Interview, 23 November 2018)

> Ontario has taken some initiative at individual universities doing this sort of thing [providing grants], and they do have the odd taskforce here and there, but they have not been robust in their provincial, province-wide policy making and initiatives in and around Indigenous achievement. /... / Not even close to the Western provinces. (Interview, 9 March 2018)

Institutional strategic plans were seen as helpful in prioritizing Indigenous research. Once an area is declared a priority, funding is then allocated. The following comment linking increased research funding to Indigenous strategic plans illustrates this point:

> *There's various ways that it [research] is supported and it's encouraged. For example, at the [name of the institution], we have a strategic plan that specifically outlines Indigenous engagement. So, Indigenous research and knowledge is being supported that way, very specifically.* (Interview, 10 April 2019)

More importantly, an improvement was also noticed in the knowledge around Indigenous epistemologies and methodologies among the Tri-Council committee members who make decisions on Indigenous grant applications:

> *SSHRC for, I'm going to say, for about a decade, has had differing levels of commitment, and in a sense, it has improved over time. They are falling in line with others in changing the terminologies. Now, that is an investment in a sense, not just because they're targeting particular research projects, but those adjudicators they select to do this sort of work are those who are, themselves, more learned in the areas for which they're adjudicating, which wasn't always the case. And that, itself, is perhaps one of the more important things that, I think, they contributed to.* (Interview, 9 March 2018)

While the knowledge among Tri-Council adjudication committees was viewed positively, the Research Ethics Board decisions at individual universities often remain problematic. The limited number of Indigenous faculty on campus has left the decision-making capacity primarily in the hands of non-Indigenous individuals. Crucial to the structure of those committees is the knowledge and awareness of non-Indigenous peoples participating in adjudication work. Indigenous research methods still tend to be measured, challenged, and problematized based on western criteria. The need to constantly justify and educate others on Indigenous research methodologies was perceived as time-consuming and an additional barrier to Indigenous faculty members' research activities. A research participant commented:

> *We have an Indigenous research ethics circle there, but there is a lot of internal political issues and sometimes it is hard. Sometimes, because of the lack of Indigenous researchers at the institution, there are people who sometimes sit on that board that do not have the Indigenous research experience required. I guess that*

is more of a barrier than support. I had to justify my decision to do my research through Indigenous research methodologies. (Interview, 14 February 2018)

While overall the opportunities for research funding through federal projects have increased, there is a difference in the ways in which individual faculty members are able to access those opportunities. There were some interviewed participants who were highly successful in grant applications, with several institutional and federal grants secured. A faculty member noted how they had been able to navigate the grant system by gradually building their track record towards grant success:

I do hold a SSHRC grant previous to that, which was a strong influence on the nature of the application I made for the CRC [Canada Research Chair program]. (Interview, 9 March 2018)

Another faculty member suggested having average knowledge and experience with grant applications:

I feel like I'm largely just doing the same game as anyone else where you start with the university funding and from there you work on trying to get SSHRC funding. Whether there's any particular special support for Indigenous knowledge mobilization and research, I'm not terribly familiar with them. And it would probably be just the sheer amount of information that's thrown at us. (Interview, 23 November 2018)

Some interviewees expressed being overwhelmed by the various funding opportunities, deadlines, and grants available. There was clearly a sense of the need for stronger direction, mentorship, and guidance in order to navigate the complexity of grants. A faculty member pointed out the need for stronger support from the university in regard to filtering the information that is directed to different groups:

You know, we get so many e-mails in a day talking about the things happening in the university. There seems to be a lack of curation. You know, there's a source of funding for another area that is completely in another type of discipline and another type of issue. So, I haven't actually gotten a hold of how to curate things for myself. (Interview, 23 November 2018)

There was agreement across participants that institutional research support often ends with sharing grant information. Nevertheless, support for how to write grants from Indigenous perspectives and how to engage in Indigenous research methodologies is often needed in order to excel in research projects. This skill forms a core component of the successful project:

> I don't know whether or not there is enough institutional support to ... how to work collaboratively with Indigenous communities. / ... / I'm thinking, is the institutional responsibility of let's throw some money at it but not do the pieces about how do you negotiate that into one's research agenda? (Interview, 3 December 2018)

Indigenous faculty members also noted that they were often involved in research projects as co-applicants, while they did not hold a grant as a principal investigator themselves. This tendency suggests a checkbox nature of the involvement of Indigenous faculty in universities, whereby Indigenous names are listed for the sole purpose of securing the success of the grant by others. Driven by the requirements set by ethics protocols, the involvement of an Indigenous person has become a must in grant applications involving Indigenous topics. As a result, Indigenous faculty members were often approached to be listed in the grants of non-Indigenous researchers who had better knowledge of how to navigate the funding system:

> I have two SSHRC projects. I'm not the lead on any of them, but I'm a co-applicant on [name of a person's] grant. She is not an Indigenous person, but she has done lots of research with Indigenous communities. So, she has lots of years of experience getting funding applications. And, so, this big one is like a 2.5 million. (Interview, 12 December 2018)

Such partnerships in research can be useful, as they may provide opportunities for Indigenous faculty to learn new skills, explore topics of interest, and network with other academics and organizations. On the other hand, there needs to be an awareness that commitments made to others take time away from prioritizing one's own research agenda. This dilemma points to a need for a stronger mentorship that should be available and can help early career researchers navigate their academic research trajectories better. Peer learning and networking opportunities with others were a recurring theme in faculty conversations. Indigenous faculty members commented:

> I like the networking that's happening with [name of VP Indigenous]. Unfortunately, she is leaving. And hopefully it continues happening. I want to meet more people working in similar areas. (Interview, 23 November 2018)

There is an Indigenous coordinator at the [name of the university], so it is kind of a network of Indigenous scholars, and I think that it is really important to have colleagues to support you as you are trying to bring new and emerging pedagogies and methodologies into the university. (Interview, 14 February 2018)

There was a point made about how Indigenous faculty members are typically so overworked and burdened with a variety of tasks that they have hardly any time left to help other Indigenous colleagues. A faculty member reflected on the institutional supports available:

I'm going to say none, at this point. None. Absolutely none. I've had to seek it [support] out myself. So, I've taken classes at the Centre for Advanced Teaching and Learning. So, that's been really helpful. But most of it is not an Indigenous way. And many of our Indigenous colleagues on campus, they're overworked. They've got so much going on. They are busy. When do you have time to seek out mentorship from other Indigenous faculty members? Because we're all just juggling all kinds of things. (Interview, 12 December 2018)

With slowly growing numbers of Indigenous hires and growing awareness of Indigenous knowledges, Indigenous research projects are becoming supported through various funding programs within Canadian higher education institutions. However, the funding is provided in an isolated manner, resulting from short-term opportunities, and lacks comprehensive, systematic supports. Various reports by Indigenous organizations have pointed out similar difficulties in accessing government funds, suggesting a lack of knowledge about where and how to apply and various eligibility restrictions for different types of funding (National Aboriginal Capital Corporation, 2017; National Indigenous Economic Development Board, 2019). This points to the dire need for Indigenous research support provided in a more comprehensive and systematic way that focuses on broader supports going beyond finance. Writing support, mentorship, protected time for conducting research, and consideration of time spent in Indigenous communities and educating others on Indigenous methodologies are needed for decolonizing research practice in universities.

Perspectives on Impacting Change

Over the past decades, there has been an enormous growth in the number of books, international peer-reviewed journal articles, and other publications by Indigenous peoples about Indigenous research, Indigenous theory, and Indigenous research methodology (Battiste &

Youngblood Henderson, 2009; Smith, 2018b; Kovach, 2021). Indigenous authors have taken up a wide array of research topics from politics and archaeology to Indigenous science and engineering, education, and health (SSHRC, 2018; Smith, 2018b). Situated in the context of continuous unequal power relations within academia, the primary task of Indigenous faculty has been to enlarge the space where the production and preservation of knowledge relevant to Indigenous peoples can emerge. The increase in decolonizing approaches to research grounded in Indigenous ways helps to create a strength-based narrative that has the potential to shift the broader norms and values in an organization. This theme of expanding knowledges grounded in Indigenous theory and methods was clearly present in the interviews. The following comment provides an example of how a faculty member was developing their methodological approach that would best align with Indigenous knowledges:

> I often found that we do a bit of a disservice to people when we interview them and we retell their story. So, we lose the authenticity of the story, and we lose a lot of the emotion that the person originally shared with us when they tell their story. And, so, I wanted to have a methodology that was a lot more conducive to allowing their voice to be heard. So, I did digital storytelling. (Interview, 12 December 2018)

Another faculty member noted how Indigenous knowledges have grounded the theoretical work emerging in the field of social work:

> We've had lots of social work theories that have been rooted in Indigenous ways of knowing, and those are … those have been integrated into our curriculum. (Interview, 3 December 2018)

The emphasis on bringing forward cultural aspects of Indigenous knowledges was a central theme in the work of many Indigenous faculty members. Their research has contributed to the expansion of knowledges from Indigenous perspectives, adding a different, empowering aspect to the mainstream literature. This strengths-based perspective came forward in the following comment when a faculty member emphasized the value found in Indigenous knowledges and, thus, used their research to shape the norms and beliefs of the mainstream narrative. The faculty member commented:

> I am very interested in shining a light on Indigenous culture, beliefs, values, traditions that were brought into the business by Indigenous business people, and

how that might bring a more holistic understanding of what business could be, like, the cultural perspective. (Interview, 10 April 2019)

Another noted how the work around expanding cultural knowledge is important, as it helps to pave the way for younger generations:

I think, we're learning more and more to recognize that there is knowledge in our cultures that is very valuable. And those ways of knowing and being are really important for the next generation. (Interview, 12 December 2018)

The ways in which research creates a different narrative around Indigenous knowledges serve as a mechanism for gradually shaping mainstream organizational values, norms, and perspectives.

Opportunity to Make a Difference

Faculty members recognized that their position as professors, immersed in research, provided a platform for being intimately involved in organizational change. In the midst of broader socio-political developments, there was a recognition that it is an exciting time to do Indigenous research. Several Indigenous faculty members noted that there is currently a momentum around Indigenous knowledges in higher education, things are changing quickly, and there is an opportunity to make an impact. A faculty member commented:

I sometimes say that it's interesting ... exciting, I should say, to be a Native scholar now, because things are happening quickly and you get to have some influence. You can affect that conversation in a way that is helpful. (Interview, 9 March 2018)

Another pointed out how perspectives around Indigenous knowledges are changing and new interpretations of the knowledge pave the way for societal change. A faculty member pointed out how, for example, their work in interpreting law had allowed them to shape organizational norms:

The origins [of this research] are personal and, you know, actually getting charged for something that a few years later was recognized as an Indigenous right, on an academic level, it's interesting to look at the law. /... / I am trying to kind of interject and add something to the debates. (Interview, 23 November 2018)

As part of transformative action, the chance to engage with young people was highlighted by several participants. Youth were seen as a crucial catalyst for rebuilding capacity in Indigenous communities. Faculty members had the opportunity to work with students and disseminate research findings through teaching and research collaborations with (Indigenous) students. These connections help to create stronger awareness and excitement around the work done by Indigenous peoples, which then may help to strengthen the position of Indigenous knowledges in universities. A faculty member commented:

> *[I appreciate] the opportunity to share in my classes some of the case studies that I have come across in my research, so that students are more sensitive to the nature of Indigenous economies, the fact that it actually exists. Many Canadians aren't aware of the level, the complexity, the breadth, the depth of the activity that is going on in Canada.* (Interview, 10 April 2019)

Building capacity through increasing the number of people advocating for Indigenous research supports efforts for organizational change. One faculty member pointed out the important role of social media in connecting and strengthening the networks of Indigenous individuals. Social media platforms have become a significant mechanism that facilitates cultural awakening and activist work among Indigenous peoples:

> *I engage in social media, especially Twitter, with Indigenous activists and Indigenous scholars and Indigenous leaders, and I like what I see. There is more and more cultural production, even though it's not my area.* (Interview, 23 November 2018)

Opportunity to impact change is linked to access to higher-level decision making. The following example demonstrates how having a prestigious, federally funded research position opened up opportunities for one Indigenous faculty member to influence decisions and advocate for Indigenous interests. This faculty member reflected:

> *The current federal government has expressed an interest and has actually followed up on developing legislation to support Indigenous languages ... They [the Department of Cultural Heritage] wish to establish an Indigenous Languages Act, and they wish to apportion federal funds to be supportive of that. / ... / I've met them – in order to interface with Indigenous communities to support the development of that Act. So, I've been lucky enough to be a part of those discussions here in [name of the city], which has been great, and I've had a chance to go out to Ottawa to do a little bit of chatting there, too.* (Interview, 9 March 2018)

Overall, there was a shared understanding that there are enhanced opportunities for Indigenous faculty to have a say in institutional but also in federal-level discussions around policy and procedure involving Indigenous research. While direct opportunities may not come along often or may not be accessible to everyone, indirect opportunities to strengthen the position of Indigenous worldviews are there by using social media or dissemination of research through traditional academic channels.

Thoughts on Research Impacts

As noted earlier, Indigenous research projects often carry a different purpose compared to mainstream research projects. The focus is often on strengthening knowledge capacity; contributing to self-determination of Indigenous peoples; reconnecting to one's roots, land, and community; and creating meaningful space in academia for Indigenous knowledges. The assessment of research impact must be reflective of these purposes. Faculty members were clear that traditional ways of assessing the impact of research would not always apply to Indigenous research projects. Participants mentioned that their work could not be tracked by Google Scholar citations because the work carried a different purpose – benefiting community. One faculty member was very clear in resisting and confronting the dominant academic standards around research. This faculty member stated:

> You cannot use your systems to measure my success. Because who I am isn't because of your systems. Who I am is because of my mother, my father, my aunts, my uncles, my grandparents, my siblings, my cousins. They're all Indigenous. My strength comes from them. (Interview, 9 March 2018)

Another faculty member was more accepting of the western ways of measuring research outcomes. Their comment attests to how there are often diverse views and perspectives represented among Indigenous individuals in academia:

> I think what many [Indigenous scholars] struggle with is recognizing the customary ways in which knowledge production occurs in the academy, okay? I'm not critical of those customary ways and, in fact, I kind of like them. Peer-reviewed journals, books, and stuff. And I see what goes on at the universities, and I kind of appreciate what they do. (Interview, 9 March 2018)

Generally, however, the conversations unfolded around how often traditional academic ways might not support the primary purpose of Indigenous research: benefiting the community. The outcomes of such research, guided by Indigenous communities, should be relevant and practical to these communities. Mainstream tools for research dissemination, such as peer-reviewed published articles, will not have the same applicability or relevance to Indigenous communities as they do to people in academia. The following quote best illustrates this thought:

> *If my work is relevant to a particular population and I promise community "X" that I am going to, in a reciprocal way for their participation in research, make my work available to them, am I really going to send them an esoteric research report that was published in journal "X"? I could do that. I could do, or I could be looking at other means of knowledge mobilization that is useful to them, right?* (Interview, 9 March 2018)

Comments regarding the impact of research were clearly made in relation to its influence on people: helping practitioners working in local communities, supporting research participants themselves (often from Indigenous communities), but also assisting colleagues in academia. These answers corresponded to the work done by Linda Tuhiwai Smith (2018b), who noted that Indigenous research strives to make transformational difference to the situation and condition of Indigenous peoples.

Resisting the dominant discourses and strengthening Indigenous knowledge capacity by creating different narratives around Indigenous history and culture was another key theme among several responses:

> *One, that's important to me and that I think most about in the work that I do, is a retelling of history being brought by non-Indigenous people. That's the kind of work I engage in, and that, I think, I find the most rewarding.* (Interview, 23 November 2018)

> *I would like to research Indigenizing education, Indigenizing education as a panacea to all the ills that befall on Indigenous people.* (Interview, 14 February 2018)

Research impact was seen also through contribution to theoretical knowledge – for example, to the knowledge on language revitalization, to make sure the richness of Indigenous languages gets safeguarded and paid more attention. The survival of languages was directly linked to the survival of Indigenous peoples as distinct cultural groups in Canada. A faculty member reflected:

> *Oh, well, heuristics or theories that will lead to language support, possibly retention. At the very least, a description of where we're at with public education, where we're at with the confluence of different uses across communities with the language, and incisive exploration of endangered languages. At the very least I*

would like to offer some support, theoretical support, for communities and peoples
who wish to save languages. (Interview, 9 March 2018)

Sometimes broader change starts with changes in oneself. Several faculty members mentioned reconnecting to their roots through their work. As many had grown up away from their cultural communities, with limited exposure to their Indigenous heritage, re-creating those connections to land and community had become essential. They learned about Indigenous history in Canadian public schools through books written from the western perspective, resulting in a distorted view of Indigenous history. Their research projects provided them with an opportunity to rethink the history of their people, situate their own individual experiences, and re-theorize ideas from Indigenous perspectives. Participants mentioned that they had a need to get a better grasp on the knowledge that had not been readily available to them. Only then could they hope to be beneficial to their people. Indigenous researchers often do not have the privilege of building on existing knowledge as other academics do. They must start building the knowledge from the ground up, applying new reconceptualization of knowledges associated with Indigenous peoples. Participants reflected on their experiences as follows:

It [research] was such a process of coming to know. Coming to know myself but
then also coming to know the literature and coming to know the ideas that were
out there. And, then hopefully moving forward. /... / I hope, you know, there will
be some benefits to my community. (Interview, 4 December 2018)

Non-Indigenous systems have been pretty effective in disconnecting Indigenous
people from family community, culture, language, land. Been very effective. And
I found that out with my research, as well. So, it basically mirrors my experience.
(Interview, 12 December 2018)

The connection between a person's own life experience and trauma and their specific research agenda was apparent in several cases. For example, one faculty member reflected how their research in social work around the topic of children in care was driven by their own lived experience growing up in care, away from their parents and community. Their current research project was used for healing purposes, first, to make sense of their own experience and then to try to understand how to help others in similar situations. This idea aligns with what Kuokkanen (2007a) observed as the principle of "giving back" through research – whether this means reporting back to the research participants, sharing the benefits of the research, bringing back new knowledge to the community, or taking the needs and concerns of the people into account when formulating new research agendas. It is all part of a broader process of decolonizing institutional expectations and mentalities in society, while restoring Indigenous perspectives.

Relationship building is at the centre of Indigenous research. Research projects are carried out with the purpose of engaging with participants over longer periods of time. These relationships are often a powerful catalyst for change for the participants as well as for the researchers. Comments were shared that attest to how a research project had made a positive contribution to its participants and their experiences. Individuals were seen to engage in a healing process in making sense of their lived experiences:

> *Well, digital storytelling as a methodology was an incredibly healing initiative for them [participants]. It brought them [the Indigenous participants] together. They developed camaraderie. /... / And, so, they developed a lot of beautiful relationships. /... / They lived with the aspects of their story and, until they actually bring that story out in their video, they sometimes never know what the message is, right. And, I think, in the process, they come to a better understanding of themselves.* (Interview, 12 December 2018)

Finally, there were comments shared that emphasized impacting non-Indigenous peoples such as other faculty members and colleagues. In these comments, there was an interest in drawing broader public attention, educating the general population, and adding new knowledge from Indigenous perspectives to topics traditionally analysed through the lens of western ways. A faculty member shared the following, emphasizing the aspect of mutual learning:

> *I have been a bridge to helping non-Indigenous people understand why things are the way they are. / ... / I have played that bridge in trying to help people understand that there were harms that were done against Indigenous people. We are just as intelligent as non-Indigenous people. And we deserve to be in the university environment, to learn from others, as well as for others to learn from us.* (Interview, 12 December 2018)

> *We make universities more responsive to Indigenous people, Indigenous knowledges and, so, be humble, and learn from us, as well.* (Interview, 12 December 2018)

> *My research has actually been very focused on creating that, both on campus and in the community, to try and bridge the divide between Indigenous and non-Indigenous people.* (Interview, 3 December 2018)

A research participant reflected on their experience as an Indigenous PhD student aiming to conduct collaborative research with their community. By pushing for an organizational change from the inside, they contributed to and potentially expedited the change occurring in their institution regarding research ethics standards. They shared how, as a graduate student, they faced constant struggles in their communication with their university's research ethics office and faculty administration and needed to create awareness of the way research is conducted from Indigenous perspectives in order to proceed. The prevalent questioning and need for constant validation of Indigenous knowledges confirmed the ingrained Eurocentric bias in the academy. They faced resistance to including an Elder on their committee and had to justify why their research needed to utilize Indigenous research methodologies and prove their validity. Furthermore, smudging as part of a research protocol was problematized and eventually denied on university premises. As a result, they had to move their research circles off site to stay true to Indigenous ways of conducting research. Their advocacy work did eventually push the institutional boundaries, and policy change followed at that institution. A different faculty member summarized the impact of Indigenous research as follows:

> *The kind of work that I do is to bring to light, and share, broaden, the range of people's awareness in this area, because I find it very narrow, if it exists at all. So, for me, that's success.* (Interview, 10 April 2019)

The idea of bringing Indigenous and western worldviews closer together was seen as one of the purposes of Indigenous research work. Adding knowledge from Indigenous perspectives helps to expand worldviews and challenge the traditional academic ways of knowing, and this will eventually make academia more relevant to a changing society. The importance of having different knowledge systems coexist was emphasized in the following comment:

> *And, so, we need to bridge the knowledge between Indigenous people and non-Indigenous institutions. So, but, doing that, we need to also – these institutions need to move over, maybe not move over, but they need to make space for that knowledge to coexist alongside western knowledge.* (Interview, 12 December 2018)

My own learning journey as a non-Indigenous researcher has been greatly impacted by these conversations with Indigenous faculty. For example, one faculty member promptly pointed out that "research" and "research agenda" are very western concepts and a western way of looking at knowledge production. This conversation pushed me to reflect more deeply on the meaning of research. The faculty member noted:

> *You're pushing the idea of research, again, and, you see, what you're going to get from somebody like me is a lot of stories. And you're going to have to figure it out yourself.* (Interview, 9 March 2018)

This conversation encouraged me to find answers to my questions through my own deeper reflection on their experiences, which created a powerful impact on my personal learning journey in engaging with Indigenous research and knowledges. Such personal conversations constantly occurring within the walls of higher education institutions are precisely the little steps that drive decolonial organizational change. While involving significant emotional labour, these conversations push boundaries in the understanding of what research is, what values it carries, and what purpose it serves.

Conclusion

Research projects by Indigenous faculty are often driven by different purposes compared to mainstream research. The primary goal of Indigenous research is to make a positive impact on Indigenous peoples by strengthening and reinvigorating their communities. To protect Indigenous peoples from negative impacts of research projects and to return to them control over research, new ethical standards have been developed, initiated by Indigenous peoples. Research principles that are grounded in the values of Indigenous ownership, control, access, and possession of research data are imperative in this work. Tri-council funding agencies as well as institutional research boards have followed the community guidelines of ethical research standards, ensuring that these standards are implemented consistently.

A key purpose for Indigenous research projects is to directly support efforts of self-determination and self-governance. This work is critical by nature, as the questions driving such research challenge the dominant perspectives and power relations in universities. This work also focuses on bringing awareness to the existing hegemonies and practices that have cemented the Eurocentric privilege in our higher education institutions. Research projects focusing on Indigenous topics create an opportunity to reconceptualize, build, and strengthen this work. These research agendas have a transformative nature, as this work adds pressure to the system to change.

The conversations with Indigenous faculty brought forward the aspect of learning: learning about themselves as Indigenous individuals, learning about the experiences of others, and calling others to learn from Indigenous worldviews. When people engage in reflective decolonial learning, they can refine their understanding of the core values, beliefs, and norms that ground our world, organizations, and institutions. Learning from Indigenous research projects has opened ways to reshape the narratives associated with Indigenous peoples. Demonstrating and sharing the beauty of Indigenous knowledges through interactions with others (e.g., students, colleagues, research participants) is gradually working towards impacting views and changing organizational behaviours. Overall, Indigenous faculty members have had a significant impact on the way in which research relating to Indigenous peoples is conducted in Canadian higher education institutions. Their work continues to influence and shape our understandings of relevant research, pointing out ideas and new normative values that can form the foundation of systemic organizational change.

Innovation

I think innovation would mean trying to build something new out of something that's already there. Indigenous people have been doing that since contact.

(Interview, 14 February 2018)

Innovation is a concept prominently ingrained in the fabric of the contemporary university. Innovation is something universities strive for; it is connected to contributing to the knowledge economy, creating new jobs, pursuing competitiveness, and adopting an economic growth agenda. Often innovation equals institutional excellence. Articulated as a core institutional value, innovation is featured in institutional strategic plans in the context of research excellence, teaching excellence, and new curriculum and program development. As noted by the University of Alberta (2016, pp. 12, 18): "excellence is both a goal and an attitude / ... / research excellence drives innovation and advances society." The concept of innovation is usually associated with scientific discovery or technological advancement emerging from research collaborations with industry and the private sector. Innovation tends to be coupled with the ideas of productivity, commercialization, and profits, aiming to achieve economic advantage over others. As such, innovation serves as a highly colonial concept that furthers the already existing power hierarchies in universities. When it comes to Indigenous innovation, the institutional strategic plans remain largely silent. Indigenous innovation does not seem to exist in the context of Canadian higher education. While some Indigenous strategic plans make mention of embedding Indigeneity into all facets of university life, including innovation, only a few institutional strategic plans of U15 universities mention contributions of Indigenous knowledges to innovation. The University of

Manitoba sees innovative research, scholarship, teaching, and learning emerging from Indigenous knowledges and perspectives (University of Manitoba, 2015, p. 10). Similarly, the University of Ottawa recognizes that introducing Indigenous principles into all disciplinary teaching programs can lead to effectively supporting students' learning while also promoting innovation through new forms of knowledge production (University of Ottawa, 2019, p. 15). This limited uptake of Indigenous innovation in policy documents demonstrates an extremely narrow and inequitable view of innovation that disassociates Indigenous knowledges and people from capabilities to innovate. As such, innovation is another highly politicized concept that powerfully shapes how Indigenous knowledges are viewed and positioned in higher education activities, including funding decisions. There is a need for more diverse perspectives on innovation that help to bring forward voices from the margins and move away from exploitative views associated with an innovation agenda. In particular, there is a pressing need to decolonize the western framings of innovation, so that it is grounded in Indigenous experience and can work towards strengthening Indigenous knowledges. It is important to reassess what counts as innovation in higher education contexts and what values are shaping its narrative.

Indigenous Innovation

Indigenous peoples are inherently innovators, as their historical survival in rough environmental and social conditions under the colonial regime has depended on it. The literature is clear that Indigenous innovation should be understood as distinctive, already at the centre, and as theory, process, and practice that:

a) is driven by Indigenous people (i.e., those who are accountable to their local community);
b) seeks to restore, reclaim, protect, maintain, and revitalize local Indigenous knowledges linked with Indigenous cultural practices and languages;
c) draws from local Indigenous knowledge systems;
d) is equipped to conscientiously respond to imperialism and its strategies, including colonization and capitalism;
e) creates spaces where metanarratives are problematized, approaches evaluated and reevaluated, and tensions appropriately addressed;
f) opens, expands, and rebuilds dialogue within and between Indigenous communities;

g) explores and builds connections with other knowledge systems (i.e., western modern science);

h) is concerned with how Indigenous people benefit and for how long (Huaman, 2015, pp. 5–6).

The perspective articulated by many scholars (Battiste, 2002; Cheek, 1992; Gumbo, 2015) is that Indigenous innovation is inherently cultural (not commercial) and includes a body of culturally relevant knowledge that provides methods and means to improve quality of life for Indigenous peoples. The research literature also suggests that Indigenous innovation is primarily connected to preserving Indigenous heritage through Indigenous people (re)learning their cultural ways of knowing and being (Hindle & Lansdowne, 2005; Huaman, 2015). As such, innovation in Indigenous contexts is often understood as "looking back" and not necessarily as "looking forward" (Hindle & Lansdowne, 2005). It is often about healing and recovery from the colonial past. A faculty member supported this perspective, sharing that:

> Innovation is almost everything that we do today to retain, or restore, our traditions, our cultures, and our languages. /… / So, innovation is finding new ways, outside of the context of a traditional lifestyle for Indigenous people, of restoring those things. /… / It's how we restore and retain knowledge, language, and cultural systems, you know, in this contemporary setting. (Interview, 22 November 2018)

A broader perspective on Indigenous innovation also includes technological advances that emerge from Indigenous cultural knowledge and are aimed at solving problems facing Indigenous communities. Seemann (2000) argued that Indigenous communities' approaches to problem solving are holistic, characterized by the intertwining of culture, technology, and environment. Examples of such innovation include technologies such as beading; textile, jewellery, and brasswork manufacture; food technologies (fermentation, frying, drying); and technological knowledge in agriculture, fishing, forestry, astronomy, renewable energy, atmospheric management techniques, knowledge transmission systems, architecture, medicine, and pharmacy, all informed by Indigenous knowledges (Gumbo, 2015). Obikeze (2011) described Indigenous technology in terms of tangible devices (e.g., knives, fishing nets, machines, electronic devices) and intangible devices (e.g., songs, jokes, ideas, skills, methodologies, organizations). In the Canadian context, there are many examples of Indigenous innovation. For instance, the T'Sou-ke First Nation in British Columbia has established a solar power system that generates clean energy for their community, reducing dependence on fossil fuels (British Columbia Assembly of First Nations, 2020). Similarly, the Mi'kmaq community in Nova Scotia has introduced a tidal energy project, utilizing the power of the tides to generate electricity (Nova Scotia, 2012). Indigenous knowledge systems have played a vital role in environmental conservation and land management. For instance, the Haida Nation in British Columbia has implemented a marine resource stewardship program known as the Haida Gwaii Watchmen (Coastal First Nations, web). This initiative combines traditional knowledge with modern conservation practices to protect the coastal ecosystems and cultural sites of the Haida people. Inuit of Nunavut are known for their art, including carvings from soapstone and bone. According to Battiste (2002), Indigenous knowledge comprises the complex set of technologies developed and sustained by Indigenous civilizations.

Several scholars have found parallels between Indigenous innovations and mainstream theorization of social innovation (Alexiuk, 2013; Sengupta et al., 2015). The mutually aligned ideas touch upon collective action, creativity, and facilitating processes of learning. For example, Alexiuk (2013) has argued that Indigenous innovation can be viewed as a unique type of social innovation continually informed by the application of Indigenous knowledges to promote the resurgence of these knowledges and related practices, as guided by the wisdom of the ancestors. Peredo et al. (2019, p. 112) approached Indigenous social innovation as a distinct concept that is defined as "a novelty informed by ancestral knowledge and practices, in some product, practice, technology or other phenomenon with social and cultural impact, developed and implemented by the Indigenous in accordance with their worldviews." Social innovation and Indigenous innovation both have social transformational agendas with a clear emphasis on knowledge and reconstruction of meaning within social systems. Indigenous innovation addresses holistic health and well-being and often has a strong link to sustainability and social justice agendas. Alexiuk (2013) also has argued that emphasizing such connections between these two knowledge systems may be useful, as those practices will lead to relationship building and knowledge integration that are culturally appropriate and collaboration-focused.

Critical scholars have noted that, in order to decolonize the concept of innovation, it needs to be addressed as a contextual social and political process (McGowan et al., 2020; Pecis & Berglund, 2021; Peredo et al., 2019). Social framing of innovation helps us to move away from the idea of innovation being predominantly technology-centred, white, and male. It allows us to bring forward Indigenous experiences and examine the structures and institutional arrangements that create and contribute to the systemic inequalities that have emerged from mainstream framings of innovation (Pecis & Berglund, 2021). Pecis and Berglund (2021) argued that innovation, in its true meaning, is a revolutionary act for the common good, which includes both economic and social development, filled with aspirations for positive change. Indigenous innovation, from a socio-political perspective, has been found to serve the purpose of pursuing intergenerational and decolonial justice (Tamtik, 2020; Vunibola & Scobie, 2022). There is a stream of literature that views Indigenous practices for self-determination as a distinct form of innovation (Alfred & Corntassel, 2005; Corntassel, 2012). The latter perspective is linked to a political aspect of innovation, pointing to how identity plays into who is expected to innovate and for what purpose. Bringing forward socio-political perspectives from the margins helps to position Indigenous peoples as innovators and emphasizes the necessity of a value shift in terms of how innovation is typically perceived.

The theme of transformation associated with Indigenous innovation can be connected to decolonization. Sengupta et al. (2015) argued that Indigenous innovation should be understood in broader terms as creating shifts in power dynamics between Indigenous and non-Indigenous people, and thus serving as a form of decolonization. Decolonization does not mean a return to a static version of Indigenous culture that reflects or attempts to revive a particular past time period, but rather tends to include inputs from contemporary Indigenous knowledges that reflect current contexts of time and space. For example, Indigenous innovation may seek to improve democracy in decision making and return authority and power over traditional lands to Indigenous peoples (Westley et al., 2006). Another example of Indigenous innovation is Indigenous knowledges leading decolonization processes within mainstream organizations, including higher education institutions. The shifting logic of innovation centred on transformative change was communicated by Indigenous faculty on several occasions. When reflecting on the institutional impact of Indigenous innovation, they often mentioned the theme of transformational change:

> *I think we've pushed people to think … We've been the consciousness … We've been the environmental consciousness. We've been the spiritual consciousness. We've been the cultural consciousness. We've been the consciousness of what happened through colonization, decolonizing consciousness. Those are all … if you want to call it, creativity.* (Interview, 9 March 2018)

This perspective of broader transformation of human behaviours and values was expressed by two faculty members. One commented: *"[For innovation] I would use words like initiatives that transform, would fit more ... because innovation, to a certain extent, I would see it as you do this and then it stops, versus transformation, which is a long process"* (interview, 3 December 2018). Another faculty member saw Indigenous innovation as transformational activity, new ways of making sense of the world, and disruption of the structures of normative categorical thinking. They suggested: *"[Innovation,] it's like shifting people, paradigms, shapes. I think we've been very innovative in being shape shifters. You know – tricksters, shape shifters"* (interview, 9 March 2018).

Scholars have pointed to the series of strategies with a critical decolonial nature that would allow Indigenous knowledges to shape dominant institutional structures and thus contribute to Indigenous innovation. These strategies are *reframing, discovering, restoring, unsettling,* and *protecting* (Alexiuk, 2013; Alfred, 2009; Regan, 2011; Smith, 1999). *Reframing* allows the questioning and confrontation of colonial values, beliefs, and assumptions and encourages change at higher levels (Moore & Westley, 2011). The *discovering* strategy helps to explore Indigenous and mainstream knowledge systems and examine how they may work together to achieve development goals that advance well-being and opportunity for Indigenous peoples (Smith, 1999). *Restoring* takes place when Indigenous people bring with them an ancient knowledge that demonstrates their distinctive form of knowing as well as its dynamics – that is, its capacity to recreate itself and resist western hegemony. *Unsettling* is a project unique to settler allies and has been described by Regan (2011) as engagement in disruptive, uncomfortable experiences that expose internal colonial values and beliefs. These processes can lead to unsettling experiences, enhanced intercultural understandings, and, most often, an understanding of the ignorance settler Canadians have towards Indigenous ways, views, and practices (Regan, 2011). *Protecting* safeguards the integrity of Indigenous knowledges and does not allow sacred pedagogy to be compromised. Engaging in these strategies would strike a balance between knowledge systems. This balance could lead to innovative approaches to intractable problems, resulting in novel and mutually beneficial alternatives.

Finding a Common Ground

At first glance, there seems to be an epistemological and ontological disconnect between the mainstream perception of innovation and Indigenous knowledges. Indeed, because innovation is strongly associated with the neoliberal narrative of technological progress, commercialization, and profits, this concept does not seem to align well with Indigenous worldviews. When Indigenous individuals were asked to describe what innovation means to them, some mentioned that the word is *"very business, technology driven"* or *"I associate innovation with scientific discovery."* It was also seen to be *"contradictory"* and *"a misnomer."* One person reflected: *"I most often think of this idea of progress that innovation is tied to, but this may be my own colonized thoughts around what it means to be Indigenous and what it means to be innovative"* (interview, 4 December 2018). Another commented: *"I have a problem with these big, new terminologies that get thought up by those in western-thinking frameworks"* (interview, 9 March 2018). My conversation partners had a hard time suggesting an Indigenous word for innovation, noting that *"I cannot think of one,"* *"it wouldn't be a word that I would use regularly,"* and it was *"not a word that I know of."* The following suggestion was made to describe the essence of innovation: *"mâmaskâc – a Cree word for somebody that does amazing things"* (interview, 9 March 2018). Clearly, the word "innovation" is grounded in mainstream scientific and technological narratives and does not translate directly into Indigenous languages.

While there seems to be an epistemological divide between how Indigenous and western colonial worldviews perceive the concept of innovation, there are important similarities in their ontological understandings of it. These similarities allow for a common ground where higher education institutions can critically assess their perspective on innovation and consider alternatives. One commonality that is represented in both worldviews is the association of innovation with *creativity*. In the mainstream scholarly literature, innovation is typically related to the combination of new or existing knowledge in a novel creative way, which may lead to a new product, process, or service (Borrás & Edquist, 2014). Along these lines, most institutional strategic plans have emphasized the importance of creativity, which is seen to lead to new knowledge and the discovery, generation, and dissemination of new ideas and different ways of thinking (and thus innovation) (e.g., University of Alberta, 2016; University of Calgary, 2017a; Dalhousie University, 2015; University of Saskatchewan, 2018; University of Toronto, 2018; University of Waterloo, 2013). Indigenous individuals similarly highlighted the aspect of creativity in knowledge creation. One individual noted: *"[When thinking of innovation] I just think of creativity"* (interview, 14 February 2018). Another summarized creativity as follows: *"Innovation, to me, is trying to take something that is old, whether it be an idea or maybe something material, and then trying to transform it into something different"* (interview, 4 December 2018). Both worldviews see creativity as a valuable quality that can lead to improvement and a better life.

Another commonality associated with innovation is the idea that it is not necessarily discipline-bound. The interconnectedness of knowledge, research methods, ecosystems, peoples, places, and multiple sources of knowledge forms the foundation of Indigenous knowledges. Indigenous knowledges have always existed holistically, incorporating empirical knowledge, spiritual knowing, experiences, and normative knowledge based on community values. As a system, Indigenous knowledges constantly adapt to the dynamic interplay of changing empirical knowledge and societal values. Western approaches to knowledge creation have similarly started to let go of disciplinary boundaries in the pursuit of innovation. Interdisciplinarity has been perceived as "a catalyst for innovation" (University of Ottawa, 2019, p. 5). Interdisciplinarity as an institutional goal has been highlighted in most institutional strategic plans, emphasized by support for interdisciplinary research (e.g., Dalhousie University, 2015; McGill University, 2017; University of Waterloo, 2013; University of Western Ontario, 2014) and interdisciplinary programs and learning experiences (University of Alberta, 2016). This shared idea of interdisciplinarity aligns well with Indigenous perspectives of knowledge connection, which helps to form a shared base for mutual understanding.

Innovation is pursued with the all-encompassing intent of bettering our lives and finding solutions to bigger societal problems that need to build on various knowledges. This thread of innovation, associated with solving complex societal challenges, has been a cross-cutting theme among institutional strategic plans (e.g., Université Laval, 2017; University of Manitoba, 2015; McGill University, 2017; McMaster University, 2018; University of Saskatchewan, 2018; UBC, 2018b; University of Waterloo, 2013; University of Western Ontario, 2014). Universities have pointed to the need to contribute to areas such as aging populations (Dalhousie University, 2015), environmental problems (Dalhousie University, 2015; University of Ottawa, 2019), financial challenges (Queen's University, 2018), and critical issues around poverty, housing, and public health. Innovation clusters have been established in environmental and energy sectors, transportation, and political systems (University of Toronto, 2018). A faculty member commented: "*Indigenous innovation would be thinking about how to bring ideas and values of the past into the present to address certain problems and create certain solutions*" (interview, 4 December 2018). This perspective aligns with the idea that Indigenous innovation involves a process of healing, recovery, and reconciliation. Innovation associated with decolonization was a unique theme represented in the strategic plan of the University of Saskatchewan (2018). A faculty member shared this perspective, noting that innovation is connected to decolonization in higher education spaces and would constitute a shift in the way higher education institutions currently operate: *"If they [higher education institutions] want to include us, then that's going to require innovation on their part. Do they really want that? I don't know"* (interview, 14 February 2018).

Indigenous innovation is grounded in balanced relationships and reciprocal efforts to solve shared societal problems. It emphasizes collaboration and respectfully working together, not individual gain or competitive advantage. Such a fundamental shift in philosophy allows for building on mutual strengths and creating a shared path forward, overlooking any disciplinary, administrative, or political boundaries. Indigenous faculty members tended to agree that there are significant benefits to working together in a respectful way, building on each other's strengths in moving forward. The following quotes summarize this perspective well:

> *Bringing in the best of Indigenous worldviews and the best of non-Indigenous worldviews to me is innovation. Being able to draw the strengths from both and creating something new that will speak to many people.* (Interview, 14 February 2018)

> *I think that because we are seeing a lot of non-Indigenous scholars already engaging in some of these creative things makes it easier, makes it something that is more accepted.* (Interview, 14 February 2018)

Overall, there are important connections and promising parallels between the two worldviews when it comes to thinking about innovation. There is an enormous potential in Canada to build on the two knowledge systems in order to address societal problems that are a concern for all. Viewing innovation from a perspective of shared gain and not of individual advantage would be an innovation in itself. Higher education institutions have a crucial role in recognizing this potential for triggering normative shifts in how innovation is understood, opening up a different path forward.

Faculty Perspectives on Impacting Change

From the conversations with Indigenous faculty members, it became apparent that Indigenous knowledges are already broadening the mainstream logic of innovation by gradually carving spaces for different norms and values to emerge. Following the logic of Indigenous innovations emerging from the processes of *reframing*, *discovering*, *restoring*, *unsettling*, and *protecting*, there are several examples that show how Indigenous initiatives are already transforming our higher education institutions. While these activities may not necessarily be innovative by Indigenous standards, they demonstrate the importance of viewing knowledge in a non-hierarchical way by creating relationships and connections between knowledge systems as opposed to referring to Indigenous knowledge as "new." Scholars have cautioned against the association of Indigenous innovation with novelty, as it risks the commodification of Indigenous knowledges and practices within mainstream higher education spaces (McGregor et al., 2010). It is important to remember that Indigenous innovations flow directly from Indigenous knowledges to address Indigenous interests – active protection of Indigenous ways, views, and practices resists the misuse of sacred knowledge and pedagogies. Furthermore, it is important to make this distinction, as Indigenous knowledges are sought by Indigenous groups to build resilience against the status quo and bring forward transformation (McGregor et al., 2010).

An example of how Indigenous knowledges have shifted and broadened the institutional logic of pedagogical innovation in universities is the introduction of alternative ways of gaining knowledge. Moving beyond textbook knowledge and incorporating land-based pedagogy and research into university practices is considered innovative and now highly encouraged in higher education settings. As a pedagogical practice, land-based knowledge has always existed in Indigenous communities. Incorporating this into Canadian higher education institutions helps to invigorate these cultural practices and thus serve the interests of Indigenous communities. A faculty member reflected:

> *We're using this terminology all over Canada now about land-based research. We used to call it Indigenous Science, you know, 20 years ago. /… / I don't look at it as going back to the past; I look at it as bringing the past forward to the present. /… / It's multidimensional, you know, in a sense that it's our history, it's our stories, it's where we are today, and what we're doing with tradition today. Not necessarily what we did with tradition yesterday, which I think is what mostly is thought of tradition today.* (Interview, 22 November 2018)

This example shows how traditional knowledges have been restored, reframed, and taken up in a unique way in higher education spaces. These pedagogical practices help to centre Indigenous knowledges in academia and rebuild relationships between the two knowledge systems.

A different conversation partner talked about how several social work theories have been grounded in Indigenous ways of knowing, and how these are inherently integrated into university curriculum. A couple of people mentioned new Indigenous programs as examples of innovation, relating them to the restoration of Indigenous knowledges and reframing of mainstream knowledges. One highly successful programmatic development has emerged at McGill University, where the university offers a Bachelor of Education degree that is delivered exclusively in the Listuguj Mi'gmaq First Nations community in northeastern Quebec (McGill Reporter, 2018). The program is infused with Mi'gmaq values, and courses are taught by Listuguj community members with master's degrees and doctorates as well as by McGill professors and course lecturers. An integral component of the program is unsettling values – creating enhanced awareness and offering training to the non-Indigenous community – which is helping to shift norms and values in academia. The universities' efforts to frame these initiatives as programmatic innovations have added political momentum and attracted financial support, which are helpful for sustaining a broader normative shift across higher education spaces.

The conceptual approach of two-eyed seeing (Bartlett et al., 2012; Martin, 2012) was brought up in conversations. This approach mindfully acknowledges and respects a diversity of perspectives between worldviews. Only by not perpetuating the dominance of one over another can one build mutual understanding. One faculty member reflected on how they grounded their work in the two-eyed seeing approach when writing their doctoral dissertation. They reflected:

> *Looking at my graduate research, I developed an [name of the program] – a university program – and again it had the balance of the two approaches, so I had to creatively create and deliver this program that will speak to Indigenous communities and that also aligns with the academic requirements, which sometimes makes you feel like you are fitting a circle into a box or something.* (Interview, 14 February 2018)

As demonstrated, Indigenous knowledges have been pushing the boundaries of what counts as valid knowledge in academia, predominantly by looking at the histories of systems that emerged from the colonial past and ways to decolonize them. However, the contributions of Indigenous individuals should also be associated with contemporary, technology-driven developments in energy renewal and water protection programs. Indigenous individuals, as active users of various social media platforms, have also been pushing the boundaries of usage and norm of such platforms. There are many examples where Indigenous people have created their own video or board games, focusing on the reclamation of cultural narratives, emphasizing Indigenous history and languages, and imagining different futures for their people. Some of these games operate in Indigenous languages, encouraging players to engage with their linguistic heritage. These innovative uses of media platforms in general illustrate their potential for redefining Indigeneity in contemporary contexts and demonstrate how traditions can adapt and benefit from evolving technologies that have not been designed with Indigenous languages in mind. A faculty member commented:

> With social media, Indigenous peoples can carve their own space and be innovative with free rein, without having to worry as much about majority society's perceptions of what Indigeneity is. That's what I like the most, I think, in that you see in some of these innovative areas, which I find on some level reassuring. (Interview, 23 November 2018)

The unique immersive interactivity that social media platforms offer enables Indigenous people to share and reflect on their experiences in a culture that generally distorts or silences them. On these new platforms, Indigenous people have creatively built organized action, formed new collectives, and triggered activist movements that have challenged dominant societal values and norms (Carlson & Dreher, 2018; Lumby, 2010). These are just a few select examples that demonstrate how Indigenous knowledges have gradually helped to transform our mainstream perspectives of what is considered an innovation.

Conclusion

This chapter has demonstrated how Indigenous knowledges have been central to the conversations around innovation, yet Indigenous innovation is often a formally unrecognized part of institutional planning. Indigenous innovation must be approached as a phenomenon in its own right. It should be understood as a creative process of transformation, driven by the innovators' cultural knowledge and lived experiences. Indigenous knowledges can be both progressive and tradition-oriented, anchored in respect for and affirmation of ancestral epistemologies and methodologies. Indigenous innovation is a concept closely connected to the processes of restoring cultural and linguistic heritage, re-creating historical narratives, and focusing on community empowerment.

The concept of innovation is a prime example of how mainstream ideologies have overlooked and marginalized Indigenous knowledges, framing and normalizing innovation uncritically in economic terms. Kuokkanen (2007a) has recalled that not every technological or academic innovation should be about the expression of progress, nor should traditions necessarily be seen as barriers to progress. She has also pointed out how higher education as a system tends to commodify and exploit Indigenous knowledges by framing them as commercialized innovations. Subsequently, the mainstream use of the word "innovation" does not directly fit with the Indigenous linguistic marker. It is easy to overlook the several common characteristics of the concept inherently shared by both Indigenous and mainstream academic worldviews – creativity, interdisciplinarity, and collaborative effort. These shared values can provide a shared foundation for both worldviews to work together and help build on each other's strengths in the pursuit of solutions to shared problems in society. To move forward, it is important to think about how to decolonize innovation, so that the concept is understood beyond western perspectives on excellence, where higher education institutions play a key role.

Decolonization happens when people in academia commit to identifying and changing systems and processes rooted in colonial ideologies that continue to oppress Indigenous peoples and their knowledges. Engaging differently with innovation is an essential step on this path. Decolonizing innovation in academia demands new ways of acting and relating to innovation and a shift in the normative foundations associated with innovation agendas. First and foremost, this process should primarily consider power and authority, questioning who currently defines innovation, how they define it, and in what ways Indigenous individuals themselves can determine if and how they want to engage with the concept. Returning control to Indigenous communities is important here. Second, shifting the norms of innovation away from purely economic grounds towards community-based social transformations informed by cultural experiences would confront patterns of consumerism that have inherently disregarded the use of land and the environment. The pursuit of individual gain has overlooked the power of the collaborative relationships that form the basis of Indigenous innovation. In this process, it is important to formally recognize (in tenure and promotion processes, and when allocating research grants and building research budgets) that the everyday, invisible contributions of individual faculty members to restorative and regenerative work with Indigenous families and communities count as innovation. As Indigenous research projects get more visibility and funding, as well as broader dissemination, there are several ways in which the processes of broader transformation can become more grounded and normalized in institutional practices. While the processes are slowly unfolding in institutional settings, there needs to be a recognition of this change and clear uptake of policies on Indigenous innovation. Decolonizing innovation requires non-Indigenous peoples to understand how the norms that have been so ingrained in academic contexts may be harmful to others and how these activities relate to the cultural, academic, social, and political aspirations of the Indigenous peoples whose lands/territories universities are located upon.

Conclusion: Indigenous Knowledges as Catalyst for Decolonial Change in Canadian Higher Education

Indigenous knowledges have become a powerful catalyst for change, impacting Canadian higher education in significant ways. The emergence of Indigenous knowledges has altered universities' governance systems, modified institutional climates, introduced new policies, changed teaching pedagogies and programming, contributed to new ways of conducting research, and begun to shift institutional innovation agendas. Indigenization efforts across Canadian universities have intensified in scope and scale with a clear emphasis on dismantling the colonial structures of universities. These important changes in the higher education sector have evolved gradually over decades without strong scholarly attention given to them. The goal of this book has been to address this gap in the literature by documenting the change, analysing its processes, and sharing the perspectives of Indigenous faculty members on these transformations. This book demonstrates how Indigenous peoples are claiming their rightful place in academia through critical work from the ground up, challenging the ways higher education institutions operate. Another goal of the book has been to highlight and acknowledge the accomplishments of Indigenous faculty, administrators, students, and staff in bringing along normative shifts in mainstream higher education. Indigenous individuals have worked to transform generally accepted and strongly established organizational norms in universities. As such, Indigenous knowledges have served as catalysts for new perspectives, ideas, and approaches, challenging the status quo of the university and sparking the momentum of change there, inspiring everyone to take action. As a result, Indigenous knowledges in academia have moved from the margins into the centre, to an area of institutional strategic importance, accompanied by funding and focused programmatic developments across many universities.

These processes of change are essentially the transformation of ingrained norms – moving away from limiting, harmful, and inequitable practices that do not align with the present-day needs of a knowledge society. The economic competitiveness agenda that has driven our society for decades is being challenged by calls from Indigenous researchers to engage in conversations around knowledge that supports sustainable living, environmental mindfulness, and collaborative relationships among people, strengthening our communities. Indigenous knowledges are grounded in these values. The emergence of Indigenous knowledges in academia has initiated critical conversations around the legal, ethical, and moral responsibilities that higher education institutions carry in society. First, the movement around Indigenous knowledges has given strong impetus for post-secondary institutions to revisit the legal frameworks around Indigenous rights, including, but not limited to, the United Nations Declaration on the Rights of Indigenous Peoples (UNDRIP, 2007), and the Constitution Act, including the Canadian Charter of Rights and Freedoms (1982). Making sure that institutional practices are not in violation of these foundational documents has become an important consideration. Second, ethical practices, particularly in relation to the ethical conduct of research impacting Indigenous groups, have initiated broader conversations around (research) integrity, honouring cultural protocols, and being mindful of who owns, accesses, and controls research data associated with Indigenous peoples. Discussions around individual and collective responsibilities to vulnerable groups have translated into new research protocols and guidelines. Finally, moral considerations around justice, equity, and fairness have become an area of institutional attention. The *Truth and Reconciliation Commission of Canada: Calls to Action* (TRC, 2015) has become a core reference point in institutional strategic plans and other documentation. Higher education institutions have embarked on the process of facilitating equity, diversity, inclusion, and decolonization as their core consideration in maintaining relevancy and legitimacy in society. These conversations have led to a broader normative recognition that post-secondary education institutions in Canada continue to operate as colonial establishments, increasing momentum around the need to establish universities that focus on anti-racism and decolonization. Indigenous scholars have played a prominent role in bringing these conversations to the forefront. They have championed the need to value community and relationship-building over the race of economic growth while moving away from a society focused on individual merit and competitiveness.

The presence of Indigenous knowledges in Canadian higher education is now considered an institutional strength. For decades, Indigenous knowledges did not have a place in Canadian higher education at all. In fact, Indigenous peoples were legally prohibited from participating in higher learning unless they gave up their Treaty rights to land, cultural heritage, and formal status. Today, Indigenous peoples are making important contributions to higher education through Indigenous programming, research and scholarship, community engagement, and institutional governance. This new strength-based perspective has unfolded as part of a gradual normative change arising from the scholarly and activist work of Indigenous peoples. Higher education institutions have started to recognize and value the capacity, skills, knowledge, connections, and potential that are grounded in Indigenous peoples and the knowledges they bring. Adopting a strength-based perspective does not mean ignoring challenges or spinning struggles into strengths. It means that non-Indigenous peoples must engage in critical decolonization, working collaboratively with Indigenous communities, in order to tackle the systematic barriers that may hinder Indigenous peoples from fully realizing their strengths.

The emergence of Indigenous knowledges has initiated processes of broader organizational change that invite us to critically examine the colonial ideology that universities and their operations are grounded on. Decolonization, conceptualized as a socio-political movement, tackles strongly established norms, values, beliefs, and behaviours in higher education. Taken-for-granted assumptions that have held true in higher education for decades about who gets to be educated, who decides what is being taught in our universities, which pedagogical approaches are appropriate, and what research brings value are changing. While a radical decolonial shift in higher education still remains a distant goal, the processes of decolonization are unfolding. The main conclusion made in this book is the fact that Indigenous knowledges are emerging strongly and independently in academia, and this change is a result of proactive and continuous ground-up work by Indigenous individuals asserting their rightful space in Canadian higher education.

Understanding the Emergence of Indigenous Knowledges in Higher Education

Creating normative change in universities has been considered an almost impossible task. Established university policies and practices are so deeply ingrained in traditional norms that they are seen to smother all attempts at Indigenous educational sovereignty (Brunette-Debassige,

2021). Nevertheless, significant advances have been made. To understand and explain how the emergence of Indigenous knowledges in higher education has evolved, we need to revisit theory. The theoretical perspective of this book regards institutional change as a social process centred on accepted norms that are grounded in the processes of learning. Norm-building activities that involve learning guide individual and collective behaviour and can lead to institutional change. The book argues that decolonization is emerging as a collective norm in higher education that has started to impact the way universities operate. Recognizing the impacts of colonialism and addressing the ongoing systems of power and privilege have become a starting point in norm-building processes. Self-determination and self-governance are the focus of these processes, which have been the main idea behind the advocacy work of Indigenous communities.

While learning starts with an individual, it is the collective that validates that learning. The concept of group influence on social norms has long been established in the literature of organizational change (Cajete, 2004; Finnemore & Sikkink, 1998; Powell & Colyvas, 2007). Group members who share common values begin critiquing established norms and promoting new, more relevant behaviours while working to overcome stakeholder resistance. This work continues until wider acceptance is reached, and the social context gets altered. At the centre of this process are attempts to modify others' perceptions of social reality. This perspective on institutional change argues that norms are actively built by calling attention to issues that have been invisible or have not been "named, interpreted and dramatized" (Finnemore & Sikkink, 1998, p. 910). As such, it highlights the role of an individual in the change process. It also focuses on the idea of building a critical mass that would accept, support, and further advocate for the norm, creating norm diffusion into policy and practice. These developments are accompanied by environmental pressures that may or may not support further transformation and wider acceptance of the norm. The emergence of Indigenous knowledges in higher education has been an example of this complex and lengthy process of norm dynamics that involves active norm building by individuals, accompanied by socio-political developments that have either delayed or accelerated this work.

The advocacy work to support Indigenous self-determination in Canada has been continuing for decades, but only recently have universities started to implement changes with tangible results. Yet those outcomes have been diverse, with some institutions making further gains than others. Universities are often referred to as loosely coupled systems based on the decentralized and autonomous decision-making structure they entail. Higher education institutions are not uniform organizations but rather vibrant and dynamic entities that serve multiple and sometimes conflicting purposes. That would explain their diversity in adapting to institutional change. Conceptualizing higher education institutions as living, multilayered organizations sheds light on the impact of their internal and external environments, sharing of information, and receptiveness to various socio-economic pressures. The examination of functional, social, and political pressures coming from the environment helps to clarify the processes around adapting to Indigenous knowledges. The functional pressures involving changing demographics and increased demand for higher education access are important. The demographic data show rapid expansion of Indigenous populations in Canada since the 1950s, a trend that continues today (see Romaniuc, 2003; Statistics Canada, 2016). Furthermore, the population of Indigenous peoples is nearly a decade younger compared to the rest of Canada (Statistics Canada, 2019). This trend has been reflected in higher education through expanding student access and participation rates of Indigenous individuals starting in the late 1960s. The initial increased access to higher education was possible partly because the federal government created post-secondary funding programs for Indigenous students, and Indigenous students had increased high school completion rates (Pidgeon, 2019). However, the predominant expectation for Indigenous students was to assimilate into the mainstream culture, erasing Indigenous ways of knowing. The current inconsistency among higher education institutions offering Indigenous programming stemmed from the limited federal–provincial direction for governing the Indigenous post-secondary education sector. As a result, some higher education institutions started to offer additional supports and new programming (e.g., teacher education programs and Native Studies programs), while others did not. From the 1970s onwards, a small number of Indigenous scholars began working in universities as faculty members. While the number of Indigenous students and faculty is slowly increasing, issues around the limited cultural relevancy of higher education programming and decision making involving Indigenous peoples remain.

The socio-political pressures emerging from critical scholarly work have been another significant factor in organizational change. Impactful work from Indigenous scholars emerged around the 1980s and 1990s with critical works published by Indigenous scholars such as Marie Battiste, Linda Tuhiwai Smith, Apela Colorado, Gregory Cajete, and others. This stream of literature became a foundational body of scholarship on Indigenous theories, epistemologies, and methodologies, centring on the need for decolonization. Since then, the norms around Indigenous knowledges from strength-based perspectives started to advance and be more strongly linked to Indigenous empowerment and self-determination. Higher education institutions have started to incorporate such knowledges into their policy work by creating Indigenous advisory committees, task forces, and councils to help bring in Indigenous perspectives to university operations, including strategic planning and programmatic supports from the 1990s onward.

These developments within academia have been accompanied by broader political pressures around Indigenous and human rights. The role of Indigenous norm shapers supporting the rights-based perspective is described in the following quote by Marie Battiste (2013b, p. 1): "Recognizing those basic rights was a 25 years struggle for Indigenous leaders and activists like Grand Keptin Alex Denny, George Manuel, Harold Cardinal, Wilton Littlechild and many others in Canada and throughout the Indigenous world." Furthermore, engagement in the larger political scene with the federal government has served as an important mechanism for applying normative pressures. International declarations such as United Nations Declarations of Rights of Indigenous People (UNDRIP) have been another step towards strengthening Indigenous rights at the global scale. Education, including higher education, as a path for Indigenous self-determination and self-governance has been consistently articulated in a series of policy documents such as the Wahbung position paper (Manitoba Indian Brotherhood, 1971), *Indian Control over Indian Education* by the National Indian Brotherhood (1972), the Royal Commission on Aboriginal Peoples (RCAP) reports (1996), and the Assembly of First Nations report *First Nations Control of First Nations Education* (2010). Most impactful to organizational change has been the work of the Truth and Reconciliation Commission's *Calls to Action* (TRC, 2015), which has put significant pressure on various societal organizations, including educational organizations, through its calls to address established power hierarchies in society and focus on amending relationships with Indigenous communities. As a result, most universities have developed new Indigenous strategic plans or updated existing ones, where the lead is taken by Indigenous communities. These strategies have been important in norm-building processes, as they clearly centre on returning control to Indigenous communities and building their capacity as self-governing people. The documents focus on colonialism as an ongoing ideology that keeps perpetuating harmful conditions for Indigenous communities and the need for this to change. These documents have led the way towards more formal, policy-focused venues for advocacy work.

Participants in this research attested to various other, more recent socio-political events that have had an impact on their lives and have influenced their work. Increased concerns over missing and murdered Indigenous women and girls, with the public attention created by the case of Tina Fontaine in Winnipeg, were mentioned. This case was seen to raise renewed awareness of the need for a national-level inquiry into systemic racism towards Indigenous peoples. The case of Colten Boushie in Saskatchewan was mentioned in association with inherent bias towards Indigenous peoples in the justice system in Canada. It was seen to influence more critical work around racial discrimination against Indigenous people. The finding of the remains of Indigenous children on various residential school sites across Canada was viewed as an additional driver of work revealing the extent of injustices performed against Indigenous peoples. Other social movements such as Idle No More and Black Lives Matter were seen as adding environmental pressures on higher education institutions to remain collectively responsible for revisiting the structures of colonialism and shaping the conversations around inequities embedded in the higher education system.

The Importance of Individual Efforts

The ground-up work carried out by Indigenous individuals involved in higher education institutions (faculty members, administrators, students, and staff) forms a significant pillar of the direct pressure for normative change. The role of Indigenous faculty has been a particular focus of this book, highlighting how daily, seemingly insignificant activities have created an important impetus for organizational change. While individuals may feel powerless in the process, each of them has had a subtle influence on the rigid system, which has collectively led to significant results. Several themes emerged from the interviews related to individual strategies that have impacted broader institutional transformation.

Grounding oneself in Indigenous knowledges. This theme was shared among most of the participants, suggesting that Indigenous knowledges provided them strong grounding and direction in their work. Indigenous knowledges have become a form of particular social and cultural capital in higher education, opening up opportunities for adding value to the organization. Indigenous knowledges were seen to help secure a purpose, agency, and voice for Indigenous faculty, reinforcing the norms and values associated with Indigenous identity. Many shared a sense of deeper purpose as they carried out research agendas, knowing that higher education is currently lacking a strong Indigenous knowledge base. Research publications written from Indigenous perspectives play a vital role in enhancing Indigenous knowledges but also in shaping discourses, problematizing widely accepted views, and confronting assumptions. Engaging and further developing Indigenous theoretical and conceptual frameworks and methodologies helps to advance different ways of knowing, placing value on the critical dialogue and systemic inquiry that serve as foundational elements for shifting norms. Strengthening Indigenous perspectives helps Indigenous faculty members to situate themselves in a unique space where they have a distinct position and increasing power of influence in higher education.

Confronting western mainstream norms. Another theme that emerged from the interviews was the need to actively confront western norms bestowed upon Indigenous individuals. In higher education settings, this tends to occur not only in informal conversations but also in formal meetings. There was a raised consciousness expressed around the grassroots activism that must occur daily in order to shift practices that do not resonate with Indigenous cultural perspectives. The theme of educating others was a prominent one. Indigenous faculty members often commented on having to educate others when in meetings, advocating for different policy approaches, and confronting and explaining why standard practices would not be appropriate. This advocacy contributes to deeper-level normative organizational change that targets core beliefs and values. As academia tends to view itself as a catalyst for positive social change, association with harmful behaviours towards Indigenous peoples is inherently problematic and has led to openness towards new norms among non-Indigenous peoples. The daily acts of resistance shared by research participants demonstrated how they had worked to refuse colonial attempts to erase or assimilate Indigenous peoples. However, finding the mental and physical energy to constantly carry out this activist work takes an emotional toll. Faculty members shared their experiences with fatigue and feelings of numbness and defeat, which could lead to resignations. This theme speaks to the price Indigenous individuals often must pay in the process of being advocates for new organizational norms in academia.

Dealing with failure. Recognizing and accepting failure was an underlying theme associated with individual attempts to bring forward change in universities. Frustration and sadness were feelings frequently shared in the conversations, pointing to the rigidity of the system and bureaucracy that has been difficult to overcome. Sometimes in these discussions, personal failures were approached as learning opportunities that would allow the building of knowledge and competencies for the future. At other times, failures were seen as inevitable and something that people should get used to. In situations where administrative encounters, for example, were perceived as highly disrespectful and directly undermining Indigenous individuals' cultural ways of knowing, these failures became motivation for further work. These encounters at times inspired almost a personal mission to make a change. The examples included changing research ethics, honouring Elders, confronting racist attitudes, and attempting to make Indigenous perspectives strongly visible. This perspective aligns with the symbolism of the trickster, whereby the trickster is often confronted with failure for ignoring certain rules and practices (Archibald, 2008), yet is focused on reconnecting with cultural teachings as a source for moving forward. The source of strength and empowerment for Indigenous individuals comes from witnessing positive change and seeing and celebrating success. In particular, such strength can come from the success of Indigenous youth when they feel empowered by learning about their heritage and having a stronger voice in academia when reclaiming their cultural perspectives.

Capacity through collaboration. The theme of collaboration to strengthen the position of Indigenous knowledges in academia was present in the interviews. Exchanging expertise and information among non-Indigenous and Indigenous faculty members through either formal or informal networks was represented. Social media plays a role in connecting individuals and developing networks. Connecting with others helps to share experiences with wider audiences and encourage discussions. Being able to advocate among students for the values brought by Indigenous knowledges was another important action often mentioned. Youth in general were seen as a crucial group that needs to be awakened and persuaded to be part of the general momentum around Indigenous knowledges. Witnessing how institutions of higher learning can become a platform for political activism for Indigenous youth, as they create their own stories and combat stereotypes and prejudice, has become a powerful source of motivation for Indigenous faculty in working towards normative shifts. Working together has helped to create a stronger collective voice that can serve as a pressure point for normative change. There was also a recognition that the numbers of Indigenous faculty are still relatively low, and stronger efforts to build a critical mass are needed. Building on each other's strengths was also mentioned in relation to working together with non-Indigenous peoples, so that everyone is contributing and playing their part in the process. Collaborating with high-level stakeholder groups that have power and authority helps to provide further access to decision making and shapes the process. As a result, Indigenous knowledges are gradually becoming associated with progress, innovation, and relevance, attracting larger groups of individuals to the work of applying pressure to universities to change.

Institutionalization of norms on Indigenous terms. Norm-building literature speaks about institutionalization, in which activities and norms are accepted and worked into organizational policy, procedure, and structures. While this development is unfolding in Canadian higher education, with universities changing their policies in relation to Indigenous initiatives, the nature of the activities seems significant. The processes of institutionalization are developing on Indigenous terms. There is an emphasis on ensuring that Indigenous knowledges will not get diluted or, once again, taken over by the dominant cultural group. An example of how Indigenous groups were able to stand their ground regarding policy change was shared by Jacquie Ottmann, professor and vice-provost Indigenous Engagement at the time at the University of Saskatchewan, during her presentation at Congress 2021 (Ottmann, 2021). She shared a story of how she led the development of a new institutional strategic plan with the Indigenous community. The intent was to gift the final document to the university. The idea of gifting was first rejected by administrators, who noted that, in university settings, documents get adopted and not gifted. Only after a while, following lengthy conversations and resistance, was this approach recognized by the university's Board of Governors, which then led to change in the language used in policy documents. As is evident from this example and others shared in the book, change can happen on Indigenous terms where Indigenous peoples are the ones leading these processes, making sure that their values stay intact.

This book combined examinations of both internal and external processes to understand the emergence of Indigenous knowledges in higher education, demonstrating how normative organizational change has unfolded. The process has not been a clear linear path but rather a multilayered and complex dynamic evolving over several decades with gradually increasing momentum. Individual stories and experiences are important components in this, as they help to shed light on the complexity of the power dynamics and nuances involved in the process. This understanding is important for clarifying our own position in these processes, and questioning and shifting our values and perspectives, which can further shift the norms and structures of higher education institutions.

Decolonial Institutional Change

The normative shift prompted by Indigenous peoples is centred on returning control that would support self-governance and rebuilding the capacity of distinct communities, their cultural traditions, and their languages. This work focuses on empowering Indigenous peoples by connecting to their land and roots, leading eventually to self-determination. Prioritizing decolonization is a key in these developments. As all these aspects require profound change in individually and collectively ingrained norms, values, and behaviours, it is crucial to examine one's privilege and its role in the ongoing structures of colonial ideology. These processes do not happen quickly but take time and willingness to engage. For this reason, there is still a considerable variety in how universities are accepting decolonization as a new norm. This normative confusion has been playing out in higher education in different ways, with individuals and institutions often struggling to find a suitable narrative and action plan to align themselves with. In most cases, the predominant institutional responses have unfolded around Indigenous inclusion (Gaudry & Lorenz, 2018), making space for alternative ways of knowing but leaving systems and structures unaffected. In other cases, the core institutional narrative has unfolded around reconciliation. Reconciliation as an approach aims to find a balance and build consensus around Indigenous and other ways of knowing. The goal is to collaboratively create a path forward for reconciling relationships between the universities and Indigenous communities in a way that supports and strengthens the Indigenous communities. Decolonization approaches are calling for foundational, structural shifts in the academy, completely overturning present academic norms grounded in the structures and systems that have created barriers for Indigenous and other minoritized groups. These discussions have spread out into larger debates and institutional attention around equity and diversity, with universities starting to use the language of Indigenization and decolonization as an overarching goal to move towards. As Gaudry and Lorenz (2018) noted, this transformative vision of Indigenization may be too radical, and, at least for now, more modest goals of increasing Indigenous student enrolment and hiring more Indigenous faculty and staff have been the reality. The perspectives of the Indigenous faculty members shared in this book align with the viewpoint of limited institutional interest in radical decolonization. There are examples of some institutions more readily willing to engage in decolonization with a focus on anti-racism agendas and criticality around the structural and systemic change that is needed in higher education. Overall, there seems to be turmoil occurring within many institutions without a strong consensus or clarity on the next steps to navigate these transformations.

Continuing the Conversation towards Decolonial Institutional Change

The most significant step in navigating this transformation is the impetus towards prioritizing decolonization as an important way forward. In the Canadian context, this perspective has been largely driven by the emergence of Indigenous knowledges in higher education. Still, the processes of decolonization and Indigenization that have started to develop in our institutional settings are only the beginning of this shift. The change is still unfolding; universities and colleges are trying to find ways of adapting to the environmental pressures, with differing results. The question becomes how these processes that are currently unfolding can lead to sustainable structural change in higher education. Isolated events may sometimes trigger cascading effects on an organizational scale, but long-term sustainability of those efforts needs strategic efforts. Sustaining organizational capacity, motivation, and commitment to work with Indigenous individuals is imperative for making our higher education system more equitable for Indigenous knowledges. Significant work has already been accomplished by Indigenous communities; now it is time for non-Indigenous individuals to take an active role in securing the continuous sustainability of this momentum.

In moving forward, higher education institutions have an important decision to make – whether to support Indigenous inclusion or whether to fully support Indigenous sovereignty. While Indigenous inclusion assumes making space for Indigenous knowledges within the original institutional structure, Indigenous sovereignty aims to alter the system and tackle reform at a deeper level. In inclusion, by creating a space, we are allowing Indigenous knowledges to exist in the university, but only in marginal spaces with clearly defined parameters established by the dominant cultural group. The deeper-level transformation of Indigenous sovereignty targets the structures of higher education. Pedri-Spade (2018) noted that trying to "Indigenize" universities without dismantling systems of oppression changes nothing and rather creates conditions where Indigenous peoples are further marginalized in ways that are gendered and racialized. Furthermore, Aguilera Black-Bear and Tippeconnic (2015, p. 5) pointed out that Indigenous educational sovereignty is considered imperative to the cultural sovereignty and survival of Indigenous communities. The question becomes – are we ready to move from the inclusive approaches that are prevalent in higher education today, to a level of structural systemic change that is aiming for decolonization?

Beck and Pidgeon (2020, pp. 399–400) have argued that decolonizing the policies and practices of higher education requires further relational change focused on the following: 1) *respect for different ways of knowing and being* – questioning what we know, how we know it, what normative assumptions we are making, and how they relate to different ways of knowing); 2) *responsibility to land and people* – considering our social, cultural, and physical locations, and understanding how we benefit from the lands we are working on and what protocols we subsequently need to respect as a visitor or host on Indigenous lands; 3) *reciprocal relationships* – reflecting on the quality, purpose, intention, and goals in working with others; are we being reciprocal in not only considering gains but also sharing our offerings in return, respecting the sharing of knowledges, accepting that each person involved in the relationship has something to contribute and something to learn; 4) *relevant policies, programs, and services* – policies must clearly articulate the intent of decolonization and what shifts are needed to make our policies and programs holistic and relevant to the educational experiences of all. This is a process that requires committed efforts from both Indigenous and non-Indigenous peoples.

Guided by this framework, the first focus should be learning at **the individual level**, recognizing our own role and responsibility in contributing to sustainable change in higher education. As a starting point, having a stronger knowledge of the history of colonial practices in Canada is important. A willingness to notice and question established beliefs and standard norms held in higher education in relation to Indigenous knowledges is important. Pitawanakwat and Pedri-Spade (2022) have noted that moving forward in higher education requires non-Indigenous peoples to make what is familiar to them strange. It requires an understanding that what seems familiar and to work so well excludes and causes harm to others. It is important to re-evaluate the core norms and values that have worked so well for some, understanding that the norms underlying our higher education systems and institutional structures have been deeply oppressive and inequitable to Indigenous peoples.

At **the institutional level**, the change requires learning to reorient conventional power structures through changing our governance system, recognizing and acting against the overall power hierarchies in the organizational structures as well as within academic disciplines. Based on the research literature and supported by the findings shared in this book, the following directions at the organizational level may be helpful for higher education leaders to consider in moving forward in the spirit of decolonization:

- Recognize that all levels of education in Canada are affected by ongoing colonialism and racism;
- Establish anti-racist institutional cultures supported by strategic policies;
- Make structural change an explicit policy priority (analysing barriers and continuously engaging in reflective dialogue for implementation);
- Allocate dedicated resources and continuous budget lines for Indigenous activities from university budgets;
- Hire more Indigenous faculty with dedicated teaching and comprehensive supports;
- Identify and remove various physical and mental artifacts in university contexts that were, and still are, harmful to Indigenous peoples;
- Self-engage in learning and educating ourselves on Indigenous history, perspectives, and languages, which helps to facilitate organizational transformation from within (Cote-Meek, 2014; Pardy & Pardy, 2020; Pidgeon, 2016; Pitawanakwat & Pedri-Spade, 2022).

These processes centre on one core theme – learning. Learning and unlearning, where the focus is on the root causes of the problem, accompanied by changes in attitudes, values, beliefs, and individual daily practices, can bring about sustainable organizational change. These perspectives point to the important work higher education institutions must take on. This work requires a heightened level of humility and responsibility on the part of academia, supported by finance and policy. As Pitawanakwat and Pedri-Spade (2022, p. 30) noted, "At the heart of this work will remain the importance of kinship, of *being in good relations* with one another and the lands and waters as our living relatives." The academy is a site where powerful and sustainable transformations can occur that influence our whole society moving forward. Let's go then and lead by example!

References

Absolon, K. (2010). Indigenous wholistic theory: A knowledge set for practice. *First Peoples Child & Family Review, 5*(2), 74–87. https://doi.org/10.7202/1068933ar.

Absolon, K., & Willett, C. (2004). Aboriginal research: Berry picking and hunting in the 21st century. *First Peoples Child & Family Review, 1*(1), 5–17. https://doi.org/10.7202/1069581ar.

AFN (Assembly of First Nations). (2018). *First Nations post-secondary education.* https://www.afn.ca/wp-content/uploads/2018/07/PSE_Fact_Sheet_ENG.pdf.

AFN (Assembly of First Nations). (2010). *First Nations control of First Nations education.* https://education.afn.ca/afntoolkit/wp-content/uploads/2021/04/2010-AFN-First-Nations-Contol-of-First-Nations-Education_sm.pdf.

Aguilera Black-Bear, D., & Tippeconnic III, J.W. (Eds.). (2015). *Voices of resistance and renewal: Indigenous leadership in education.* University of Oklahoma Press.

Ahenakew, C. (2016). Grafting Indigenous ways of knowing onto non-Indigenous ways of being: The (underestimated) challenges of a decolonial imagination. *International Review of Qualitative Research, 9*(3), 323–40. https://doi.org/10.1525/irqr.2016.9.3.323.

Alexiuk, E. (2013). Exploring the common ground between social innovation and Indigenous resurgence: Two critical Indigenist case studies in Indigenous innovation in Ontario, Canada [Master's thesis, University of Waterloo]. UWSpace. https://uwspace.uwaterloo.ca/handle/10012/7579.

Alfred, T. (2009). *Peace, power, righteousness: An* Indigenous manifesto (2nd ed). Oxford University Press.

Alfred, T., & Corntassel, J. (2005). Being Indigenous: Resurgences against contemporary colonialism. *Government and opposition, 40*(4), 597–614. https://doi.org/10.1111/j.1477-7053.2005.00166.x.

Andersen, C., & O'Brien, J. (2017). Sources and methods in Indigenous Studies. In C. Andersen & J.M. O'Brien (Eds.), *Sources and methods in Indigenous studies* (pp. 1–12). Routledge Taylor & Francis Group. https://doi .org/10.4324/9781315528854.

Andreotti, V., Ahenakew, C., & Cooper, G. (2011). Epistemological pluralism: Ethical and pedagogical challenges in higher education. *AlterNative: An International Journal of Indigenous Peoples, 7*(1), 40–50. https://doi .org/10.1177/117718011100700104.

Andreotti de Oliveira, V., Stein, S., Ahenakew, C., & Hunt, D. (2015). Mapping interpretations of decolonization in the context of higher education. *Decolonization: Indigeneity, Education & Society, 4*(1).

Annus, E. (2011). The conditions of Soviet colonialism. *Interlitteraria, 16*(2), 441–59. https://www.ceeol.com/search/article-detail?id=258804.

Ansloos, J., Stewart, S., Fellner, K., Goodwill, A., Graham, H., McCormick, R., … & Mushquash, C. (2019). Indigenous peoples and professional training in psychology in Canada. *Canadian Psychology/Psychologie canadienne, 60*(4), 265–80. https://doi.org/10.1037/cap0000189.

âpihtawikosisân (23 September 2016). Beyond territorial acknowledgements. https://apihtawikosisan.com/2016/09/beyond-territorial -acknowledgments/.

Archibald, J.A. (2008). An Indigenous storywork methodology. In J.G. Knowles & A.L. Cole (Eds.), *Handbook of the arts in qualitative research: Perspectives, methodologies, examples, and issues* (pp. 371–93). SAGE Publications.

Archibald, J.A., & Bowman, S.S. (1995). Honoring what they say: Postsecondary experiences of First Nations graduates. *Canadian Journal of Native Education, 21*(1), 1–247.

Argote L., & Miron-Spektor, E. (2011). Organizational learning: From experience to knowledge. *Organization Science, 22*, 1123–37. https://doi .org/10.1287/orsc.1100.0621.

Argyris, C., & Schön, D.A. (1997). Organizational learning: A theory of action perspective. *Reis, 77/78*, 345–8. https://doi.org/10.2307/40183951.

Asher, L., Curnow, J., & Davis, A. (2018). The limits of settlers' territorial acknowledgments. *Curriculum Inquiry, 48*(3), 316–34. https://doi.org/10 .1080/03626784.2018.1468211.

Austin, I., & Jones, G.A. (2015). *Governance of higher education: Global perspectives, theories, and practices*. Routledge.

Aveling, N. (2013). "Don't talk about what you don't know": On (not) conducting research with/in Indigenous contexts. *Critical Studies in Education, 54*(2), 203–14. https://doi.org/10.1080/17508487.2012.724021.

Bailey, K.A. (2016). Racism within the Canadian university: Indigenous students' experiences. *Ethnic and Racial Studies, 39*(7), 1261–79. https://doi .org/10.1080/01419870.2015.1081961.

Ball, J., & Janyst, P. (2008). Enacting research ethics in partnerships with Indigenous communities in Canada: "Do it in a good way". *Journal of Empirical Research on Human Research Ethics, 3*(2), 33–51. https://doi.org/10.1525/jer.2008.3.2.3.

Ball, S.J. (2003). The teacher's soul and the terrors of performativity. *Journal of Education Policy, 18*(2), 215–28. https://doi.org/10.1080/0268093022000043065.

Barker, A.J. (2012). Already occupied: Indigenous peoples, settler colonialism and the Occupy movements in North America. *Social Movement Studies, 11*(3–4), 327–34. https://doi.org/10.1080/14742837.2012.708922.

Bartlett, C., Marshall, M., Marshall, A. (2012). Two-eyed seeing and other lessons learned within a co-learning journey of bringing together Indigenous and mainstream knowledges and ways of knowing. *Journal of Environmental Studies and Sciences, 2*, 331–40. https://doi.org/10.1007/s13412-012-0086-8.

Battiste, M. (2000). *Reclaiming Indigenous voice and vision.* UBC Press.

Battiste, M. (2001). Decolonizing the university: Ethical guidelines for research involving Indigenous populations. In L.M. Findlay & P.M. Bidwell (Eds.), *Pursuing academic freedom: Free and fearless* (pp. 190–203). UBC Press.

Battiste, M. (2002). *Indigenous knowledge and pedagogy in First Nations education: A literature review with recommendations.* National Working Group on Education and the Minister of Indian Affairs Indian and Northern Affairs Canada (INAC). https://www.afn.ca/uploads/files/education/24._2002_oct_marie_battiste_indigenousknowledgeandpedagogy_lit_review_for_min_working_group.pdf.

Battiste, M. (2005). Indigenous knowledge: Foundations for First Nations. *WINHEC: International Journal of Indigenous Education Scholarship,* (1), 1–17. https://journals.uvic.ca/index.php/winhec/article/view/19251.

Battiste, M. (2007). Research ethics for protecting Indigenous knowledge and heritage: Institutional and researcher responsibilities: Chapter 5. In N.K. Denzin & M.D. Giardina (Eds.), *Ethical futures in qualitative research: Decolonizing the politics of knowledge* (pp. 111–35). Routledge.

Battiste, M. (2013a). *Decolonizing education: Nourishing the learning spirit.* Purich Publishing.

Battiste, M. (2013b). *You can't be the doctor if you're the disease: Eurocentrism and Indigenous renaissance* [CAUT Distinguished Academic Lecture]. ResearchGate. https://www.researchgate.net/profile/Marie_Battiste/publication/279577148_You_can't_be_the_global_doctor_if_you're_the_colonial_disease/links/598a50380f7e9b9d44c9c995/You-cant-be-the-global-doctor-if-youre-the-colonial-disease.

Battiste, M. (2016). Research ethics for protecting Indigenous knowledge and heritage: Institutional and researcher responsibilities. In M. Battiste (Ed)., *Ethical futures in qualitative research* (pp. 111–32). Routledge.

Battiste, M. (2018). Reconciling Indigenous Knowledge in education: Promises, possibilities, and imperatives. In M. Spooner & J. McNinch (Eds.), *Dissident knowledge in higher education* (pp. 123–48). University of Regina Press.

Battiste, M., Bell, L., & Findlay, L.M. (2002). Decolonizing education in Canadian universities: An interdisciplinary, international, Indigenous research project. *Canadian Journal of Native Education, 26*(2), 82–95. https://doi.org/10.14288/cjne.v26i2.195923.

Battiste, M., & Youngblood, J. (2000). *Protecting Indigenous knowledge and heritage: A global challenge.* UBC Press.

Battiste, M. & Youngblood Henderson, J. (2009). Naturalizing Indigenous knowledge in Eurocentric education. *Canadian Journal of Native Education, 32*(1), 5–18. https://doi.org/10.14288/cjne.v32i1.196482.

Battiste, M.A., & Barman, J. (Eds.). (1995). *First Nations education in Canada: The circle unfolds.* UBC Press.

Bauman, G.L. (2002). Developing a culture of evidence: Using institutional data to identify inequitable educational outcomes [Doctoral dissertation, University of Southern California]. USC Digital Library. http://digitallibrary.usc.edu/cdm/ref/collection/p15799coll16/id/273970.

Becher, T., & Trowler, P.R. (2001). *Academic tribes and territories.* McGraw-Hill Education (UK).

Beck, K., & Pidgeon, M. (2020). Across the divide: Critical conversations on decolonization, Indigenization, and internationalization. In M. Tamtik, R.D. Trilokekar, & G.A. Jones (Eds.), *International education as public policy in Canada* (pp. 384–406). McGill-Queen's University Press.

Beitman Brener, N. (2017). *Report on Indigenous professional and graduate students: A perspective on the future of Aboriginal students at* Queen's University. https://sgps.ca/wp-content/uploads/2017/05/Report-on-Indigenous-Professional-and-Graduate-Students.pdf.

Bhopal, K., & Pitkin, C. (2020). "Same old story, just a different policy": Race and policy making in higher education in the UK. *Race Ethnicity and Education, 23*(4), 530–47. https://doi.org/10.1080/13613324.2020.1718082.

Billy Minnabarriet, V. (2012). Aboriginal post-secondary education in British Columbia: Nicola Valley Institute of Technology [Doctoral dissertation, University of British Columbia]. UBC Theses and Dissertations. https://open.library.ubc.ca/cIRcle/collections/ubctheses/24/items/1.0103447.

Bopp, J., Bopp, M., Brown, L., & Lane, P. (2004). *The sacred tree.* Twin Lakes, WI: Lotus Press.

Bopp, M., Brown, L., & Robb, J. (2017). Reconciliation within the academy: Why is Indigenization so difficult? *Four Worlds Centre for Developmental Learning.* http://www.fourworlds.ca/news.html.

Borrás, S., & Edquist, C. (2014). Innovation policy for knowledge production and R&D: The investment portfolio approach (No. 2014/21). Lund

University, CIRCLE-Center for Innovation, Research and Competences in the Learning Economy. https://ideas.repec.org/p/hhs/lucirc/2014_021 .html.

Boyce, M.E. (2003). Organizational learning is essential to achieving and sustaining change in higher education. *Innovative Higher Education, 28*(2), 119–36. https://doi.org/10.1023/B:IHIE.0000006287.69207.00.

Brandon University. (6 May 2021). *Senator Mary Jane McCallum appointed as new Brandon University Chancellor.* https://www.brandonu.ca /news/2021/05/06/senator-mary-jane-mccallum-appointed-as-new -brandon-university-chancellor/.

Brant, J.R. (2017). Journeying toward a praxis of Indigenous maternal pedagogy: Lessons from our sweetgrass baskets [Doctoral dissertation, Brock University]. Brock University Digital Repository. https://dr.library .brocku.ca/bitstream/handle/10464/13126/Brock_Brant_Jennifer_2017 .pdf?sequence=1&isAllowed=y.

Brayboy, B.M.J. (2005). Toward a tribal critical race theory in education. *Urban Review, 37*, 425–46. https://doi.org/10.1007/s11256-005-0018-y.

Brayboy, B.M.J., Fann, A.J., Castagno, A.E., & Solyom, J.A. (2012). Postsecondary education for American Indian and Alaska Natives: Higher education for nation building and self-determination: ASHE Higher Education Report 37(5). John Wiley & Sons.

Brayboy, B.M.J., & Maughan, E. (2009). Indigenous knowledges and the story of the bean. *Harvard Educational Review, 79*(1), 1–21. https://doi.org/ 10.17763/haer.79.1.l0u6435086352229.

British Columbia Assembly of First Nations (2020). T'Sou-ke First Nation: A leader in the innovative use of renewable energy in Canada. https:// www.bcafn.ca/priority-areas/climate-emergency/climate -emergency-videos/tsou-ke-first-nation-leader-innovative.

Brown, W. (2015). *Undoing the demos: Neoliberalism's stealth revolution.* MIT Press.

Brunette-Debassige, C. (2021). The trickiness of settler colonialism: Indigenous women administrators' experiences of policy in Canadian universities [Doctoral dissertation, University of Western Ontario]. Scholarship@Western. https://ir.lib.uwo.ca/etd/7702.

Brunette-Debassige, C., & Viczko, M. (2022). Critical perspectives for educational leadership and policy in higher education. In *The* Palgrave Handbook on Critical Theories of Education (pp. 261–82). Cham: Springer International Publishing. https://doi.org/10.1007/978-3-030-86343-2_15.

Bundale, B. (22 June 2018). *Halifax professor resigns over university's failure to "indigenize the academy".* Toronto Star. https://www.thestar.com /halifax/2018/06/22/halifax-professor-resigns-over-universitys-failure -to-indigenize-the-academy.htm.

Cajete, G. (1999). Igniting the sparkle: An Indigenous science education model. Skyland, NC: Kivaki Press.

Cajete, G. (2000). *Native science: Natural laws of interdependence.* Clear Light.

Cajete, G. (2004). Philosophy of Native science. In A. Waters (Ed.), *American Indian thought: Philosophical essays* (pp. 45–57). Wiley.

Calderón, D. (2006). One-dimensionality and Whiteness. *Policy Futures in Education, 4*(1), 73–82. https://doi.org/10.2304/pfie.2006.4.1.73.

Calderón, D. (2011). Locating the foundations of epistemologies of ignorance in education ideology and practice. In E. Malewski & N. Jaramillo (Eds.), *Epistemologies of ignorance in education* (pp. 105–27). Information Age Publishing.

Calderón, D. (2014). Speaking back to manifest destinies: A land education-based approach to critical curriculum inquiry. *Environmental Education Research, 20*(1), 24–36. https://doi.org/10.1080/13504622.2013.865114.

Cannon, M.J. (2013). Changing the subject in teachers education: Indigenous, diasporic and settler colonial relations. In M. Smith (Ed.), *Transforming the academy. Indigenous education, knowledges and relations* (pp. 52–7). E-Book.

Capper, C.A. (2018). *Organizational theory for equity and diversity: Leading integrated, socially just education.* Routledge. https://doi.org/10.4324/9781315818610.

Carlson, B., & Dreher, T. (2018). Introduction: Indigenous innovation in social media. *Media International Australia, 169*(1), 16–20. https://doi.org/10.1177/1329878X18803.

Carr-Wiggin, A., Ball, T., Lar-Son, K., & MacLeod, L. (2017). *Raising Indigenous librarians: A Canadian internship story.* IFLA. http://library.ifla.org/1765/1/169-carr-wiggin-en.pdf.

Castellano, M., Davis, L., & Lahache, L. (Eds.). (2001). *Aboriginal education: Fulfilling the promise.* UBC Press.

Castellano, M.B. (2000). Updating Aboriginal traditions of knowledge. In G.J.S. Dei, D.G. Rosenberg, & B.L. Hall (Eds.), *Indigenous knowledges in global contexts: Multiple readings of our world* (pp. 21–36). University of Toronto Press.

Castellano, M.B. (2014). Ethics of Aboriginal research. In W. Teayes et al. (Eds.), *Global bioethics and human rights: Contemporary issues* (pp. 273–89). Rowman & Littlefield Publishers.

CAUT (Canadian Association of University Teachers). (2017). *Guide to acknowledging First Peoples & traditional territory.* https://www.caut.ca/sites/default/files/caut-guide-to-acknowledging-first-peoples-and-traditional-territory-2017-09.pdf.

CAUT (Canadian Association of University Teachers). (2018a). *Underrepresented* & underpaid diversity & equity among Canada's post-secondary *education teachers.* https://www.caut.ca/sites/default/files/caut_equity_report_2018-04final.pdf.

CAUT (Canadian Association of University Teachers). (2018b). *CAUT report on Board of Governors structures at thirty-one Canadian universities*. https:// www.caut.ca/sites/default/files/caut-report-board-of-governors -structures-at-thirty-one-canadian-universities_2018-05.pdf.

CAUT (Canadian Association of University Teachers). (2019). *Annual report 2018–2019*. https://www.caut.ca/sites/default/files/annual_report _2018-19.pdf.

CBCNews. (12 February 2018a). *Dalhousie only seeking racially visible, Indigenous candidates for senior job*. https://www.cbc.ca/news/canada/nova -scotia/dalhousie-university-recruitment-management-racially-visible -indigenous-1.4531723.

CBCNews. (6 December 2018b). *U of M Indigenous leader resigns, says administration frustrated anti-racism efforts*. https://www.cbc.ca /news/canada/manitoba/university-manitoba-indigenous -provost-resignation-1.4936274.

CBCNews. (24 February 2020). *Diversity push doubles the number of minorities studying education at U of M*. https://www.cbc.ca/news/canada/manitoba /diversity-university-of-manitoba-education-faculty-1.5467647.

CCAB (Canadian Council for Aboriginal Business). (2016). *Promise and prosperity: The 2016 Aboriginal business survey*. https://www.ccab.com /wp-content/uploads/2016/10/CCAB-PP-Report-V2-SQ-Pages.pdf.

Census Canada. (2016). The Aboriginal languages of First Nations people, Métis and Inuit. https://www12.statcan.gc.ca/census-recensement/2016 /as-sa/98-200-x/2016022/98-200-x2016022-eng.cfm.

Champagne, D. (2013). UNDRIP (United Nations Declaration on the Rights of Indigenous Peoples): Human, civil, and Indigenous rights. *Wicazo Sa Review, 28*(1), 9–22. https://www.muse.jhu.edu/article/506184.

Cheek, D.W. (1992). Thinking constructively about science, technology and society education. State University of New York.

Chen, K.-H. (2010). *Asia as method: Toward deimperialization*. Duke University Press.

Chou, M.H., & Ravinet, P. (2017). Higher education regionalism in Europe and Southeast Asia: Comparing policy ideas. *Policy and Society, 36*(1), 143–59. https://doi.org/10.1080/14494035.2017.1278874.

Christian, D. (2017). Gathering knowledge: Indigenous methodologies of land/place-based visual storytelling/filmmaking and visual sovereignty [Doctoral dissertation, University of British Columbia]. UBC Theses and Dissertations. https://open.library.ubc.ca/cIRcle/collections/ubctheses /24/items/1.0343529.

Clapcott, J., Ataria, J., Hepburn, C., Hikuroa, D., Jackson, A.M., Kirikiri, R., & Williams, E. (2018). Mātauranga Māori: Shaping marine and freshwater futures. *New Zealand Journal of Marine and Freshwater Research, 52*(4), 457–66. https://doi.org/10.1080/00288330.2018.1539404.

Clark, B.R. (1983). *The higher education system: Academic organization in cross-national perspective*. University of California Press.

Clark, D.A., Kleiman, S., Spanierman, L.B., Isaac, P., & Poolokasingham, G. (2014). "Do you live in a teepee?" Aboriginal students' experiences with racial microaggressions in Canada. *Journal of Diversity in Higher Education, 7*(2), 112–25. https://doi.org/10.1037/a0036573.

Claxton, N.X. (2020). Chapter 5: Indigenous land-based healing pedagogies. In N.J. Harper & W.W. Dobud (Eds.), *Outdoor therapies: An introduction to practices, possibilities, and critical perspectives* (pp. 52–64). Routledge. https://doi.org/10.4324/9780429352027.

Coastal First Nations (web). Coastal Guardian Watchmen. https://coastalfirstnations.ca/our-stewardship/coastal-guardian-watchmen/

Coburn, C.E. (2003). Rethinking scale: Moving beyond numbers to deep and lasting change. *Educational Researcher, 32*(6), 3–12. https://doi.org/10.3102/0013189X032006003.

Constitution Act, 1982. Part I: Canadian Charter of Rights and Freedoms. http://laws-lois.justice.gc.ca/eng/const/page-15.html.

Corntassel, J. (2011). Indigenizing the Academy: Insurgent education and the role of Indigenous intellectuals. Federation for the Humanities and Social Sciences. https://www.ideas-idees.ca/blog/indigenizing-academy-insurgent-education-and-roles-indigenous-intellectuals.

Corntassel, J. (2012). *Re-envisioning resurgence: Indigenous pathways to decolonization and sustainable self-determination*. UVicSPACE: Research and Learning Repository. https://dspace.library.uvic.ca/bitstream/handle/1828/12471/Corntassel_Jeff_Decolonization_2012.pdf?sequence=3.

Cote-Meek, S. (2014). *Colonized classrooms: Racism, trauma and resistance in post-secondary education*. Fernwood Publishing.

Cote-Meek, S., & Moeke-Pickering, T. (Eds). (2020). Decolonizing and Indigenizing education in Canada. Canadian Scholars.

Coulthard, G.S. (2014). *Red skin, white masks: Rejecting the colonial politics of recognition*. Minneapolis: Minnesota.

CRC (Canada Research Chair). (n.d.-a). *Program statistics.* https://www.chairs-chaires.gc.ca/about_us-a_notre_sujet/statistics-statistiques-eng.aspx#3.

CRC (Canada Research Chair). (n.d.-b). *Program details.* https://www.chairs-chaires.gc.ca/program-programme/index-eng.aspx.

CRCP (Canada Research Chairs Program) (web). Program representation statistics. https://www.chairs-chaires.gc.ca/about_us-a_notre_sujet/statistics-statistiques-eng.aspx#a3.

Crocker, R.K. (2022). *Religion and schooling in Canada: The long road to separation of Church and State*. University of Ottawa Press.

Daes, E. (1993). *Study on the protection of the cultural and intellectual property rights of Indigenous peoples* (Paper presented at the Sub-Commission on Prevention of Discrimination and Protection of Minorities, Commission on Human Rights, United Nations Economic and Social Council). United Nations Digital Library. https://digitallibrary.un.org/record/170886?ln=en.

Daigle, M. (2019). The spectacle of reconciliation: On (the) unsettling responsibilities to Indigenous peoples in the academy. *Environment and Planning D: Society and Space, 37*(4), 703–21. https://doi.org/10.1177/0263775818824342.

Dalhousie University. (2015). *Dalhousie University plan*. https://cdn.dal.ca/content/dam/dalhousie/pdf/about/Strategic-Planning/UniversityPlan-Online.pdf.

Dalhousie University. (2017). *Employment equity policy*. https://cdn.dal.ca/content/dam/dalhousie/pdf/dept/university_secretariat/policy-repository/EmploymentEquityPolicy2017October2-v2.pdf.

Daniels, E.A. (2011). Racial silences: Exploring and incorporating critical frameworks in the social studies. *Social Studies, 102,* 211–20. https://doi.org.10.1080/00377996.2011.558938.

Datta, R. (2019). Sustainability: Through cross-cultural community garden activities. *Local Environment, 24*(8), 762–76. https://doi.org/10.1080/13549839.2019.1641073.

Davidson, P., & Jamieson, R. (19 November 2018). Advancing reconciliation through post-secondary education. Policy Options. Retrieved from https://policyoptions.irpp.org/magazines/november2018/advancing-reconciliation-through-post-secondary-education/.

Debassige, B., & Brunette-Debassige, C. (2018). Indigenizing work as "willful work": Towards Indigenous transgressive leadership in Canadian universities. *Cultural and Pedagogical Inquiry 10*(2), 119–38. https://doi.org/10.18733/cpi29449.

Deer, F. (2020). The Indigenous achievement agenda and identity politics in university administration: Navigating faculty recruitment in an era of institutional change. In E.A. Samier & P. Milley (Eds.), *Educational administration and leadership identity formation* (pp. 103–16). Routledge.

Dei, G.J.S. (2000). Rethinking the role of Indigenous knowledges in the academy. *International Journal of Inclusive Education, 4*(2), 111–32. https://doi.org/10.1080/136031100284849.

Dei, G.J.S. (2008). Indigenous knowledge studies and the next generation: Pedagogical possibilities for anti-colonial education. *Australian Journal of*

Indigenous Education, *37*(Suppl.), 5–13. https://doi.org/10.1375 /S1326011100000326.

DiMaggio, P.J., & Powell, W.W. (1983). The iron cage revisited: Institutional isomorphism and collective rationality in organizational fields. *American Sociological Review*, *48*, 147–60.

Dion, S.D. (2007). Disrupting molded images: Identities, responsibilities and relationships – teachers and Indigenous subject material. *Teaching Education*, *18*(4), 329–42. https://doi.org/10.1080/10476210701687625.

Dlamini, S.N. (2002). From the other side of the desk: Notes on teaching about race when racialised. *Race Ethnicity and Education*, *5*(1), 51–66. https://doi .org/10.1080/13613320120117199.

Doharty, N., Madriaga, M., & Joseph-Salisbury, R. (2021). The university went to "decolonise" and all they brought back was lousy diversity double-speak! Critical race counter-stories from faculty of colour in "decolonial" times. *Educational Philosophy and Theory*, *53*(3), 233–44. https://doi.org /10.1080/00131857.2020.1769601.

Donald, D. (2009). Forts, curriculum, and Indigenous métissage: Imagining decolonization of Aboriginal-Canadian relations in educational contexts. *First Nations Perspectives*, *2*(1), 1–24.

Donald, D. (2012). Indigenous métissage: A decolonizing research sensibility. *International Journal of Qualitative Studies in Education*, *25*(5), 533–55. https://doi.org/10.1080/09518398.2011.554449.

Donald, D. (2021). We need a new story: Walking and the wâhkôhtowin imagination. *Journal of the Canadian Association for Curriculum Studies*, *18*(2), 53–63. https://doi.org/10.25071/1916-4467.40492.

Dorion, J., & Yang, K.R. (2000). Métis post-secondary education: A case study of the Gabriel Dumont Institute. In M. Brant Castellano, L. Davis, & L. Lahache (Eds.), *Aboriginal education: Fulfilling the promise* (pp. 176–89). UBC Press.

Dua, E., & Bhanji, N. (2012). Exploring the potential of data collected under the Federal Contractors Programme to construct a national picture of visible minority and Aboriginal faculty in Canadian universities. *Canadian Ethnic Studies*, *44*(1), 49–74. https://doi.org/10.1353/ces.2012.0001.

Eastman, J., Jones, G.A., Trottier, C., & Bégin-Caouette, O. (2022). *University governance in Canada: Navigating complexity*. McGill-Queen's University Press.

Ellermann, A., & O'Heran, B. (2021). Unsettling migration studies: Indigeneity and immigration in settler colonial states. In *Research handbook on the law and politics of migration* (pp. 21–34). Edward Elgar Publishing. https://doi.org/10.4337/9781789902266.00011.

Episkenew, J.A. (2013). Indigenizing university administration or Tâwaw cî? (Take 2). In M. Smith (Ed.), *Transforming the academy. Indigenous education, knowledges and relations* (pp. 64–8). E-Book.

Farnel, S., Koufogiannakis, D., Laroque, S., Bigelow, I., Carr-Wiggin, A., Feisst, D., & Lar-Son, K. (2018). Rethinking representation: Indigenous peoples and contexts at the University of Alberta Libraries. *International Journal of Information, Diversity, & Inclusion, 2*(3), 9–25. https://www.jstor.org/stable/48644435.

Farrell-Morneau, A.L. (2014). Memengwaawid, to be a butterfly: An Indigenous exploration of Northwestern Ontario Anishinawbe and Muskego or Ininiw sacred stories and teachings in a contemporary novel [Doctoral dissertation, Lakehead University]. Lakehead University Knowledge Commons. https://knowledgecommons.lakeheadu.ca/bitstream/handle/2453/569/MorneauA2014d-1b.pdf?sequence=1&isAllowed=y.

Final Report of the Minister's Working Group on Education. (2002). *Our children: Keepers of the sacred knowledge.* Department of Indian Affairs and Northern Development Canada. https://www.afn.ca/uploads/files/education/23._2002_dec_jeffrey_and_jette_final_report_to_min_national_working_group_ourchildrenkeepersofthesacredknowledge.pdf.

Finnemore, M., & Hollis, D.B. (2016). Constructing norms for global cybersecurity. *American Journal of International Law, 110*(3), 425–79. https://doi.org/10.1017/S0002930000016894.

Finnemore, M., & Sikkink, K. (1998). International norm dynamics and political change. *International Organization, 52*(4), 887–917. https://www.jstor.org/stable/2601361.

First Peoples Group (2022). *"Gii-ikidonaaniwan". "It has been said".* Queen's University *Indigenous identity project. Final report.* https://www.queensu.ca/indigenous/sites/oiiwww/files/uploaded_files/FPG%20Queens%20Report%20Final%20July%207.pdf.

Fitznor, L. (2005). Aboriginal educational teaching experiences: Foregrounding Aboriginal/Indigenous knowledges and processes. University of Manitoba. http://citeseerx.ist.psu.edu/viewdoc/download?doi=10.1.1.128.6337&rep=rep1&type=pdf.

Fitznor, L. (2017). The power of Indigenous knowledge: Naming and identity and colonization in Canada. In *Indigenous peoples' wisdom and power* (pp. 51–77). Routledge.

FNIGC (First Nations Information Governance Centre). (2014). *The First Nations principles of OCAP®.* https://fnigc.ca/ocap-training/.

Fontaine, L.S. (2017). Redress for linguicide: Residential schools and assimilation in Canada. *British Journal of Canadian Studies, 30*(2), 183–205. https://www.muse.jhu.edu/article/670700.

Fontaine, L.S. (2018). Our languages are sacred: Finding constitutional space for Aboriginal language rights [Doctoral dissertation, University of Manitoba]. MSpace. http://hdl.handle.net/1993/32864.

Foucault, M. (1980). Power/knowledge: Selected interviews and other writings 1972–1977. Ed. C. Gordon. Pantheon.

Foucault, M. (1983). *This is not a pipe.* University of California Press.

Friesen Lepp, H. (2018). "We are all relations": An Indigenous course requirement (ICR) experience. *International Journal for Talent Development and Creativity, 6*(1&2), 189–270.

Fulcrum News. (2020). *First draft of U of O's Indigenous Action Plan revealed.* https://thefulcrum.ca/news/first-draft-of-u-of-os-indigenous -action-plan-revealed/.

Gallop, C.J., & Bastien, N. (2016). Supporting success: Aboriginal students in higher education. *Canadian Journal of Higher Education, 46*(2), 206–24. https://doi.org/10.47678/cjhe.v46i2.184772.

Gamble, T. (18 June 2021). *New Masters of Indigenous Education program seeks to incorporate Indigenous knowledge at UBC.* The Ubyssey. https://www .ubyssey.ca/news/new-masters-of-indigenous-education-program/.

Gaudry, A., & Lorenz, D. (2018). Indigenization as inclusion, reconciliation, and decolonization: Navigating the different visions for indigenizing the Canadian Academy. *AlterNative: An International Journal of Indigenous Peoples, 14*(3), 218–27. https://doi.org/10.1177/1177180118785382.

Goddard, J.T., & Foster, R.Y. (2002). Adapting to diversity: Where cultures collide: Educational issues in northern Alberta. *Canadian Journal of Education/Revue canadienne de l'éducation*, 1–20. https://doi.org/10.2307/ 1602185.

González, R.G., & Colangelo, P. (2010). The development of Indigenous higher education: A comparative historical analysis between Australia, Canada, New Zealand, and the US, 1880–2005. *Journal of American Indian Education*, 3–23. http://www.jstor.org/stable/43608577.

Government of Canada (2018). Budget 2019. Chapter 3: Advancing reconciliation. Retrieved from https://budget.gc.ca/2019/docs/plan /chap-03-en.html.

Grafton, E., & Melançon, J. (2020). Chapter 8. The Dynamics of Decolonization and Indigenization in an Era of Academic "Reconciliation". In S. Cote-Meek & T. Moeke-Pickering (Eds)., *Decolonizing and indigenizing education in Canada* (pp. 135–53). Canadian Scholars.

Grande, S. (2015). *Red pedagogy: Native American social and political thought.* Rowman & Littlefield.

Grande, S. (2018). Refusing the university. In E. Tuck & K.W. Yang (Eds.), *Toward what justice?* (pp. 47–65). Routledge.

Gregory, D., Pijl-Zieber, E.M., Barsky, J., & Daniels, M. (2008). Aboriginal nursing education in Canada: An update. *Canadian Nurse, 104*(4), 24–8. PMID: 18488764.

Grosfoguel, R. (2013). The structure of knowledge in westernised universities: Epistemic racism/sexism and the four genocides/epistemicides. *Human Architecture: Journal of the Sociology of Self-Knowledge, 1*(1), 73–90.

Gumbo, M.T. (2015). Indigenous technology in technology education curricula and teaching. In P.J. Williams, A. Jones, & C. Buntting (Eds.), *The future of technology education* (pp. 57–75). Singapore: Springer.

Gunstone, A. (2013). Indigenous leadership and governance in Australian universities. *International Journal of Critical Indigenous Studies, 6*(1), 1–11. https://doi.org/10.5204/ijcis.v6i1.108.

Gusa, D.L. (2010). White institutional presence: The impact of Whiteness on campus climate. *Harvard Educational Review, 80*(4), 464–90. https://doi.org/10.17763/haer.80.4.p5j483825u110002.

Haig-Brown, C. (2010). Indigenous thought, appropriation, and non-Aboriginal people. *Canadian Journal of Education/Revue Canadienne de l'éducation, 33*(4), 925–50. http://www.jstor.org/stable/canajeducrevucan.33.4.925.

Haig-Brown, C., & Hodson, J. (2009). Starting with the land: Toward Indigenous thought in Canadian education. In P.A. Woods & G.J. Woods (Eds.), *Alternative education for the 21st century* (pp. 167–87). Palgrave Macmillan.

Haig-Brown, C., & Hoskins, T.K. (2019). Indigenous teacher education in Canada and Aotearoa New Zealand. In *Oxford research encyclopedia of education*. https://doi.org/10.1093/acrefore/9780190264093.013.746.

Hampton, R. (2016). Racialized social relations in higher education: Black student and faculty experiences of a Canadian university [Doctoral dissertation, McGill University]. https://escholarship.mcgill.ca/concern/theses/q237hv236.

Hancock, R.L., Moran, R., Newman, C., Walsh, A., & Rogers, S. (2021). Editorial remarks: Conversations with Indigenous Knowledges. *KULA: Knowledge Creation, Dissemination, and Preservation Studies, 5*(1), 1–3. https://doi.org/10.18357/kula.204.

Hart, M.A. (2010). Indigenous worldviews, knowledge, and research: The development of an Indigenous research paradigm. *Journal of Indigenous Voices in Social Work, 1*(1), 1–16. http://hdl.handle.net/10125/12527.

Hayward, A., Sjoblom, E., Sinclair, S., & Cidro, J. (2021). A new era of Indigenous research: Community-based Indigenous research ethics protocols in Canada. *Journal of Empirical Research on Human Research Ethics,* 1–15. https://doi.org/10.1177/15562646211023705.

Henry, F. (2012). Indigenous faculty at Canadian universities: Their stories. *Canadian Ethnic Studies, 44*(1), 101–32. https://doi.org/10.1353/ces.2012.0005.

Henry, F., Dua, E., James, C.E., Kobayashi, A., Li, P., Ramos, H., & Smith, M. (2017a). *The equity myth:* Racialization and Indigeneity at Canadian universities. UBC Press.

Henry, F., Dua, E., Kobayashi, A., James, C., Li, P., Ramos, H., & Smith, M.S. (2017b). Race, racialization and Indigeneity in Canadian universities. *Race*

Ethnicity and Education, 20(3), 300–14. https://doi.org/10.1080/13613324 .2016.1260226.

Henry, F., & Tator, C. (2012). Interviews with racialized faculty members in Canadian universities. *Canadian Ethnic Studies, 44*(1), 75–99. https://doi .org/10.1353/ces.2012.0003.

Henry, R., & Tait, C. (2023). Indigenous identity fraud: An interview with Caroline Tait. *Aboriginal Policy Studies, 10*(2). 10.5663/aps.v10i2.29424.

Herbert, J. (2010). Indigenous studies: Tool of empowerment within the academe. *Australian Journal of Indigenous Education, 39*(S1), 23–31. https:// doi.org/10.1375/S1326011100001101.

Higgins, J. (2007). Institutional culture as keyword. *Review of higher education in South Africa: Selected themes*, 97–123. Retrieved from https:// citeseerx.ist.psu.edu/viewdoc/download?doi=10.1.1.148.3863&rep=rep1 &type=pdf.

Hindle, K., & Lansdowne, M. (2005). Brave spirits on new paths: Toward a globally relevant paradigm of Indigenous entrepreneurship research. *Journal of Small Business & Entrepreneurship, 18*(2), 131–41. https:// doi.org/10.1080/08276331.2005.10593335.

Hirji, F., Jiwani, Y., & McAllister, K.E. (2020). On the margins of the margins: #CommunicationSoWhite – Canadian style. *Communication, Culture & Critique, 13*(2), 168–84. https://doi.org/10.1093/ccc/tcaa019.

Horne, C., & Mollborn, S. (2020). Norms: An integrated framework. *Annual Review of Sociology, 46*, 467–87. https://doi.org/10.1146/annurev-soc-121919 -054658.

Huaman, E.S. (2015). Indigenous-minded innovation in shifting ecologies. In E.S. Huaman & B. Sriraman (Eds.), *Indigenous innovation: Universalities and peculiarities* (pp. 1–9). Sense Publishers.

Hurtado, S., Clayton-Pedersen, A.R., Allen, W.R., & Milem, J.F. (1998). Enhancing campus climates for racial/ethnic diversity: Educational policy and practice. *Review of Higher Education, 21*(3), 279–302. https:// doi:10.1353/rhe.1998.0003.

Hurtado, S., Griffin, K.A., Arellano, L., & Cuellar, M. (2008). Assessing the value of climate assessments: Progress and future directions. *Journal of Diversity in Higher Education, 1*(4), 204–21. https://doi.org/10.1037/a0014009.

Hutchings, S. (2014). Introduction: Indigenous knowledges impacting the environment. *AlterNative: An International Journal of Indigenous Peoples, 10*(5), 445–9. https://doi.org/10.1177/117718011401000501.

Indigenomics Institute. (n.d.). *100 billion.* http://indigenomicsinstitute .com/100-billion/.

Indigenous Connect. (n.d.). *Migizii Agamik.* University of Manitoba. https:// umanitoba.ca/admin/indigenous_connect/5558.html.

Inuit Tapiriit Kanatami. (2018). *National Inuit strategy on research: Implementation plan*. https://www.itk.ca/wp-content/uploads/2018/09 /ITK_NISR_Implementation-Plan_Electronic-Version.pdf.

Iseke-Barnes, J. (2009). Unsettling fictions: Disrupting popular discourses and trickster tales in books for children. *Journal of the Canadian Association for Curriculum Studies, 7*(1), 24–57. https://jcacs3.journals.yorku.ca/index .php/jcacs/article/view/17988.

ITAC (Indigenous Tourism Association of Canada). (2019). *Accelerating Indigenous tourism growth in Canada: Five-year strategic plan update* 2019–2024. https://indigenoustourism.ca/corporate/wp-content/uploads/2019/03/18 -10-Accelerating-Tourism-Growth-Booklet-v7.pdf.

Iverson, S.V.D. (2005). A policy discourse analysis of US land-grant university diversity action plans [Doctoral dissertation, University of Maine]. DigitalCommons@UMaine. https://digitalcommons.library.umaine.edu /cgi/viewcontent.cgi?article=2798&context=etd.

Janzen, M. (2019). Breathing life into the territorial acknowledgement. *TCI (Transnational Curriculum Inquiry), 16*(2), 74–81. https://doi.org/10.14288 /tci.v16i2.192298.

Jimmy, E., Andreotti, V., & Stein, S. (2019). Towards braiding. Musagetes Foundation. https://artseverywhere.ca/wp-content/uploads/2019/07 /Braiding_ReaderWeb.pdf.

Jones, G.A. (1998). The idea of a Canadian university. *Interchange, 29*, 69–80. https://doi.org/10.1023/A:1007452504974.

Jones, G.A. (2002). The structure of university governance in Canada: A policy network approach. In A. Alberto, G.A. Jones, & B. Karseth (Eds.), *Governing higher education: National perspectives on institutional governance* (pp. 213–34). Springer.

Jones, G.A. (2013). The horizontal and vertical fragmentation of academic work and the challenge for academic governance and leadership. *Asia Pacific Education Review, 14*(1), 75–83. https://doi.org/10.1007 /s12564-013-9251-3.

Jungic, V., & Thompson, S. (2020). SFU Academic Summer Camp for Aboriginal Students 2014–2018. *Journal of STEM Outreach, 3*(1), 1–10. https://doi.org/10.15695/jstem/v3i1.04.

Kaljundi, L. (2022, April). Decolonise that – Estonian identity as Indigenous and/or white. https://www.ashadecolder.com/decolonise -that-estonian-identity-as-indigenous-and-or-white.

Kanu, Y., (2011). *Integrating Aboriginal perspectives into the school curriculum: Purposes, possibilities, and challenges*. University of Toronto Press.

Kezar, A., & Eckel, P.D. (2002). The effect of institutional culture on change strategies in higher education: Universal principles or culturally responsive

concepts? *Journal of Higher Education, 73*(4), 435–60. https://doi.org
/10.1080/00221546.2002.11777159.

Kimmerer, R. (2013). *Braiding sweetgrass: Indigenous wisdom, scientific knowledge and the teachings of plants.* Milkweed Editions.

King, H. (2018). An Anishinaabe politics of the international: Odaenuah, Akina, miniwaa Gchi'naaknigewin (Doctoral dissertation, McMaster University). http://hdl.handle.net/11375/27622.

Kirkness, V.J., & Barnhardt, R. (1991). First Nations and higher education: The four R's – Respect, relevance, reciprocity, responsibility. *Journal of American Indian Education, 30*(3), 1–15.

Kirmayer, L.J., Brass, G.M., Holton, T., Paul, K., Simpson, C., & Tait, C. (2007). *Suicide among Aboriginal people in Canada.* The Aboriginal Healing Foundation. http://www.ahf.ca/downloads/suicide.pdf.

Klein, U. (2016). Gender equality and diversity politics in higher education: Conflicts, challenges and requirements for collaboration. *Women's Studies International Forum, 54,* 147–56. https://doi.org/10.1016/j.wsif.2015.06.017.

Kobayashi, A. (2018). Now you see them, how you see them: Women of colour in Canadian academia. In F. Henry & C. Tator (Eds), *Racism in the Canadian university. Demanding social justice, inclusion, and equity* (pp. 60–75). University of Toronto Press.

Kovach, M. (2009). *Indigenous methodologies: Characteristics, conversations, and contexts.* University of Toronto Press.

Kovach, M. (2010). Conversation method in Indigenous research. *First Peoples Child & Family Review: An Interdisciplinary Journal Honouring the Voices, Perspectives, and Knowledges of First Peoples through Research, Critical Analyses, Stories, Standpoints and Media Reviews, 5*(1), 40–8. https://doi.org
/10.7202/1069060ar.

Kovach, M. (2021). *Indigenous methodologies: Characteristics, conversations, and contexts.* 2nd edition. University of Toronto Press.

Kristoff, T., & Cottrell, M. (2021). Supporting First Nations and Métis post-secondary students' academic persistence: Insights from a Canadian First Nations–affiliated institution. *Canadian Journal of Higher Education, 51*(2), 46–60. https://doi.org/10.47678/cjhe.vi0.188993.

Kuokkanen, R. (2007a). *Reshaping the university: Responsibility, Indigenous epistemes, and the logic of the gift.* UBC Press.

Kuokkanen, R. (2007b). The gift logic of Indigenous philosophies in the academy. In G. Vaughan (Ed.), *Women and the gift economy: A radically different worldview is possible* (pp. 71–83). Inanna Publications and Education.

Kuokkanen, R. (2019). *Restructuring relations: Indigenous self-determination, governance, and gender.* Oxford University Press.

Ladson-Billings, G. (2006). From the achievement gap to the education debt: Understanding achievement in US schools. *Educational Researcher, 35*(7), 3–12. https://doi.org/10.3102/0013189X035007003.

Ladson-Billings, G., & Tate, W.F. (1995). Toward a critical race theory of education. *Teachers College Record, 91*(1), 47–68. https://doi.org /10.1177/016146819509700104.

Lakehead University. (n.d.). *Indigenous course requirement.* https://www .lakeheadu.ca/indigenous/icr.

Lambert, J. (2013). *Digital storytelling: Capturing lives, creating community* (4th ed.). Routledge.

Lather, P. (1991). Getting smart: Feminist research and pedagogy with/in the postmodern. Routledge.

Latulippe, N., & Klenk, N. (2020). Making room and moving over: Knowledge co-production, Indigenous knowledge sovereignty and the politics of global environmental change decision-making. *Current Opinion in Environmental Sustainability, 42*, 7–14. https://doi.org/10.1016/j.cosust.2019.10.010.

Laurentian University (2021). National Indigenous Peoples Day. Retrieved from https://laurentian.ca/national-indigenous-peoples-day.

Lavallée, L. (2007). Physical activity and healing through the medicine wheel. *Pimatisiwin, 5*(1), 127–53. https://journalindigenouswellbeing.co .nz/media/2018/10/7_Lavallee.pdf.

Lavallée, L. (2009). Practical application of an Indigenous research framework and two qualitative Indigenous research methods: Sharing circles and Anishnaabe symbol-based reflection. *International Journal of Qualitative Methods, 8*(1), 21–40. https://doi.org/10.1177/160940690900800103.

Lavallée, L. (2020a). Chapter 7. Is decolonization possible in the academy? In S. Cote-Meek & T. Moeke-Pickering (Eds.), *Decolonizing and indigenizing education in Canada* (pp. 117–33). Canadian Scholars.

Lavallée, L. (2020b). Resisting exotic puppetry: Experiences of Indigenous women leadership in the academy. In T. Moeke-Pickering, S. Cote-Meek, & A. Pegoraro (Eds.), *Critical reflections and politics on advancing women in the academy* (pp. 21–32). IGI Global.

Lee, J.T. (2023). Romanticizing decolonization and Asian epistemology: Reflections on identity and space. *Asia Pacific Education Review, 24*(2), 1–11. https://doi.org/10.1007/s12564-023-09835-3.

Lees, A., Tropp Laman, T., & Calderón, D. (2021). "Why didn't I know this?": Land education as an antidote to settler colonialism in early childhood teacher education. *Theory into Practice, 60*(3), 279–90. https://doi.org/10 .1080/00405841.2021.1911482.

Louie, D.W. (2019). Aligning universities' requirements of Indigenous academics with the tools used to evaluate scholarly performance and grant tenure and promotion. *Canadian Journal of Education/Revue canadienne de l'éducation, 42*(3), 791–815. https://www.jstor.org/stable/26891585.

Louie, D.W., Poitras-Pratt, Y., Hanson, A.J., & Ottmann, J. (2017). Applying Indigenizing principles of decolonizing methodologies in university classrooms. *Canadian Journal of Higher Education/Revue canadienne d'enseignement supérieur, 47*(3), 16–33. https://doi.org/10.7202/1043236ar.

Lowan-Trudeau, G. (2012). Methodological métissage: An interpretive Indigenous approach to environmental education research. *Canadian Journal of Environmental Education (CJEE), 17*, 113–30.

Lumby, B.L. (2010). *Cyber-Indigeneity: Urban Indigenous identity on Facebook.* University of Wollongong, Research Online. https://ro.uow.edu.au/cgi /viewcontent.cgi?referer=https://scholar.google.com/scholar?hl=en&as _sdt=0%2C5&q=lumby+2010%2C+indigenous&btnG=&httpsredir=1 &article=2271&context=artspapers.

Maeße, J. (2017). The elitism dispositif: Hierarchization, discourses of excellence and organizational change in European economics. *Higher Education, 73*(6), 909–27. https://doi.org/10.1007/s10734-016-0019-7.

Manitoba Indian Brotherhood. (1971). *Wahbung:* Our tomorrows.

Marsden, M., & Henare, T.A. (1992). *Kaitiakitanga: A definitive introduction to the holistic world view of the Māori.* Ministry for the Environment, Australia.

Martin, D.H. (2012). Two-eyed seeing: A framework for understanding Indigenous and non-Indigenous approaches to Indigenous health research. *Canadian Journal of Nursing Research Archive, 44*(2), 20–43.

Masta, S. (2019). Challenging the relationship between settler colonial ideology and higher education spaces. *Berkeley Review of Education, 8*(2). https://doi.org/10.5070/B80037547.

Mattern, A. (2013, Fall). The best is yet to come: Aboriginal teacher education programs thriving. *Green & White: University of Saskatchewan Alumni Magazine,* 22–3. https://greenandwhite.usask.ca/documents/pdf /GandW%20fall2013.pdf.

McAllister, T.G., Beggs, J.R., Ogilvie, S., Kirikiri, R., Black, A., & Wehi, P.M. (2019). Kua takoto te mānuka: Mātauranga Māori in New Zealand ecology. *New Zealand Journal of Ecology, 43*(3), 1–7. https://doi.org/10.20417 /nzjecol.43.41.

McCaffrey, S. (2013). Locating my Indian self in the academy's tenure process. In M. Smith (Ed)., *Transforming the academy. Indigenous education, knowledges and relations* (pp. 69–74). E-Book.

McGill Reporter (16 April 2018). Training the next generation of Indigenous teachers. Retrieved from https://reporter.mcgill.ca/training-the -next-generation-of-indigenous-teachers/.

McGill University. (2017). *Provost's task force on Indigenous Studies and Indigenous Education: Final report.* https://www.mcgill.ca/provost/files /provost/final_report_-_clean_-_270617.pdf.

McGowan, K., Kennedy, A., El-Hussein, M., & Chief, R.B. (2020). Decolonization, social innovation and rigidity in higher education. *Social Enterprise Journal, 16*(3), 299–316. https://doi.org/10.1108/SEJ-10-2019-0074.

McGregor, D. (2004). Coming full circle: Indigenous knowledge, environment, and our future. *American Indian Quarterly, 28*(3/4), 385–410. http://www.jstor.org/stable/4138924.

McGregor, D., Bayha, W., & Simmons, D. (2010). "Our responsibility to keep the land alive": Voices of northern Indigenous researchers. *Pimatisiwin: A Journal of Aboriginal and Indigenous Community Health, 8*(1), 101–23.

McKay, D.L. (2021). Real Indians: Policing or protecting authentic Indigenous identity? *Sociology of Race and Ethnicity, 7*(1), 12–25. https://doi.org/10.1177/2332649218821450.

McMaster University. (n.d.). *Harvey E. Longboat Graduate Scholarship for First Nations, Inuit and Métis Students.* https://gs.mcmaster.ca/current-students/scholarships/harvey-e-longboat-graduate-scholarship-for-first-nations-inuit-and-metis-students/.

McMaster University. (2018). *Research for a brighter world: Strategic plan for research 2018–2023.* https://research.mcmaster.ca/research/strategic-plan-for-research-2018-2023/.

McMaster University. (2021). Indigenous Strategic Directions. https://miri.mcmaster.ca/wp-content/uploads/2023/03/McMaster_Indigenous StrategicDirections.pdf.

Memorial University. (2020a). *Memorandum of understanding between* Memorial University of Newfoundland *and Memorial University of Newfoundland Faculty Association.* http://munfa.ca/wp/wp-content/uploads/2020/10/Indigenous-Cluster-Hire-MOU-April-16-2020-signed_Redacted.pdf.

Memorial University. (2020b). *Research impacting Indigenous groups policy.* https://www.mun.ca/research/Indigenous/RIIG_Policy-2020.pdf

Mertens, D.M. (2005). *Research and evaluation in education and psychology: Integrating diversity with quantitative, qualitative, and mixed methods* (2nd ed.). Sage Publications.

Meyer, H.D., & Rowan, B. (2006). Institutional analysis and the study of education. In H.D. Meyer & B. Rowan (Eds.), *The new institutionalism in education* (pp. 1–13). SUNY Press.

Mignolo, W.D. (2011). Geopolitics of sensing and knowing: On (de)coloniality, border thinking and epistemic disobedience. *Postcolonial Studies, 14*(3), 273–83. https://doi.org/10.1080/13688790.2011.613105.

Mohamed, T., & Beagan, B.L. (2019). "Strange faces" in the academy: Experiences of racialized and Indigenous faculty in Canadian universities. *Race Ethnicity and Education, 22*(3), 338–54. https://doi.org/10.1080/13613324.2018.1511532.

Moore, M.L., & Westley, F. (2011). Public sector policy and strategies for facilitating social innovation. *Horizons: The Public Policy Journal.* https://

issuu.com/gfbertini/docs/public_sector_policy_and_strategies _for_facilitati.

Morcom, L.A. (2017). Indigenous holistic education in philosophy and practice, with wampum as a case study. *Foro de Educación, 15*(23), 121–38. doi: http://dx.doi.org/10.14516/fde.572.

More, A.J. (1981). *Native teacher education: A survey of Native Indian and Inuit teacher education projects in Canada* [Paper presentation]. Canadian Indian Teacher Education Projects (CITEP) Conference, Vancouver, Canada. https://files.eric.ed.gov/fulltext/ED249029.pdf.

Moses, E. (2012). Dancing with Chikapesh: An examination of Eeyou stories through three generations of storytellers [Unpublished doctoral dissertation, McGill University]. Library and Archives Canada. https://www.collectionscanada.gc.ca/obj/thesescanada/vol2/QMM /TC-QMM-114159.pdf.

Mzinegiizhigo-kwe Bédard, R.E. (2018). *"Indian in the Cupboard"*: Lateral violence and Indigenization of the academy. In C. Cho, J. Corkett, and A. Steele (Eds), *Exploring the toxicity of lateral violence and microaggressions*. Palgrave Macmillan, Cham. https://doi.org/10.1007/978-3-319-74760-6_5.

Nakata, M. (2007). The cultural interface. *Australian Journal of Indigenous Education, 36*(S1), 7–14. https://doi.org/10.1017/S1326011100004646.

National Aboriginal Capital Corporation. (2017). *Aboriginal entrepreneurship in Canada*. https://nacca.ca/report-shows-aboriginal-entrepreneurs-face -significant-barriers-in-financial-ecosystem/.

National Indian Brotherhood. (1972). *Indian control of Indian education* [Policy paper]. http://www.avenir-future.com/pdf/maitrise%20indienne%20 de%20l%27éducation%20ang.pdf.

Nichols, J. (2018). Unsettling Canada's colonial constitution. A response to the question of domestic law and the creation of an access and benefit-sharing regime. In C. Oguamanam (Ed.), *Genetic resources, justice and reconciliation: Canada and global access and benefit sharing* (pp. 63–79). Cambridge University Press.

Nicoll, F. (2004). "Are you calling me a racist?": Teaching critical whiteness theory in Indigenous sovereignty. *Borderlands, 3*(2). Retrieved from http:// www.borderlands.net.au/vol3no2_2004/nicoll_teaching.htm.

NIEDB (National Indigenous Economic Development Board). (2019). *The Indigenous economic progress report*. http://www.naedb-cndea.com /wp-content/uploads/2019/06/NIEDB-2019-Indigenous-Economic -Progress-Report.pdf.

Nova Scotia (web). Mi'kmaq Community develops renewable energy project. https://novascotia.ca/news/release/?id=20120210004.

Nutley, S.M., Walter, I., & Davies, H.T. (2007). *Using evidence: How research can inform public services*. Policy Press.

Obikeze, D.S. (2011). Indigenous knowledge systems and the transformation of the academy in Africa: The CULPIP Model. http://citeseerx.ist.psu.edu/viewdoc/download?doi=10.1.1.164.4272&rep=rep1&type=pdf.

Oliver, C. (1992). The antecedents of deinstitutionalization. *Organization Studies, 13*, 563–88. https://doi.org/10.1177/017084069201300403.

Olsen J. (2007). The institutional dynamics of the European university. In P. Maassen & J. Olsen (Eds.), *University dynamics and European integration.* Springer. https://doi.org/10.1007/978-1-4020-5971-1_2.

Onkwehonwe Rising. (2020). *"Whose land?" The trials and tribulations of territorial acknowledgement.* https://onkwehonwerising.wordpress.com/2016/10/18/whos-land-the-trials-and-tribulations-of-territorial-acknowledgement/.

Ontario's Universities. (2020). *Lighting the fire: Experiences of Indigenous faculty in Ontario universities.* https://ontariosuniversities.ca/indigenous-faculty-ontario-universities.

Ottmann, J. (1 June 2021). *Revising the accord for Indigenous education.* The Canadian Association for the Study of Indigenous Education Edmonton, Alberta. Virtual.

Ottmann, J., & Jeary, J. (2016). Assessment practices and aboriginal students. In S. Scott, D.E. Scott, & C.F. Webber (Eds.), *Leadership of assessment, inclusion, and learning* (pp. 327–63). Springer, Cham.

Ottmann, J., & Pritchard, L. (2010). Aboriginal perspectives and the social studies curriculum. *First Nations Perspectives, 3*(1), 21–46.

Pardy, L., & Pardy, B. (2020). Decolonizing non-Indigenous faculty and students: Beyond comfortable diversity. In *Decolonizing and Indigenizing education in Canada* (pp. 229–45). Canadian Scholars.

Parent, A. (2017). Visioning as an integral element to understanding Indigenous learners' transition to university. *Canadian Journal of Higher Education, 47*(1), 153–70.

Peach, L., Richmond, C.A., & Brunette-Debassige, C. (2020). "You can't just take a piece of land from the university and build a garden on it": Exploring Indigenizing space and place in a settler Canadian university context. *Geoforum, 114*, 117–27. https://doi.org/10.1016/j.geoforum.2020.06.001.

Pecis, L., & Berglund, K. (2021). Hidden in the limelight: A feminist engagement with innovation studies. *Organization, 28*(6), 993–1017. https://doi.org.10.1177/13505084211015380.

Pedri-Spade, C. (2018). *A bag worth a pony: The art of the Ojibwe bandolier bag* (Marcia G. Anderson) [Review]. *Transmotion, 4*(1), 153–55. http://www.mnhs.org/mnhspress/books/bag-worth-pony.

Pennock, L., Jones, G.A., Leclerc, J.M., & Li, S.X. (2015). Assessing the role and structure of academic senates in Canadian universities, 2000–2012. *Higher Education, 70*(3), 503–18. https://doi.org/10.1007/s10734-014-9852-8.

Peredo, A.M., McLean, M., & Tremblay, C. (2019). Indigenous social innovation: What is distinctive? And a research agenda. In G. George, T. Baker, P. Tracey, & H. Joshi (Eds.), Handbook *of inclusive innovation*, 107–28. Edward Elgar Publishing.

Pete, S. (2016). 100 ways: Indigenizing & decolonizing academic programs. *Aboriginal Policy Studies*, 6(1), 81–9. https://doi.org/10.5663/aps.v6i1.27455.

Pidgeon, M. (2008). Pushing against the margins: Indigenous theorizing of "success" and retention in higher education. *Journal of College Student Retention*, 10, 339–60. https://doi.org/10.2190/CS.10.3.e.

Pidgeon, M. (2014). Moving beyond good intentions: Indigenizing higher education in British Columbia universities through institutional responsibility and accountability. *Journal of American Indian Education*, 53(2), 7–28. https://www.muse.jhu.edu/article/798538.

Pidgeon, M. (2016). More than a checklist: Meaningful Indigenous inclusion in higher education. *Social Inclusion*, 4(1), 77–91. https://doi.org/10.17645/si.v4i1.436.

Pidgeon, M. (2019). Aboriginal higher education and Indigenous students. In W. Archer & H.G. Schuetze (Eds.), *Preparing students for life and work: Policies and reforms affecting higher education's principal mission* (pp. 42–63). Brill Sense.

Pidgeon, M., Archibald, J.A., & Hawkey, C. (2014). Relationships matter: Supporting Aboriginal graduate students in British Columbia, Canada. *Canadian Journal of Higher Education*, 44(1), 1–21.

Pidgeon, M., & Hardy Cox, D. (2005). Perspectives of Aboriginal student services professionals: Aboriginal student services in Canadian universities. *Journal of Australian & New Zealand Student Services*, 25, 3–30.

Pitawanakwat, B.T., & Pedri-Spade, C. (2022). Indigenization in universities and its role in continuing settler-colonialism. *Janus Unbound: Journal of Critical Studies*, 1(2), 12–35. https://doi.org/10.2021/ju.v1i2.2377.

Povey, R., Trudgett, M., Page, S., & Coates, S.K. (2022). Paying-it-forward: Indigenous leadership in American higher education. *Race Ethnicity and Education*, 26(2), 240–56. https://doi.org/10.1080/13613324.2022.2033197.

Powell, W.W., & Colyvas, J.A. (2007). The new institutionalism. In S.R. Clegg & J.R. Bailey (Eds.), *The international encyclopedia of organization studies*, 976–9. Sage.

Preston, J.P. (2016). Education for Aboriginal peoples in Canada: An overview of four realms of success. *Diaspora, Indigenous, and Minority Education*, 10(1), 14–27. https://doi.org/10.1080/15595692.2015.1084917.

Queen's University. (2018). Strategic research plan 2018–2023: Excellence in research through diversity of thought and understanding research brings Queen's to the world and the world to Queen's. https://www.queensu.ca/strategicplanning/research.

Queen's University. (2023). Global Engagement Strategic Plan. https://www
.queensu.ca/international/sites/ovpiwww/files/uploaded_files
/Queens-University-Global-Engagement-Strategic-Plan-2023-2028-Final
-Accessible%20().pdf.

Radio Canada. (12 January 2017). *5 M$ pour le pavillon des Premiers-Peuples du
campus de Val-d'Or de l'UQAT.* https://ici.radio-canada.ca/nouvelle
/1010434/annonce-uqat-val-dor-pavillon-premiers-peuples-abitibi.

Rae Scott, B. (2020). Chapter 3: Decolonization through Métissage. In S. Cote-
Meek & T. Moeke-Pickering (Eds.),*Decolonizing and Indigenizing education in
Canada* (pp. 31–49). Canadian Scholars.

Ragoonaden, K., & Mueller, L. (2017). Culturally responsive pedagogy:
Indigenizing curriculum. *Canadian Journal of Higher Education, 47*(2), 22–46.

Rancic, M. (11 May 2022). Ryerson University officially changes its name to
Toronto Metropolitan University. https://www.universityaffairs
.ca/news/news-article/ryerson-university-officially-changes-its-name
-to-toronto-metropolitan-university/#:~:text=Français-,Ryerson%20
University%20officially%20changes%20its%20name%20to%20Toronto%20
Metropolitan%20University,advocacy%2C%20consultation%20and%20
committee%20work.&text=Following%20a%20years%2Dlong%20
process,Ryerson%20University%20in%20late%20April.

RCAP (Royal Commission on Aboriginal Peoples). (1996). *Report of the Royal
Commission on Aboriginal Peoples.* https://www.bac-lac.gc.ca/eng/discover
/aboriginal-heritage/royal-commission-aboriginal-peoples/Pages/final
-report.aspx.

RCAP (Royal Commission on Aboriginal Peoples). (1993). Ethical Guidelines
for Research). https://www.wrrb.ca/sites/default/files/15.%20RCAP
_Guidelines_1993.pdf.

Regan, P. (2011). *Unsettling the settler within: Indian residential schools, truth
telling, and reconciliation in Canada.* UBC Press.

Regnier, R. (1994). The sacred circle: A process pedagogy of
healing. *Interchange, 25,* 129–44. https://doi.org/10.1007/BF01534540.

Restoule, J., Mashford-Pringle, A., Chacaby, M., Smillie, C., Brunette, C., &
Russel, G. (2013). Supporting successful transitions to post-secondary
education for Indigenous students: Lessons from an institutional
ethnography in Ontario, Canada. *International Indigenous Policy Journal,
4*(4). https://doi.org/10.18584/iipj.2013.4.4.4.

Richards, J. (2014). *Are we making progress? New evidence on Aboriginal education
outcomes in provincial and reserve schools (April 30, 2014)* [Commentary No.
408]. C.D. Howe Institute. https://papers.ssrn.com/sol3/papers
.cfm?abstract_id=2431380.

Robinson, R. (2023). Indigenous post-secondary institutes in British
Columbia, Canada: Exemplars of Indigenous control over Indigenous
education. *Canadian Journal of Education/Revue canadienne de l'éducation.*

Romaniuc, A. (2003). Aboriginal population of Canada: Growth dynamics under conditions of encounter of civilisations. *Canadian Studies in Population [ARCHIVES]*, 75–115. http://www3.brandonu.ca/cjns/20.1 /cjnsv20no1_pg95-137.pdf.

Sabatier, P.A. (1986). Top-down and bottom-up approaches to implementation research: A critical analysis and suggested synthesis. *Journal of Public Policy, 6*, 21–48. https://doi.org10.1017/S0143814X00003846.

Sabzalian, L. (2019). The tensions between Indigenous sovereignty and multicultural citizenship education: Toward an anticolonial approach to civic education. *Theory & Research in Social Education, 47*(3), 311–46. https://doi.org/10.1080/00933104.2019.1639572.

Saini, R., & Begum, N. (2020). Demarcation and definition: Explicating the meaning and scope of "decolonisation" in the social and political sciences. *Political Quarterly, 91*(1), 217–21. https://doi.org/10.1111/1467-923X.12797.

Samson, N. (10 September 2020). *Memorial has a new record-setting Indigenous research policy.* University Affairs/Affaires universitaires. https://www .universityaffairs.ca/news/news-article/memorial-has-a-new-record-setting-indigenous-research-policy/.

Sasakamoose, J., & Pete, S.M. (2015). Towards Indigenizing university policy: Education matters. *Journal of Teaching and Learning, 3*(1), 1–15.

Schneider, B., González-Romá, V., Ostroff, C., & West, M.A. (2017). Organizational climate and culture: Reflections on the history of the constructs in the *Journal of Applied Psychology. Journal of Applied Psychology, 102*(3), 468–82. https://doi.org/10.1037/apl0000090.

Schorkowitz, D. (2019). Was Russia a colonial empire?. In D. Schorkowitz et al. (Eds), *Shifting forms of continental colonialism: Unfinished struggles and tensions* (pp. 117–47). Palgrave Macmillan Publishers.

Scott, W.R. (2005). Institutional theory: Contributing to a theoretical research program. *Great Minds in Management: The Process of Theory Development, 37*(2), 460–84.

Scully, A. (2012). Decolonization, reinhabitation and reconciliation: Aboriginal and place-based education. *Canadian Journal of Environmental Education, 17*, 148–59.

Seemann, K. (2000). Technacy education: Towards holistic pedagogy and epistemology in general and Indigenous/crosscultural technology education. *Technology Teacher, 5*, 41–51.

Sengupta, U., Vieta, M., & McMurtry, J.J. (2015). Indigenous communities and social enterprise in Canada. *Canadian Journal of Nonprofit and Social Economy Research, 6*(1), 104–23. https://doi.org/10.22230/cjnser.2015v6n1a196.

Shahjahan, R. (2011). Engaging the faces of "resistance" and social change from decolonizing perspectives: Toward transforming neoliberal higher education. *Journal of Curriculum Theorizing, 27*(3), 273–86.

Shahjahan, R.A., Estera, A.L., Surla, K.L., & Edwards, K.T. (2022). "Decolonizing" curriculum and pedagogy: A comparative review across disciplines and global higher education contexts. *Review of Educational Research, 92*(1), 73–113. https://doi.org/10.3102/00346543211042423.

Shanahan, T. (2015). The role of the federal government in postsecondary education. In T. Shanahan, M. Nilson, & L. Broshko (Eds), *Handbook of Canadian higher education law* (pp. 17–36). McGill-Queen's University Press.

Sheridan College. (2020). *Research guidelines with Indigenous peoples*. https://source.sheridancollege.ca/cgi/viewcontent.cgi?article=1002&context=non faculty_cei_publications.

Shewaga, J. (2019). *USask confirms record enrolment in 2018/19*. University of Saskatchewan. https://news.usask.ca/articles/general/2019/usask -confirms-record-enrolment-in-201819.php.

Simpson, L.B. (2014). Land as pedagogy: Nishnaabeg intelligence and rebellious transformation. *Decolonization: Indigeneity, Education & Society, 3*(3).

Simpson, L.B. (2016). Indigenous resurgence and co-resistance. *Critical Ethnic Studies, 2*(2), 19–34. https://doi.org/10.5749/jcritethnstud.2.2.0019.

Simpson, L.R. (1999). *The construction of traditional ecological knowledge, issues, implications and insights*. MSpace. http://hdl.handle.net/1993/2210.

Simpson, L.R. (2004). Anticolonial strategies for the recovery and maintenance of Indigenous knowledge. *American Indian Quarterly, 28*(3/4), 373–84. http://www.jstor.org/stable/4138923.

Smith, G., & Webber, M. (2018). Transforming research and Indigenous education struggle. In E. McKinley & L. Smith (Eds.), *Handbook of Indigenous education*. Springer.

Smith, G.H. & Smith, L.T. (2018). Doing Indigenous work: Decolonizing and transforming the academy. In E.A. McKinley & L.T Smith (Eds.), *Handbook of Indigenous education* (pp. 1075–1101).

Smith, L.T. (1999). *Decolonizing methodologies: Research and Indigenous peoples*. Zed Books.

Smith, L.T. (2012). *Decolonizing methodologies: Research and Indigenous peoples* (2nd ed.). Zed Books.

Smith, L.T. (2013). *Decolonizing methodologies: Research and Indigenous peoples*. Zed Books.

Smith, L.T. (2018a). *Decolonizing methodologies: Research and Indigenous peoples*. Zed Books.

Smith, L.T. (2018b). The art of the impossible: Defining and measuring Indigenous research? Chapter 2 In J. McNinch & M. Spooner (Eds.), *Dissident knowledge in higher education* (pp. 21–40). University of Regina Press.

Smith, L.T. (2021). *Decolonizing methodologies: Research and Indigenous peoples*. Zed Books.

Smith, L.T., Tuck, E., & Yang, K.W. (Eds.). (2018). *Indigenous and decolonizing studies in education: Mapping the long view*. Routledge.

Smith, M.S. (2017). 10 disciplinary silences: Race, Indigeneity, and gender in the social sciences. In F. Henry et. al. (Eds)., *The equity myth: Racialization and Indigeneity at Canadian universities* (pp. 239–62). UBC Press.

Smith, M.S. (2019). *The diversity gap in 2019: Canadian universities* [Infographic series on U15 Presidents' Leadership Teams or Cabinets, U15 Deans, U15 Leadership Pipeline, Equity Diversity Intersectionality Decoloniality]. Academic Women's Association of the University of Alberta. https://uofaawa.wordpress.com/awa-diversity-gap-campaign/.

SSHRC (Social Sciences and Humanities Research Council). (n.d.-a). *Definitions of terms: Indigenous research*. https://www.sshrc-crsh.gc.ca/funding-financement/programs-programmes/definitions-eng.aspx#a11.

SSHRC (Social Sciences and Humanities Research Council). (n.d.-b). *Indigenous research statement of principles*. https://www.sshrc-crsh.gc.ca/about-au_sujet/policies-politiques/statements-enonces/indigenous_research-recherche_autochtone-eng.aspx.

SSHRC (Social Sciences and Humanities Research Council). (2018). *Toward a successful shared* future *for Canada: Research insights from the knowledge systems, experiences and aspirations of First Nations, Inuit and Métis peoples*. https://www.sshrc-crsh.gc.ca/society-societe/community-communite/ifca-iac/03-aboriginal_peoples_in_Canada_report-les_peuples_autochtones_en_Canada_rapport-eng.pdf.

SSHRC (Social Sciences and Humanities Research Council). (2019). *Setting new directions to support Indigenous research and research training in Canada*. https://www.canada.ca/content/dam/crcc-ccrc/documents/strategic-plan-2019-2022/sirc_strategic_plan-eng.pdf.

Staples, K., Klein, R., Southwick, T., Kinnear, L., Geddes, C., & Gingell, J. (2021). Indigenization and university governance: Reflections from the transition to Yukon University. *Tertiary Education and Management, 27*(3), 209–25. https://doi.org/10.1007/s11233-021-09073-5.

Starblanket, G. (2019). The numbered treaties and the politics of incoherency. *Canadian Journal of Political Science/Revue canadienne de science politique, 52*(3), 443–59, https://doi.org/10.1017/S008423919000027.

Statistics Canada. (2016a). *Data tables, 2016 census*. https://www12.statcan.gc.ca/census-recensement/2016/dp-pd/dt-td/index-eng.cfm.

Statistics Canada. (2016b). *2016 Census topic: Aboriginal peoples*. https://www12.statcan.gc.ca/census-recensement/2016/rt-td/ap-pa-eng.cfm.

Statistics Canada. (2017). *Upgrading and high school equivalency among the Indigenous population living off reserve*. https://www150.statcan.gc.ca/n1/pub/75-006-x/2019001/article/00013-eng.htm.

Statistics Canada. (2018). Aboriginal population profile, 2016 census. Retrieved from https://www12.statcan.gc.ca/census-recensement/2016

/dp-pd/abpopprof/details/page.cfm?Lang=E&Geo1=&Code1=&
Data=Count&SearchText=Canada&SearchType=Begins&B1=All&
SEX_ID=1&AGE_ID=1&RESGEO_ID=1.

Statistics Canada. (2019). *First Nations people, Métis and Inuit in Canada: Diverse and growing populations*. https://www150.statcan.gc.ca/n1/pub/89-659 -x/89-659-x2018001-eng.htm.

Statistics Canada. (2021). Postsecondary Student Information System (PSIS). https://www23.statcan.gc.ca/imdb/p2SV.pl?Function=getSurvey &Id=1495204.

Statistics Canada. (2022). Statistics on Indigenous peoples. https://www .statcan.gc.ca/en/subjects-start/indigenous_peoples.

Statistics Canada. (2023). An update on the socio-economic gaps between Indigenous Peoples and the non-Indigenous population in Canada: Highlights from the 2021 Census. https://www.sac-isc.gc.ca/eng/16909097 73300/1690909797208#chp3-6.

St. Denis, V. (2011). Silencing Aboriginal curricular content and perspectives through multiculturalism: "There are other children here." *Review of Education, Pedagogy, and Cultural Studies, 33*(4), 306–17. https://doi.org/10 .1080/10714413.2011.597638.

Stein, S. (2020). "Truth before reconciliation": The difficulties of transforming higher education in settler colonial contexts. *Higher Education Research & Development, 39*(1), 156–70. https://doi.org/10.1080/07294360.2019.1666255.

Stein, S., Ahenakew, C., Jimmy, E., Andreotti, V., Valley, W., Amsler, S., & Calhoun, B. (2021). Developing stamina for decolonizing higher education: A workbook for non-Indigenous people. *Gesturing towards decolonial futures collective*. https://www.researchgate.net/profile/Sharon-Stein /publication/349781935_Developing_Stamina_for_Decolonizing _Higher_Education_A_Workbook_for_Non-Indigenous_People /links/6042cd494585154e8c7c05ea/Developing-Stamina-for-Decolonizing -Higher-Education-A-Workbook-for-Non-Indigenous-People.pdf.

Stewart-Ambo, T., & Yang, K.W. (2021). Beyond land acknowledgment in settler institutions. *Social Text, 39*(1), 21–46. https://doi.org /10.1215/01642472-8750076.

Stiegelbauer, S.M. (1996). What is an Elder? What do Elders do?: First Nation Elders as teachers in culture-based urban organizations. *Canadian Journal of Native Studies, 14*, 37–66.

Stonechild, B. (2006). *The new buffalo: The struggle for Aboriginal post-secondary education in Canada*. University of Manitoba Press.

Styres, S.D. (2017). Pathways for remembering and recognizing Indigenous thought in education: Philosophies of Iethi'nihsténha Ohwentsia'kékha *(land)*. University of Toronto Press.

Styres, S. (2019). Pathways for remembering and (re) cognizing Indigenous thought in education. In Tomlins-Jahnke et al. (Eds)., *Indigenous education: New directions in theory and practice* (pp. 39–62). University of Alberta Press.

Styres, S., Zinga, D., Bennett, S., & Bomberry, M. (2010). Walking in two worlds: Engaging the space between Indigenous community and academia. *Canadian Journal of Education/Revue canadienne de l'éducation, 33*(3), 617–48. https://doi.org/10.2307/canajeducrevucan.33.3.617.

Tamtik, M. (2020). Informing Canadian innovation policy through a decolonizing lens on Indigenous entrepreneurship and innovation. *Canadian Journal of Higher Education, 50*(3), 63–78. https://doi.org/10.47678/cjhe.vi0.188773.

Tamtik, M., & Guenter, M. (2019). Policy analysis of equity, diversity and inclusion strategies in Canadian universities: How far have we come? *Canadian Journal of Higher Education/Revue canadienne d'enseignement supérieur, 49*(3), 41–56. https://doi.org/10.7202/1066634ar.

Tankard, M.E., & Paluck, E.L. (2016). Norm perception as a vehicle for social change. *Social Issues and Policy Review, 10*(1), 181–211. https://doi.org/10.1111/sipr.12022.

Taner, S. (1999). The evolution of Native Studies in Canada: Descending from the ivory tower. *Canadian Journal of Native Studies, 19*(2), 289–319.

TCPS2 (Tri-Council Policy Statement). (2018). Chapter 9: Research involving the First Nations, Inuit and Métis Peoples of Canada. https://ethics.gc.ca/eng/tcps2-eptc2_2018_chapter9-chapitre9.html.

Teillet, J. (2022). Indigenous identity fraud. A report for the University of Saskatchewan. https://leadership.usask.ca/documents/about/reporting/jean-teillet-report.pdf.

Thambinathan, V., & Kinsella, E.A. (2021). Decolonizing methodologies in qualitative research: Creating spaces for transformative praxis. *International Journal of Qualitative Methods, 20*, https://doi.org.16094069211014766.

Thornton, P.H. (2004). *Markets from culture: Institutional logics and organizational decisions in higher education publishing.* Stanford University Press.

TRC (Truth and Reconciliation Commission of Canada). (2015). *Calls to action.* http://www.trc.ca/websites/trcinstitution/File/2015/Findings/Calls_to_Action_English2.pdf.

Trent University. (n/d). *Indigenous course requirement (ICR).* https://www.trentu.ca/indigenous/icr.

Tuck, E., & McKenzie, M. (2015). Relational validity and the "where" of inquiry: Place and land in qualitative research. *Qualitative Inquiry, 21*(7), 633–8. https://doi.org/10.1177/1077800414563809.

Tuck, E., & Yang, K.W. (2012). Decolonization is not a metaphor. *Decolonization: Indigeneity, Education & Society, 1*(1), 1–40. https://doi.org/10.25058/20112742.n38.04.

Tuck, E., & Yang, K.W. (2014). R-words: Refusing research. In D. Paris & M.T. Winn (Eds.), *Humanizing research: Decolonizing qualitative inquiry with youth and communities* (pp. 223–48). SAGE.

Tuck, E., & Yang, K.W. (Eds.). (2018). *Toward what justice?: Describing diverse dreams of justice in education.* Routledge.

UBC (University of British Columbia). (n.d.). *First Nation Long House.* https://www.library.ubc.ca/archives/bldgs/firstnationlonghouse.htm.

UBC (University of British Columbia). (2018a). *Indigenous student is the first to defend her dissertation off-campus and "on land".* https://www.grad.ubc.ca/advance/2018/4/indigenous-student-first-defend-her-dissertation-campus-land.

UBC (University of British Columbia). (2018b). *Shaping UBC's next century: Strategic plan 2018–2028.* https://strategicplan.ubc.ca.

UBC (University of British Columbia). (2020). *UBC Indigenous strategic plan.* https://indigenous.ubc.ca/indigenous-engagement/indigenous-strategic-plan/.

UM Today. (11 February 2016). *Faculty of Education's Diversity Policy approved by Senate.* https://news.umanitoba.ca/faculty-of-educations-diversity-policy-approved-by-senate/.

UNDRIP (United Nations Declaration on the Rights of Indigenous Peoples) (13 September 2007). https://www.un.org/development/desa/indigenouspeoples/declaration-on-the-rights-of-indigenous-peoples.html.

Université de Montréal (2018). *Plan d'action en matière d'équité, de diversité et d'inclusion pour le programme des chaires de recherche du Canada* [*Action plan for equity, diversity and inclusion for the Canada Research Chairs Program*]. https://www.chairs-chaires.gc.ca/program-programme/srp-prs/montreal-eng.pdf.

Université Laval. (2017). *Dare, inspire, achieve, building the future together 2017–2022 strategic plan.* https://www.ulaval.ca/fileadmin/notre_universite/Strategic-Plan-2017-2022-UL.pdf.

Universities Canada. (2013). *Creating opportunities in education for Aboriginal students.* https://www.univcan.ca/wp-content/uploads/2015/07/aboriginal-students-report-2013.pdf.

Universities Canada. (2018). *Advancing reconciliation through higher education: 2017 survey findings.* https://www.univcan.ca/wp-content/uploads/2018/10/Indigenous_survey_findings_2017_factsheet_25Apr_.pdf.

Universities Canada. (2019). *Equity, diversity and inclusion at Canadian universities: Report on the 2019 national survey.* https://www.univcan.ca/wp-content/uploads/2019/11/Equity-diversity-and-inclusion-at-Canadian-universities-report-on-the-2019-national-survey-Nov-2019-1.pdf.

Universities Canada Online Database. (n.d.). *Indigenous programs and services directory.* https://www.universitystudy.ca/indigenous-programs-and-%20services-directory.

University News. (18 June 2020). *UBC appoints the Honourable Steven Lewis Point as next Chancellor*. University of British Columbia. https://news.ubc .ca/2020/06/18/ubc-appoints-the-honourable-steven-lewis-point -as-next-chancellor/.

University of Alberta. (2016). *For the public good: Institutional strategic plan*. https://www.ualberta.ca/strategic-plan/index.html.

University of Calgary. (2017a). *ii' taa'poh'to'p: Together in a good way: A journey of transformation and renewal Indigenous strategy*. https://live-ucalgary. ucalgary.ca/sites/default/files/teams/136/Indigenous%20Strategy _Publication_digital_Sep2019.pdf.

University of Calgary. (2017b). *Eyes high strategy 2017–2022*. https://www .ucalgary.ca/eyeshigh.

University of Calgary News. (31 March 2021). *UCalgary launches Provost's Postdoctoral Awards for Indigenous and Black scholars*. https://news.ucalgary .ca/news/ucalgary-launches-provosts-postdoctoral-awards-indigenous -and-black-scholars.

University of Manitoba. (2014). *Framework for research engagement with First Nation, Metis, and Inuit Peoples*. https://umanitoba.ca/faculties/health _sciences/medicine/media/UofM_Framework_Report_web.pdf.

University of Manitoba. (2015). *Taking our place: University of Manitoba strategic plan* 2015–2020. https://umanitoba.ca/sites/default/files/2020-06/um -strategic-plan-2015-2020.pdf.

University of Manitoba. (2019). *University of Manitoba Indigenous senior leadership report and recommendations to the Provost and Vice-President (Academic)*. https://umanitoba.ca/sites/default/files/2020-06/isl_report _final.pdf.

University of Manitoba. (4 November 2020). *November 4, 2020* [Senate meeting minutes]. http://umanitoba.ca/governance/sites/governance/files/2020 -12/2020_11_04_Senate%20Minutes.pdf.

University of Manitoba (7 April 2021). *Agenda, April 7, 2021* [Senate meeting agenda]. https://umanitoba.ca/governance/sites/governance/files/2021 -03/2021_04_07_Senate_agenda_reduced.pdf.

University of New Brunswick (web). Wabanaki Bachelor of Education. A four-year program in elementary education specializing in Wabanaki languages, cultures and worldviews. Retrieved from https://www.unb.ca /mwc/programs/wabanaki-bed.html.

University of Ottawa. (2019). Indigenous action plan 2019–2024. https://www .uottawa.ca/indigenous/sites/www.uottawa.ca.indigenous/files/uottawa _iap_english_revisedjun192020.pdf.

University of Ottawa. (2020). *Indigenous action plan 2019–2024*. https://www .uottawa.ca/indigenous/sites/www.uottawa.ca.indigenous/files/uottawa _iap_english_revisedjune292020.pdf.

University of Regina. (2 October 2019). *University of Regina sees largest enrolment increase in 37 years* [News release]. https://www.uregina.ca/external/communications/releases/current/nr-1022019.html.

University of Saskatchewan. (1998). A framework for planning at the University of Saskatchewan https://www.usask.ca/ipa/documents/planning/framework_for_planning.pdf.

University of Saskatchewan. (2008). *Recommendations for ethical research with Indigenous peoples – draft*. https://ethicshub.ca/wp-content/uploads/2020/05/84-Principles-and-Guidelines-for-Ethical-Research-with-Indigenous-Peoples.pdf.

University of Saskatchewan. (2018). University plan 2025: Strategic framework and narrative. https://plan.usask.ca.

University of Saskatchewan. (2020). https://indigenous.usask.ca/documents/lets-fly-up-together.pdf.

University of Saskatchewan. (2022). *deybwewin | taapwaywin | tapwewin: Indigenous truth*. https://policies.usask.ca/policies/operations-and-general-administration/deybwewin-taapwaywin-tapwewin.php#Policy.

University of Saskatchewan Council. (2012). *2012 February 20 council agenda: Updates*. https://governance.usask.ca/documents/council/agenda/2011-2012/2012%20Feb%20council%20agenda.pdf.

University of Toronto. (n.d.). *Provost's postdoctoral fellowship program*. https://www.sgs.utoronto.ca/awards/provosts-postdoctoral-fellowship-program%E2%80%8B/.

University of Toronto. (2018). Excellence, innovation, leadership: The University of Toronto strategic research plan 2018–23. https://research.utoronto.ca/reports-publications-metrics/institutional-strategic-research-plan.

University of Victoria. (2003). *Protocols & principles for conducting research in an Indigenous context*. http://icwrn.uvic.ca/wp-content/uploads/2013/08/igovprotocol.pdf.

University of Waterloo. (2013). Strategic plan 2013: A distinguished past – A distinctive future. https://uwaterloo.ca/strategic-plan-action-and-progress/sites/default/files/uploads/files/2013-2018_strategic_plan.pdf.

University of Western Ontario. (2014). Achieving excellence on the world stage. https://president.uwo.ca/strategic_planning/index.html.

UVic News (21 February 2018). Backgrounder: World's first Indigenous Law degree to be offered at UVic. https://www.uvic.ca/news/topics/2018+jid-indigenous-law+backgrounder.

Veracini, L. (2010). Settler colonialism. Palgrave Macmillan.

Vowel, C. (2016). *Indigenous writes: A guide to First Nations, Metis, & Inuit issues in Canada*. Portage & Main Press.

Vowel, C. (2017). *Indigenization in the time of pipelines*. âpihtawikosisân. https://apihtawikosisan.com/2017/02/indigenization-in-the-time-of-pipelines/.

Vunibola, S., & Scobie, M. (2022). Islands of Indigenous innovation: Reclaiming and reconceptualising innovation within, against and beyond colonial-capitalism. *Journal of the Royal Society of New Zealand, 52*(sup1), 4–17. https://doi.org/10.1080/03036758.2022.2056618.

Waldram, J.B. (1994). Aboriginal spirituality in corrections: A Canadian case study in religion and therapy. *American Indian Quarterly, 18*(2), 197–214. https://doi.org/10.2307/1185246.

Wark, J. (2021). Land acknowledgements in the academy: Refusing the settler myth. *Curriculum Inquiry, 51*(2), 191–209. https://doi.org/10.1080/03626784.2021.1889924.

Warkentin, C. (23 April 2021). *Three decades after opening, First Nations Longhouse construction will be complete by end of* 2021. The Ubyssey. https://www.ubyssey.ca/news/ubc-longhouse-expansion-complete-2021/.

Webber, G., McVittie, J., Miller, D., & Hellsten, L. (2021). The terrain of place-based education: A primer for teacher education in Canada. *A Journal of Educational Research and Practice, 30*(1), 10–29. https://doi.org/10.26522/brocked.v30i1.777.

Weiler, H.N. (2001). Knowledge, politics, and the future of higher education: Critical observations on a worldwide transformation. In R. Hayhoe & J. Pan (Eds.), *Knowledge across cultures: A contribution to dialogue among civilizations* (pp. 25–44). Comparative Education Research Center.

Weiss, C.H., & Bucuvalas, M.J. (1980). *Social science research and decision-making*. Columbia University Press.

Western University. (2016). *Indigenous strategic plan*. https://indigenous.uwo.ca/assets/docs/pdfs/reports/Indigenous-Strat-Plan---Final.pdf.

Westley, F., Zimmerman, B., & Patton, M. (2006). *Getting to maybe: How the world is changed*. Random House of Canada.

Wheelahan, L., & Moodie, G. (2022). Gig qualifications for the gig economy: micro-credentials and the "hungry mile." *Higher Education, 83*(6), 1279–95. https://doi.org/10.1007/s10734-021-00742-3.

Wildcat, M., McDonald, M., Irlbacher-Fox, S., & Coulthard, G. (2014). Learning from the land: Indigenous land-based pedagogy and decolonization. *Decolonization: Indigeneity, Education & Society, 3*(3), i–xv.

Wilder, C.S. (2013). *Ebony and ivy: Race, slavery and the troubled history of America's universities*. Bloomsbury Press.

Wilkes, R., Duong, A., Kesler, L., & Ramos, H. (2017). Canadian university acknowledgment of Indigenous lands, treaties, and peoples. *Canadian Review of Sociology/Revue canadienne de sociologie, 54*(1), 89–120. https://doi.org/10.1111/cars.12140.

Wilson, S. (2001). What is an Indigenous research methodology? *Canadian Journal of Native Education, 25*(2), 175–9.

Wilson, S. (2003). Progressing toward an Indigenous research paradigm in Canada and Australia. *Canadian Journal of Native Education, 27*(2), 161–78. https://doi.org/10.14288/cjne.v27i2.196353.

Wilson, S. (2008). *Research is ceremony: Indigenous research methods.* Fernwood Publishing.

Wilson, W.A. (2004). Introduction: Indigenous knowledge recovery is Indigenous empowerment. *American Indian Quarterly, 28*(3–4), 359–72.

Wilson, W.A. (2013). Indigenous knowledge, anticolonialism and empowerment. In M. Smith (Ed.), *Transforming the academy: Indigenous education, knowledges and relations* (pp. 19–22). E-book.

Wolfe, P. (2006). Settler colonialism and the elimination of the Native. *Journal of Genocide Research, 8*(4), 387–409. https://doi.org/10.1080/14623520601056240.

Wright, S. (2002). The Akitsiraq law school: A unique approach to Indigenous legal education. *Indigenous Law Bulletin, 5*(19), 14–17.

Wuttunee, W. (2004). *Living rhythms: Lessons in aboriginal economic resilience and vision.* McGill-Queen's University Press.

Yang, J. (11 April 2018). Celebrated Indigenous law school dean resigns claiming systemic racism. *Toronto Star.* https://www.thestar.com/news/canada/2018/04/11/celebrated-indigenous-law-school-dean-resigns-claiming-systemic-racism.html.

York University News. (9 February 2021). *York University announces new postdoctoral program for Black and Indigenous scholars.* https://yfile.news.yorku.ca/2021/02/09/york-university-announces-new-postdoctoral-program-for-black-and-indigenous-scholars/.

Youngblood Henderson, J. (2002). Aukpachi: Empowering Aboriginal thought. In M. Battiste (Ed.), *Reclaiming Indigenous voices and vision* (pp. 248–78). UBC Press.

Zapp, M., & Ramirez, F.O. (2019). Beyond internationalisation and isomorphism – the construction of a global higher education regime. *Comparative Education, 55*(4), 473–93. https://doi.org/10.1080/03050068.2019.1638103.

Index

A letter "t" following the page number indicates a table.